# Economic Evaluation

# of Urban Renewal

# Studies of Government Finance

## TITLES PUBLISHED

# Economic Evaluation of Urban Renewal

*Conceptual Foundation of Benefit-Cost Analysis*

## JEROME ROTHENBERG

*Studies of Government Finance*

THE BROOKINGS INSTITUTION

WASHINGTON, D.C.

*HT*
*175*
*.U6*
*R6*
*1967* / *57,815*

THE BROOKINGS INSTITUTION is an independent organization devoted to nonpartisan research, education, and publication in economics, government, foreign policy, and the social sciences generally. Its principal purposes are to aid in the development of sound public policies and to promote public understanding of issues of national importance.

The Institution was founded December 8, 1927, to merge the activities of the Institute for Government Research, founded in 1916, the Institute of Economics, founded in 1922, and the Robert Brookings Graduate School of Economics and Government, founded in 1924.

The general administration of the Institution is the responsibility of a self-perpetuating Board of Trustees. The trustees are likewise charged with maintaining the independence of the staff and fostering the most favorable conditions for creative research and education. The immediate direction of the policies, program, and staff of the Institution is vested in the President, assisted by an advisory council chosen from the staff of the Institution.

In publishing a study, the Institution presents it as a competent treatment of a subject worthy of public consideration. The interpretations and conclusions in such publications are those of the author or authors and do not purport to represent the views of the other staff members, officers, or trustees of the Brookings Institution.

# Foreword

UNDER THE URBAN RENEWAL PROGRAM, which began in 1949, the federal government has had the authority to grant some $6 billion to help localities finance renewal projects. This study, which concentrates on the redevelopment aspects of the program, formulates a procedure by which a benefit-cost analysis of urban renewal can be carried out. The procedure is illustrated by an analysis of five selected urban renewal projects.

The author is Jerome Rothenberg, now Professor of Economics at the Massachusetts Institute of Technology. The project was undertaken when he was a member of the economics faculty of Northwestern University.

The author acknowledges with gratitude the constructive comments of the Reading Committee, whose members were Leo Grebler, Julius Margolis, and Richard Ruggles. He is also grateful to Robert Puth, who collected the data and performed the numerical calculations for Chapter XI; to Sylvan Kamm, who provided some key information; to Andrew Gold and Evelyn Fisher for their research assistance; and to Virginia Haaga, who edited the manuscript and prepared the index.

Anthony Downs, Angus Hone, Denis Munby, Richard Muth, Robert Strotz, and Burton Weisbrod read the manuscript and were generous and helpful in commenting upon it. The author warmly thanks Joseph A. Pechman for his unfailing encouragement and support throughout the project. He is especially grateful to his wife for her substantial help.

This volume is part of the Brookings series of Studies of Government Finance, a special program of research and education in taxa-

vii

tion and government expenditures, supervised by the National Committee on Government Finance. The Committee was established in 1960 by the trustees of the Brookings Institution, and its program is supported with funds provided by the Ford Foundation.

The views expressed in this volume are those of the author and are not presented as the views of the Ford Foundation, the National Committee on Government Finance, or the staff members, officers, or trustees of the Brookings Institution.

Kermit Gordon
*President*

*July 1967*
*Washington, D.C.*

## Studies of Government Finance

Studies of Government Finance is a special program of research and education in taxation and government expenditures at the federal, state, and local levels. This program is under the supervision of the National Committee on Government Finance appointed by the trustees of the Brookings Institution, and is supported by a special grant from the Ford Foundation.

# MEMBERS OF THE ADVISORY COMMITTEE

# Contents

xi

## Text Tables

PART ONE

# Scope and Purpose of Urban Renewal

# CHAPTER I

# Introduction and Summary

UNDER THE NATIONAL HOUSING ACT of 1949 (as amended in the Acts of 1954, 1956, 1961, 1964, and 1965),[1] the federal government became an active partner in urban renewal. The activities involved were municipal, the partnership a direct one between the federal government and the localities. Federal entry did not create the field; urban renewal in one form or another has been around for decades. But it had an important influence on the magnitude and pattern of renewal programs. First, it decreased substantially the cost of a project to the locality. Second, it called upon the locality to formulate a comprehensive "Workable Program" in depth designed to attack the overall problems that the renewal project was to solve. It can reasonably be inferred that the two together have encouraged localities to undertake larger, more complicated projects than they might have otherwise, and with a good deal more explicit soul-searching and community planning.

The federal urban renewal program involves several techniques and several types of projects. Initially the chief emphasis of the program was on residential redevelopment. Residential slums were cleared and new residential structures put in their place. In more

[1] 63 Stat. 413, 42 U.S.C. 1441-83 (1958); 68 Stat. 623, 42 U.S.C. 1450-60 (1958); 73 Stat. 672, 42 U.S.C. 1450-60 (Supp. 1960); 75 Stat. 149; 79 Stat. 474.

3

recent years, techniques other than massive land clearance for residential slums have received increasing attention—notably combinations of rehabilitation and spot clearance—and areas other than those that are predominantly residential have been brought under renewal—notably commercial, educational, and industrial.

## Evaluation of the Urban Renewal Program

This study attempts to produce an analytic framework for evaluating the urban renewal program. While the diversity of techniques and project types under the broad program complicates the problem, preeminent stress is laid here on a single type of project, a single technique—that of residential redevelopment. Originally this was the overriding focus of the urban renewal program, and it has been, and still is, the object of by far the largest part of the resource manipulation under the overall program.[2] Moreover, attention to it has a number of analytic advantages.

### Advantages of Focusing on Residential Redevelopment

First, it unearths a large number of the economic issues associated with urban renewal as a whole—many of them on a scale large enough (because of the "radicalism" of redevelopment as opposed to rehabilitation) that they can be isolated for analysis. In this it serves well as a convenient point of reference for less extreme, and less homogeneous, modifications. Second, as will be argued in more detail below, it is more amenable to general analysis than are other aspects of the program because a larger part of its benefits is at least explicable—if not immediately measurable—through welfare economic theory than are the benefits of other types of projects. Some of these others have benefits that are highly specific to particular situations. They are not easily included in a general analysis. Fi-

[2] Information is not available on the cost of predominantly residential projects, either in dollars or as a percentage of total gross project costs of all redevelopment projects. However, as of December 31, 1965, the proposed reuse was predominantly residential for 493 out of 1,133 projects for which new land uses had been reported. "Blighted residential area" was cited as the basis for urban renewal assistance to 808 out of 1,180 projects in an advanced planning stage or with contracts authorized. (U.S. Department of Housing and Urban Development).

nally, attention to residential redevelopment does not exclude attention to other techniques because the analysis constantly turns up relationships with the other programs. Residential redevelopment has important complementary relationships with some, important substitutive relationships with others. Because of its usefulness as a general analytic point of reference, it highlights the mutual associations of several of the different techniques.

Thus, an essentially systematic analysis of residential redevelopment is presented here, and from time to time the connection between the analysis and some other types of program emphasis is indicated, especially in the last two chapters. The scope of this study does not permit a full examination of the other types; but guidelines for analyzing them, as well as for evaluating the urban renewal program as a whole, are attempted.

### Need to Consider Other Aspects

The last point has another implication. Even if primary attention to residential redevelopment were intended to reflect exclusive interest in either residential problems or redevelopment as a technique, it could not be achieved successfully without considering other aspects of the urban renewal program. Other techniques are partly substitutive for redevelopment, partly complementary. Nonresidential operations sometimes enhance and sometimes interfere with residential projects. Thus, for one thing, evaluation in this policy area cannot be restricted to consideration of single specialized types of projects; it should consider the relative merits of different project *packages*. For another, an evaluation of residential redevelopment is not complete when it is compared only with the status quo. Other alternatives must be considered as well; and some of these alternatives themselves comprise other portions of the urban renewal program. So, for example, any rejection of redevelopment arising from a complete evaluation is not tantamount to rejection of urban renewal. Redevelopment might be deficient only in relation to the larger use of other techniques already included in the overall urban renewal program. With respect to both of these points then, the analysis in this book does not pretend to be complete. It offers only building blocks toward an understanding of both how project packages must be comprised to facilitate meaningful policy evaluation and how other techniques can substitute for residential redevelopment to achieve some of the large goals of urban renewal.

## Procedure Under Urban Renewal

The typical residential redevelopment project under the federal urban renewal program operates as follows: The local government (city council) draws up a Workable Program for community improvement, including blight eradication and prevention and "community improvement" through local instrumentalities like zoning, housing, building and health codes, and redevelopment. This Workable Program is submitted to the federal Renewal Assistance Administration (RAA) in the United States Department of Housing and Urban Development (HUD) for certification. Upon receipt of certification, a local urban renewal agency—the local public agency (LPA)—is designated. This may be a new body set up expressly for this purpose, or an existing government body (such as a housing department), or the local governing body as a whole. The LPA applies to the RAA to approve preliminary surveys and plans for specific projects and then the final plans for these projects. RAA approval makes the project(s) eligible for the substantial federal financial contribution stipulated in the federal program. A project proper begins with LPA designation of some blighted area as a redevelopment area. All real property within this area is then acquired by the LPA, either by negotiation or by condemnation under the right of eminent domain. The LPA is required to pay "fair value," based on two independent appraisals. Land assembly is followed by relocation of the tenants of acquired property. Households dislocated by redevelopment must be helped to find "decent, safe, and sanitary" housing elsewhere. Concrete provision by the LPA for such relocation is one of the main conditions for RAA approval of a redevelopment plan. Site clearance and preparation follow, with existing structures being demolished, the site being cleared, and improvements (streets, sewer systems, schools, lighting and other utilities) being adjusted or constructed as necessary. The final step is to dispose of the land to a private or public redeveloper (or redevelopers). The land is usually sold, or it may be leased for a long term. It is generally disposed of to a private redeveloper, and the site is usually subjected to a significant change in land use—often high-rise or large-scale upper-income and upper-middle-income housing projects. Recently there has been a trend toward using portions of such sites for modern commercial centers. If it is sold to a government body, the land is used for public housing or for other public purposes, like a park or school. Disposition completes the government's responsibility under redevelopment.[3]

## Dimensions of the Program

The role of the federal government in this process is to pass on the advance planning for the overall project, to lend working capital funds for planning, surveys, and acquisition, to compensate relocatees for their moving costs (since the 1964 legislation, this includes paying temporary rent supplements to households and cash grants to small businesses), and to finance up to two-thirds of the LPA's "net project cost."[4]

NET PROJECT COST. "Net project cost" is defined as the LPA's total expenditure on the project, less the receipts realized by selling prepared land to redevelopers. Under the 1949 act the federal government was authorized to spend $1 billion in loans and $500 million in grants over a five-year period. This was increased by a series of amendments in 1955, 1957, 1959, 1961, 1964, and 1965, so that grants may be as large as $6,150 million by 1968.[5]

NUMBER OF PROJECTS. As of December 31, 1965, 1,699 local urban renewal projects had contracts authorized by the Renewal Assistance Administration, of which 1,121 were in process or completed. For 1,109 of them the total gross project cost was $6.1 billion.

[3] For a detailed explanation of the redevelopment sequence showing the relationships among the several governmental jurisdictions involved, see statement by William L. Slayton, "Report on Urban Renewal," in *Urban Renewal,* Hearings before the Subcommittee on Housing, House Committee on Banking and Currency, 88 Cong. 1 sess. (November 1963), Pt. 2, pp. 441-45.

By an act of Congress of August 10, 1965, the independent U.S. Housing and Home Finance Agency became the Department of Housing and Urban Development. The Urban Renewal Administration, within the Agency, became the Renewal Assistance Administration in HUD.

[4] The federal government makes long-term loans available for any portions of the site that are leased rather than sold. (Ashley A. Foard and Hilbert Fefferman, "Federal Urban Renewal Legislation," *Law and Contemporary Problems,* Vol. 25 [Autumn 1960], p. 653.)

[5] The size of the grant authorization, not that of loans, becomes the convenient measure of the size of the authorized program, since "the loan authorization is a revolving fund which is replenished as loans are repaid when projects are completed." *Ibid.,* p. 655.

Proceeds from sale were expected to be $1.5 billion, or 25 percent, so that the anticipated net project cost was $4.6 billion, or 75 percent of the total. Of this amount, federal grant authorizations were $3.1 billion (50 percent of gross project cost), and local grants were $1.5 billion (25 percent of gross project cost).[6] The $3.1 billion of federal grant authorizations for urban renewal projects accounted for all but $0.2 billion of the $3.3 billion of contracts executed for all assistance under Title I of the Housing Act of 1949 and was substantially less than the total of $5.0 billion in grant reservations. Thus, federal grant authorizations had reached a level of $3.3 billion, 61 percent of the then statutory maximum. Projects were slow to get underway because of the substantial task of formulating proposals that would be approved by the agency administering the program then—the Urban Renewal Administration in the U.S. Housing and Home Finance Agency. Gradually, however, the pace of project applications, approvals, and operations has accelerated markedly. In 1950, 31 localities had projects; in 1953, 86; in 1958, 331; and by December 1965, 796. The cumulative number of projects initiated rose in this period from about 50 to more than 1,700. In the early years it was chiefly the larger cities that initiated projects, but gradually interest has spread to medium-sized and even small cities.[7]

SIZE OF THE FEDERAL PROGRAM. The federal urban renewal program is a large one. It draws on extensive federal and local governmental resources, and attracts many times as much in private development funds (for site acquisition and construction). As of June 30, 1963, for 479 projects in which some or all of the land was disposed of, the investment of private redevelopers was four times as great as the combined governmental expenses, and six times as great as the federal expenses.[8] Not only are the resources involved

---

[6] U.S. Department of Housing and Urban Development, Renewal Assistance Administration, *Urban Renewal Project Characteristics* (December 31, 1965), pp. 12-14.

[7] Slayton, *op. cit.*, pp. 408-09.

[8] *Ibid.* p. 425. The "private investment" component actually contains an additional federal involvement. Many of the mortgages that provide the financing for the private improvements are guaranteed by the Federal Housing Administration, and sometimes substantial proportions are held in the portfolio of the Federal National Mortgage Association. This latter group has been cited by Martin Anderson as being 55 percent of residential renewal mortgages and 27 percent of all private renewal construction. (*The Federal Bulldozer; a Critical Analysis of Urban Renewal, 1949-*

very substantial, their use affects tens of thousands of people in major localities and millions of people throughout the country in a way that is largely irreversible. Even a single urban renewal project can effect large-scale, often radical, changes in land-use patterns in a given city. A combination of projects for any city can significantly influence living patterns there. Such changes tend to ramify, influencing the configuration of transportation, of location of amenities, of decentralization of activities, and of urban-suburban relationships. The commitment of resources that results, linked together so broadly, would be very difficult to reverse in less than decades.

## Impact of the Program

Because the program is large and may make a deep and not easily alterable difference in urban living, it is important to be reasonably sure that it is well conceived. The sixteen years of experience can serve as a basis for evaluating the further usefulness of the program as it is now constituted. This book tries to set forth a conceptual framework in welfare economics for making this evaluation.

At the outset it must be pointed out that the task is extremely difficult. It has been claimed that numerous and diverse activities have been affected by the program. And some of the impacts are notably subtle and troublesome to pin down. Not only is quantitative measurement difficult, even qualitative judgments are hard to make for some kinds of effects. Not all the knotty problems are solved in this study, but an attempt is made to discover what many of the problems are and, where they cannot be solved, at least to set out their irreducible hard core.

DECENTRALIZATION. The ultimate concern is the overall renewal program, but the problem is approached by focusing attention on

*1962* [MIT Press, 1964], pp. 129-38.) But figures this high rest on the misconception that FNMA is a direct loan agency with permanent market commitments instead of being a secondary market facility designed to keep the market orderly by periodic buying, and selling. Since Anderson wrote his book, the percentage has declined appreciably, with FNMA selling off previously held mortgages in line with its function as a secondary facility. I am indebted to Mr. Sylvan Kamm of the Renewal Assistance Administration for this clarification.

Notwithstanding this qualification, the federal "policy resources" poured into the overall program make it one of the substantial domestic operations of the federal government.

residential redevelopment. Yet even within the category of residential redevelopment, individual projects differ markedly, largely because of the way in which the program is administered by the RAA. In part because of a lack of explicit legislative direction, in part in order to encourage widespread local participation, the RAA administers the program with maximum decentralization. The projects have been shaped by local authorities to meet their particular needs; and the selection among projects has been made by local authorities as well. The RAA has not tried to ration its available resources on the basis of some criterion of priority. For one thing, it has not generally behaved as though its authorization power were subject to resource limitations.[9] For another, it has not considered that it is authorized to pass on the wisdom of locally proposed projects. Essentially it has imposed as conditions only that a properly comprehensive, consistent Workable Program be formulated by the locality, that the specific project details be technically feasible, and that a technically feasible relocation program be undertaken.

VARIETY OF PROJECTS. The administration of the program may make it more difficult to evaluate by greatly increasing the variety of projects. But this itself constitutes a characteristic of the program that must be evaluated. The lack of centrally-imposed conditions has welfare implications if the policy incentives of the local program formulators differ systematically from those of the federal agency administering the program. This is considered at length below. Moreover, even if incentives do not diverge, the lack of any central criterion of relative priorities has an important educative effect in the planning of local projects, even in a period in which RAA imposes no overall budgeting constraints. It influences local priorities.

If the task were simply to evaluate the redevelopment program retrospectively, one might proceed by enumerating all of the individual projects in the program. Less precisely, one could try to describe an "average" experience—the "typical" project—although arriving at such an "average" without full enumeration would be tricky. But the ultimate task is to assess the desirability of the program in the future. This is more complex than generalizing about past experience. Future projects may differ from previous ones for

---

[9] When actual shortages have occurred, waiting lists have been established on a first-come, first-served basis.

two reasons: (1) There may be systematic selectivity between projects initiated in the early years after enactment of the program—say, within the first fifteen years—and those that come later. Speed may be indicative of urgency, which may in turn be indicative of the "need" for the project (although such a relationship could be obscured by the fact that by the time later projects were formulated situations might have developed to make them at least as urgent as any earlier projects). (2) As a result of the experience with earlier projects, or as a result of the exhaustion of first priority projects, changes are made in the design and character of later ones.

The first problem is not intractable. If there are any systematic differences in urgency, these should already have appeared over the sixteen years since the program was begun. Examination of the features of earlier and later projects, together with interviews with the planning authorities involved, should be enough to indicate whether or not such differences exist. Extrapolation of any trend revealed would be a reasonable way to predict the future of the program.

The second difficulty is more troublesome. The kinds of revisions that have already occurred are in the record; but the revisions and changes in emphasis to come are not clear. The best one can do is to examine the changes that have already taken place, discover by direct questioning of authorities the changes that are about to be made in projects now being drawn up, and try to determine the weaknesses remaining in present projects that might be rectified.

While it is hoped that a contribution will be made toward the prospective evaluation of the whole redevelopment program, the scope of this book precludes real consideration of the variety and temporal drift of projects. The task undertaken here is the more modest one of evaluating a single *abstract* local project. The question of variety is not omitted entirely, however. The examination of the kinds of benefits that come from the program includes also consideration of the kinds of objectives that have been set for it. The different sorts of projects that have been undertaken are investigated here, but the detailed analysis that follows applies to the classic residential project.

## Analytical Method

In Chapter XI a numerical illustration of the method of analysis applied to actual projects is presented. The data refer to a number of completed redevelopment projects in Chicago. The measurements do not pretend to represent serious empirical findings. They are advanced only to indicate how the analytic method would be applied and what difficulties might be met in collecting the appropriate data.

To simplify the exposition and facilitate comparison with other types of government expenditure programs, all of the distinctive consequences of urban renewal will be treated as "benefits," only the impact of the financing of the program being reserved for the "cost" side. Thus the "benefits" side will include some negative (undesirable) consequences as well as positive ones.[10] The overall benefit impact will be taken "net" in the sense that the two kinds of effects are consolidated. The advantage of this is that, with "costs" restricted to the impact of financing only (both real resource costs and their distributional effects), it is possible to take advantage of specialized studies of differential tax effects that do not depend on the specific government expenditure programs to which they are attached. Not every benefit-cost study should have to re-evaluate the economic effects of an income tax, a sales tax, or a property tax. It should be enough to indicate the total amount to be financed and the composition of its financing, and then quantify the overall effects by referring to the specialized—and hence standardized—tax studies. The cost side is sketched below.

The federal government, out of general revenues, pays two-thirds of the "net project cost" (defined above) and makes relocation payments to households dislocated from the redevelopment site. This is clearly the lion's share of the real resource cost of the program. The local government pays one-third of the net project cost, financed preponderantly out of local property taxes. This share may take the form of money and/or the value of improvements (utilities, etc.) put into the site by the local government *or* put anywhere so long as they are intended to function substantially for the benefit of the subsequent site uses (as, for example, a school located off the site proper but intended primarily for use by future site inhabitants). Thus each project involves a redistribution of income from the nation at large to the locality in question. And tak-

[10] The impact of government investment in this functional area on private investment should ideally be treated here.

ing the program as a whole, and accounting roughly for the incidence of federal and city tax systems, there is probably some redistribution from rural and probably suburban areas to urban areas. This should be kept in mind during the detailed analysis of benefits and their distribution.

Further attention will be paid to the cost side in the context of social discounting. However, for the reason given above, no attempt will be made to make a systematic study of the impact of financing. Moreover, since a full quantitative evaluation of particular projects is not presented, more general tax studies are not used to estimate impact magnitudes. In the empirical illustration in Chapter X net project cost figures are introduced and—together with the 2:1 sharing between federal and local sources—are used as a first-level estimate of the amount of resources expended to bring about the project objectives. Studies more expressly addressed to evaluating particular projects—*ex post* or *ex ante*—should, of course, make a more profound analysis of the real cost impact.

## Summary of Findings

The first half of this study analyzes the nature of the benefits from urban renewal. Urban renewal has varied and complicated effects (some direct, some indirect) on the lives of many people. There is no convenient market in which to observe how much the affected parties are willing to pay for the bundle of consequences. The dimensions over which renewal has its effects must be simplified in order to make progress toward benefit-cost measurement.

### Benefits of Urban Renewal

It is assumed here that the avowed or implicit goals of the program delineate the major dimensions of consequence. Particularly in the case of residential redevelopment, three goals seem most important: (1) slum elimination, (2) subsidization to enhance the competitive economic viability of central city activities within metropolitan areas, (3) subsidization to augment the financial resources of central city governments.

All three affect the level of real income as well as its distribution, but in different degrees. For the second goal, effects on distribution[11] are overwhelmingly important relative to effects on level. This is somewhat less so for the third goal. Only for the first category, however, are the income-level effects substantial relative to the distributional, though even here distributional consequences are important. In this analysis, therefore, predominant—but not exclusive—stress is laid on slum elimination.

SLUM REMOVAL BENEFITS. Benefits from slum removal are not straightforward. The existence of poverty, together with the technological characteristics of the housing industry (notably the substantial durability of housing units), make the provision of low-quality, low-quantity housing in the form of old structures a presumptively efficient market utilization of resources. In these terms, eliminating units at the low end of the housing stock and replacing less than 100 percent of them (as is usually the case) at a much higher quality level can mean a serious misallocation of resources. Through the effects on the relative composition of the stock, this can also have a regressive impact on income distribution.

But the housing market does not operate either perfectly or naturally, and slums tend to be produced out of an interplay of imperfections and external interferences in that market. Chief among these are the considerable market externalities in land use involved in "neighborhood effects," the market disabilities of many of the consumers in that sector of the market, and the discouragement to abandonment and new investment due to tax laws and the unavailability of credit to property owners in the same sector. In addition, the sheer existence of slum living patterns imposes external social costs on inhabitants and noninhabitants alike and thus adds to the suboptimality of resource allocation reflected by slums.

[11] Distribution not only among households but among activities and geographic locations and political jurisdictions. These distributional effects might be termed level-of-income effects as well, since they are often designed to fulfill certain alleged "public goals." And such fulfillment can be spoken of as increasing the "real social welfare" of the community. This meaning of "income level" is excluded here. The term is used to denote only augmentation of the fulfillment of "private goals." This does not mean that public goals have no reality or no value. It means only that welfare economic analysis is designed to make evaluations not of public-goal fulfillment but only of private-goal fulfillment. Where public goals are involved, it is for political evaluation, not for economic analysis, to call out aggregate values.

Since slums do represent suboptimal resource use, their elimination can potentially reap benefits. The problem for public policy is to determine whether the costs are low enough to warrant seeking the benefits, that is, to try to compare the benefits with the costs. Delineation of the kinds of benefits attainable is crucial. There are three main sources of benefits. The first stems from enabling resource users to take the important land-use externalities into account in their resource decisions—to "internalize the externalities." The large-scale assembly of land made economically feasible by redevelopment increases the productivity of the land in the project site by opening up additional productive options. Land can be used to take full advantage of neighborhood effects.

The second lies in the fact that removing slums and replacing them with higher-quality clusterings improves the neighborhood for nearby property and genuinely enhances its quality. This represents a positive external effect, not just a relative change in locational advantages.

The third results from the sheer destruction of slum dwellings. This forcibly decreases the total amount of slum occupancy, but is offset to varying degrees by the creation of new slums or the worsening of still-existing slums through the large-scale relocation of households dislocated by redevelopment. Whatever *net* decrease in slum occupancy occurs tends to reduce the social costs generated by slum living.

Slum removal has important effects on the structure of the housing stock that influence relative prices and can considerably affect the distribution of real income. Projects have substantial lead time, usually destroy more units than they construct, and usually replace very low quality units with high to very high quality units (although some trend toward more modest—but specialized group —replacement qualities is discernible). The result is a regressive income redistribution, with lower-income groups who consume at the lower end of the housing stock suffering most, and higher-income groups who consume at the affected higher end of the housing stock benefiting most. These distributional effects must be considered in a benefit-cost analysis, since the local government level of decision making does not have the rich range of policy instrumentalities for effecting "pure" distribution changes that is open to the federal government.

SUBSIDY TO THE CENTRAL CITY. The second and third major goals listed above—subsidization of the central city and central city government—are important chiefly for their redistribution effects. As was noted above, some of the subsidy directions reflect "social goals" and are not subject to welfare economic evaluation. But the third, relating to local government, does bear an aspect that can be treated as a level-of-income effect under welfare analysis. Just as the efficiency of private decision making about resource use can be scrutinized, so too can that of comparable public decision making. There are grounds for believing that within metropolitan areas the federalist jumble of local jurisdictions, when coupled with the continued centripetal focus of the central city for many economic activities, sometimes makes for a systematic inefficiency in resource use by the central city government. Grants from higher levels of government to the central city government in such cases decrease the degree of inefficiency. The federal urban renewal program acts as such an intergovernmental grant, because the 2:1 formula for federal-local sharing of costs makes it almost certain that increased tax assessments on redeveloped land and structures will produce more in revenues for the city government than its share of project costs. In some cases, therefore, intergovernmental subsidization results in the kind of improved overall resource use that can be called a real income gain. But these cases are not general and must be established on a case-by-case basis.

The sources of income-level (or "aggregate") benefits are: (1) increased productivity of land on the redevelopment site, (2) enhanced value of nearby land and improvements, (3) a decrease in the social costs due to slum living, and (4) increased efficiency of public decision making in some metropolitan areas. In addition, there is the regressive distributional impact deriving from the change in the structure of the housing stock. (Other distributional effects are associated, as this one is not, with subsidization of activities, locations, groups, and political jurisdictions to achieve alleged specific social goals. Such effects must be paired with the valuation of the corresponding social goals in the overall accounting and are therefore excluded from this study.)

The list of benefits given here differs importantly from that of other treatments. Since the welfare focus here is the national economy and full employment is assumed, the value of improvements on the redevelopment site is not necessarily an indicator of overall social benefit. Neither is the volume of residential construction or even of total construction, nor the total income of the affected central city. Moreover, the increase in city government revenues is not necessarily a relevant benefit. Hence, the differences between its revenue gains and its share of net project costs is not a good measure of the social value of a redevelopment project.

One implication of the analysis that led to these conclusions is that the extreme decentralization in the administration of the national program probably results in systematic departures from optimal public resource decisions. Central city governments fashion their projects with an eye toward their own constituents and the condition of their own treasuries, while these projects purposely affect wider audiences, and often in deliberately adverse ways. Some integration of decision making is warranted under the program.

### Sources and Measurement of Benefits

The second half of this study examines extensively these sources of benefit (including the relevant distributional effects) in order to measure them. All four kinds of aggregate effects, as well as the magnitude of the distributional effect, are measurable in principle; but they are difficult to measure. Some are so difficult as to seem almost unmeasurable. This is true especially of the social cost of slum living. Here some of the dimensions of impact concern "commodities" that never appear in a relevant form in any market —for example, the value of a human life or of interpersonal harmony. Other benefits are easier to measure, such as the productivity gain to site land.

This book considers all these benefits but has more to say about components easier to subject to economic analysis than about the others. Unfortunately, the categories that are difficult to quantify cannot simply be disregarded in favor of those that are more tractable. The former may in fact include the most important benefits that result from urban renewal. Therefore, this examination of the former does not terminate with the discovery that a single homogeneous value dimension (money) may not be feasible for empirical studies. Next an attempt is made to throw light on the several dimensions of consequence that can be discerned and to probe the factors that determine how measurement can be made in those dimensions.

In Chapter XI the data from five completed residential redevelopment projects in Chicago are submitted to the procedure developed in this study. This is not intended as a serious empirical study of these projects but rather as a pilot application to discover where the method will proceed easily and where serious computational difficulties will be encountered. There is little intrinsic significance in the totals because of the omissions and the oversimplified form of some of the data included, but the size of some of the components that have been more effectively measured may be considered rough approximations. The illustrations reinforce the earlier fear that satisfactory measurement will be difficult. They do point out, however, that portions of the data, while inaccessible to the very modest scope of estimation in this study, will yield substantial returns with even slightly increased effort. Portions that seem inaccessible even to larger increments of effort are also discussed. In the main, the chapter focuses on the steps that must be taken beyond the techniques it offers in order to ensure progress.

The final two chapters treat briefly various issues in the current discussions on public policy with regard to renewal. Relations among the several complementary and competitive elements in renewal policy are examined, and alternative combinations are spelled out. Some comparisons are made of the treatment in this study with other discussions in the recent policy literature. Similarities and differences are noted and explained, and some preliminary broad guidelines for public policy are suggested.

# CHAPTER II

# Criteria and Method

THE METHOD USED HERE in evaluating policy is a form of the popular applied welfare economic technique known as benefit-cost analysis.[1] In this technique the policy alternatives are specified, one of them is designated—or implicitly treated as—the base alternative, and the various consequences of the others are expressed as differences from this base. The base alternative is usually, but not always, a status quo policy. The consequences are the positive and

[1] The scope of this book precludes giving anything like a detailed exposition of benefit-cost analysis. A useful recent survey of much of the literature is given in A. R. Prest and R. Turvey, "Cost-Benefit Analysis: A Survey," *Economic Journal*, Vol. 75 (December 1965). For a systematic treatment in the context of water resource development, the field in which it has had its most extensive use, see, for example, Maynard M. Hufschmidt, John Krutilla, Julius Margolis, and Stephen A. Marglin, *Report of Panel of Consultants to the Bureau of the Budget on Standards and Criteria for Formulating and Evaluating Federal Water Resources Development* (June 30, 1961); Roland McKean, *Efficiency in Government Through Systems Analysis* (Wiley, 1958); Otto Eckstein, *Water-Resource Development; the Economics of Project Evaluation* (Harvard University Press, 1958). For a number of attempts to apply benefit-cost analysis to programs other than water resources, see Robert Dorfman (ed.), *Measuring Benefits of Government Investments* (Brookings Institution, 1965). A programmatic treatment for urban government decision making is given in Nathaniel Lichfield and Julius Margolis, "Benefit-Cost Analysis as a Tool in Urban Government Decision Making," presented at the Conference on Public Expenditure Decisions in the Urban Community, Washington, D.C. (May 15, 1962).

negative changes in well-being of everyone who is at all affected by each policy in question. Wherever possible these changes in well-being are calculated in money terms.

## An Approach to Benefit-Cost Analysis

Underlying this approach is the assumption that individual preferences (values) are accepted as the measure of changes in well-being. The money value of these changes is obtained wherever possible from actual market transactions or, where such transactions do not occur, from valuations based on actual or hypothetical transactions. No reference is made directly to "social well-being." The consequences of governmental actions are all traced back to the fulfillment of wants of individuals (or of households).

The real income level of these individuals is, strictly speaking, a vector of their well-being, but benefit-cost analysis passes beyond the injunction in Paretian welfare economics against interpersonal comparisons and aggregates the money value of real income changes across individuals. However, the extent of such aggregation is controversial. There is no generally accepted method in welfare economics for aggregating the diverse welfare effects on different individuals, since there is no generally accepted way to compare the social meaning of the well-being of different individuals or of changes in well-being. Usually the aggregate of money income of all individuals in the system is treated as "total income" (or "total output"),[2] and a distinction is made between the "level of income" and the "distribution of income." Where this is done, often the first type of change is emphasized as the important one, with any undesirable distributional changes being considered reversible through income transfer policies having little to do with the functional area under consideration. This exclusion of distribution may be useful in studies on the federal level, since the federal income tax could

[2] Since not all kinds of impact on individual welfare can be expressed in money terms, there is a problem of aggregation within each individual as well as across individuals. But this can be partly treated as is the latter problem. If, for example, we cannot give a money value to the aesthetic impact on each individual resulting from renewal, we may preserve it as a separate welfare dimension and consider how to aggregate entries in this dimension across individuals. The overall welfare comparisons will then involve matrices rather than vectors, one or more aggregate money income components, *and* one or more components for each of these supplementary dimensions.

sometimes be used to achieve the desired redistribution. But in a municipal setting, the local government has no comparable tool to affect distribution directly. Therefore, in the present instance, while it will be useful to try to indicate where the effects on total output or income occur, the distributional consequences of redevelopment projects must be included as one of their essential characteristics.

The procedure, therefore, is two-fold. On the one hand, changes in total (or aggregate) real income are indicated, with primary stress on the nature of each change and its source. Some of these changes are visible in actual market transactions and valuations, but some have to be inferred. The bases for inference are presumptive visible improvements in consumption levels and presumptive improvements in the efficiency with which resources are adapted to achieve output goals. Visible output consequences need not be observed under the latter so long as there is ground for believing that efficiency of input use is enhanced. No effort is made to locate the particular individuals who benefit (or lose) from such total income changes. On the other hand, where income redistribution is involved, the source of the redistribution is indicated and the individuals affected are identified. The latter task is not an easy one.

The difficulty is the cited absence of a generally accepted method of welfare aggregation. Thus, considerations of income distribution have generally been ignored in economic studies. Some attempts have been made to incorporate distribution in a welfare analysis,[3] and while no one has been highly successful, a benefit-cost analysis can profit from them.

A reasonable minimal procedure is to aggregate the money value of program consequences, positive and negative (net benefits), for each individual, thereby giving his net position. But empirical applicability requires additional aggregation over groups of individuals. Monetary magnitudes and other measures of the effect can, of

[3] See, for example, I. M. D. Little, *A Critique of Welfare Economics* (Oxford University Press, 1950); Franklin M. Fisher, "Income Distribution, Value Judgments, and Welfare," *Quarterly Journal of Economics,* Vol. 70 (August 1956), pp. 380-424; Robert Strotz, "How Income Ought to be Distributed: A Paradox in Distributive Ethics," *Journal of Political Economy,* Vol. 66 (June 1958), pp. 189-205; John Harsanyi, "Cardinal Welfare, Individualistic Ethics, and Interpersonal Comparison of Utility," *Journal of Political Economy,* Vol. 63 (August 1955), pp. 309-21; and Jerome Rothenberg, *The Measurement of Social Welfare* (Prentice-Hall, 1961).

course, be aggregated at will for *descriptive* purposes. The problem is to determine which types of aggregation have normative significance as well. It is assumed in this study that the social expression of value judgments about distribution are related—although by no means perfectly—to certain central social decision making processes,[4] and that in a representative democracy governmental processes bear elements of this centrality. Therefore, a form of aggregation in which the aggregated groups represent individuals who would both themselves tend to behave similarly with respect to urban renewal issues in the political process *and* be perceived by others as having to be treated similarly would tend to approximate the relative weights given to these groups in the political process. These groupings would include individuals whose fortunes society treats interchangeably. And this is, at least under the present conception of social value judgments, a basis for normative aggregation.

Aggregates of this sort may be formed by analyzing the various kinds of consequences of urban renewal projects. Each type defines a number of functional groups, for example, those greatly benefited, those seriously hurt, those essentially unaffected. These groups are identified through an analysis of the consequences. For example, one result of renewal projects is the effect on the relative stocks of low-rental and high-rental housing. Low-income families, especially in the slum area being renewed, are likely to be quite similarly affected. Another consequence may be the effect on the balance between small neighborhood commercial enterprises and large chain enterprises. To facilitate the parallel between economic and political effect, the larger impact groups may be subdivided into some of the stereotype groups most perceived in political decision making—such as poor-rich, white-nonwhite, central city dwellers-suburbanites, workers-executives, and so on. This pattern of aggregation can be followed for non-pecuniary measures of effect as well as for the pecuniary ones.

## The Advantages

The advantages of the procedure are that, at least for each well-understood effect, those affected similarly know it not simply as an

[4] See Rothenberg, *op. cit.*, Chap. 13.

individual, but as a *common,* effect, and others also perceive this. Thus the affected group has its voting dispositions influenced similarly, and others know that they must take this group disposition into account. For less definite effects of the program, the direction of political mobilization is the same, but the intensity of mobilization is less.

Social value judgments about distribution do not depend solely on relative voting power, however. When it is indicated that unaffected persons must take into account project impacts on affected groups, this does not mean that people vote only for their own well-being and are indifferent to the well-being of others. They may have preferences about overall patterns of income distribution. If so, voting results will not simply mirror an income distribution that is the counterpart of relative voting power. Our suggested subgrouping of affected individuals into "political stereotypes" facilitates the use of such preferences about distribution in actual benefit-cost applications.

Finally, the procedure for ascertaining distributional effects is distinct from that of measuring so-called aggregate net income effects. Where distributional considerations are not important in making a choice, or where the policy alternatives have similar distributional effects, the first part of the method can still be used to compute a grand total benefit-cost ratio or the difference between urban renewal and other measures having the same dimension.

## The Problems

This method has difficulties of course. First is the still-arbitrary nature of the aggregation: the nature of the interpersonal comparisons involved in the aggregation cannot be guaranteed to bear a close relation to what might be derived from the society's social welfare function if such indeed exists. This is a familiar complaint, but the rationale for aggregation does pretend to have normative thrust. The vulnerability of the method on this score depends on the degree to which the political mechanism conforms with consensual values actually held in the society. And it depends even more basically on the reader's acceptance of this whole approach to the question of normative judgments in welfare economics.

The second problem is one of dismemberment. If an individual is grouped according to how he is affected by a particular dimension of consequence, then he may be counted in more than one group if he is affected in more than one way by a particular policy. This means that the analysis will exclude most effects on each individual's well-being that stem from the interrelatedness to him of different dimensions of policy consequence. The only interactions that might still be accounted for would be those in which essentially the same collection of individuals appeared in the same set of multiple groupings. Dismemberment is admittedly a defect, but given the margin of error appearing throughout the evaluation, it is probably minor. It is, in any case, a price that will have to be paid if a simple grouping is desired.

The third problem concerns the comparability, not of individuals, but of the policy alternatives. If two alternatives have differing consequence dimensions—that is, one relates to debtors-creditors and tenants-landlords, the other to property income-labor income, commercial property-residential property—then the benefit-cost groups accounted for will differ under the two alternatives (although with some overlap). This means that unless there is some way of either disaggregating to any desired grouping or aggregating all the way to a single appropriate scalar measure of the welfare of the group, the alternatives will not be comparable. The first means essentially giving up the enormous computational advantage of grouping by consequence. The second, were it available, would make superfluous any procedure providing disaggregation. The relatively *ad hoc* procedure now under discussion is considered because a uniquely appropriate total welfare aggregation is impossible to obtain. Again the defect must be acknowledged. The problem will be minimized when the pattern of overlapping groups is easily recognizable.

To summarize, a version of benefit-cost analysis will be used that stands somewhere between an enumeration of individuals and total group aggregation. The grouping of individuals that implicitly defines the social comparability of different individuals rests on a simple pragmatic basis, not on profound welfare analysis. The method has defects in application. Nonetheless it has advantages—ease of computation and proximity to the kind of categorization that is appropriate for political decision making—and is probably the best procedure to use here.

It is important to understand that the choice of this form of benefit-cost analysis automatically decides an important question about the nature of the evaluational criterion to be used. The criterion calls for a maximization of welfare among a relevant *population*, not for a maximization of property values in the relevant area.

## The Relevant Population

The next question to be answered is: Which is the "relevant" population whose well-being should be reflected? Is it the population living and working in the redevelopment area? Or is it the population of a wider encompassing neighborhood, or the population of the city as a whole, or of the metropolitan area that includes the city, or of the entire United States? The answer to this question is not easy. Strictly speaking, since the decision-making level of the major source of financing is federal, the well-being of the entire population of the United States should be considered. But the broader population is involved chiefly in financing some of the costs of the program through taxation. The truly distinctive benefits of urban renewal, in the larger sense, are contained principally within the population of the metropolitan area where each project is located. The decision to concentrate on the benefits side of the benefit-cost analysis means that reference to the population of the United States as a whole can be omitted, on the theory that the program implicitly represents a mandate from that population to redistribute real income, by achieving certain public purposes, in favor of the population of those metropolitan areas that choose to enter the program. Thus, by implication, the program will be warranted—*relative to other potential policies*—in terms of a comparison between its overall costs and the benefits accruing to these relevant metropolitan populations. It is assumed that the federal government, as chief decision maker, values the improvement in real income of these populations in terms of the latter's own preferences, since the "federal purposes" sought are not ulterior to, but simply comprise, such improvement.

The analysis will not entirely neglect the broader United States context, however. There are important resource spillovers across metropolitan areas. Large-scale construction in one community taps national resources that might otherwise have been used in other communities. Attraction of industry to one area precludes its location elsewhere. Expansion of university and hospital facilities in one locality uses not only construction resources but also, at least in the short run, specialized manpower that would—or could—have been used elsewhere (indeed, that may have had to be attracted from use elsewhere). In such situations explicit account is taken of these alternative costs for resource use in any particular locality. The accretion of these resources for use by the locality in question is considered a net benefit only to the extent that its local use in question has a social value in excess of its value in its next most advantageous use elsewhere.

Thus, this evaluation will focus on the metropolitan population relevant for each project or cluster of projects. But it is important to note that it is the *metropolitan* population that is involved, not simply the city or neighborhood. Housing units, commercial and cultural facilities, and industrial sites in the central city have close substitutes in the suburbs. Indeed, the central city government takes explicit account of this substitutability in fashioning its renewal projects. It tries to attract middle-income and upper-income families back from the suburbs into central city housing. It tries to improve the competitive position of downtown commerce relative to outlying shopping centers. It tries to attract desirable industries either *from* outlying areas, or to the central city *instead of* to outlying areas from other metropolitan clusters.

This approach raises some fundamental problems. Within metropolitan areas most, but not all, renewal projects generally, and redevelopment projects especially, have been creatures of the central city governments. With the general absence of metropolitan government, there have been no projects planned or executed by decision makers responsible to the metropolitan area as a whole. These projects have been shaped by the central city planners, with only minimal direction from the federal government, as was indicated above. The central city decision makers are responsible to the city population alone. The outlying metropolitan population, while affected in varying degrees depending on the particular project, has no political representation in these projects. Methodologically, this introduces an important slippage in the whole procedure. It is tacit in the use of benefit-cost analysis that policy makers will be attracted to benefits and repelled by costs. But if the policy makers take no legal responsibility for a significant part of the affected population—that is, they are not responsive to their well-being—then costs to the outlying metropolitan population will not necessarily be repelling nor benefits attractive. A metropolitan benefit-cost comparison for different alternatives will be irrelevant to the decision makers insofar as costs and benefits to that population have been included. Yet the attempt to solve this by computing benefits and costs only for the politically represented population leads to the dilemma that the analysis must, nonetheless, be inclusive enough to answer to the national interest; and this implies that the well-being of every significantly affected group of Americans must be included. The more inclusive metropolitan criterion is chosen here at the risk of being jurisdictionally irrelevant at present.

This choice is important. There are grounds for believing that central city and metropolitan evaluations may diverge markedly. All types of renewal projects affect the attractiveness of central city sites *relative* to suburban sites as locations for various activities—residential, commercial, industrial, and cultural. They typically involve subsidizing the enhancement of the former relative to—and often at the expense of—the latter. Thus, at the core of these projects is an important element of competition between city and suburbs. Except insofar as this sweetening of the city is meant to attract members of the suburban population to subsidized resource use in the city (as under residential projects), this engenders a competitive relationship between the respective populations. So their valuations of project benefits can differ greatly.

The implication of a significant divergence between the scope of planning responsibility and that of project effect is that planning choices may well be seriously suboptimal. Hence, a supplementary purpose in the decision to focus on the broader population is to throw into relief the consequence of operating the program within the present set of jurisdictional boundaries. It serves, therefore, as further evidence of the desirability of additional techniques of governmental cooperation and/or integration on a metropolitan level.

It might be argued that this procedure is a serious weakness in the study. While the metropolitan focus is theoretically appropriate, there is no real likelihood that anything like metropolitan government is attainable within the near—and relevant—future. Thus, a study with such a focus might be irrelevant to the needs of present decision makers. But this is not the case. It must not be forgotten that the conception of the overall program is federal, and the major burden of financing is federal. The extreme decentralization of administration, whereby all important characteristics of actual projects are determined locally, stems partly from the belief that localities know their own needs best (as well as from the belief that localities would stay out of the program if significant federal intervention were the price of participation). But the conception of the program does not require such nearly complete absence of federal guidelines. Indeed, the very increase in the program's popularity makes it likely that additional federal guidelines will be necessary. As the total local demand begins to exceed the resources available, so that capital rationing is required, some criteria of the relative desirability, or the relative urgency, of different projects will have to be formulated and applied at the federal level. These criteria could easily take into account the extent to which the project counts transfers at the expense of the outlying population as benefits, or transfers benefiting the outlying population as costs, or neglects other important effects on the remainder of the metropolitan population. Information transmitted to localities about the inclusion of metropolitan effects in the federal criterion for aid would influence central city planners in formulating projects to meet their needs. This need not prevent localities from fashioning projects to fit the particularities of their problems.

But there is a more important objection to this approach. Much of the explanation and justification of the program from official sources, and much of the actual experience with it indicates that a major purpose (or perhaps *the* major purpose) of the program is to revitalize the central city by improving the financial situation of the central city government. This improvement would come by increasing the tax base of the city government and decreasing its unnecessary expenditures. Slum removal is an objective in this context because slums are alleged to cost the city a large amount in public services while providing only a small tax base. In other words, the government "loses" money on slums. Elimination of slums through redevelopment is alleged to decrease the costs and increase the tax base. Similarly, improvement of the city's commercial attractiveness increases tax revenues without resort to tax rate increases. Also attraction of additional "desirable" industries adds to the tax rolls a property use that typically adds much to the tax base while requiring a low level of public services and thus earns a "profit" for the city government.

At the heart of the renewal program, therefore, is an intention to help the central city and its government. What better way than to allow the governmental representatives of the community to plan the betterment of both and to subsidize implementation of the plan? Thus the limited perspective of the central city may from this point of view be the very substance of one of the public goals of the federal program. To adopt a wider perspective would appear to conflict with the spirit of the program.

Although this suggestion has merit, acceptance would be undesirable. Subsidization of cities and city governments is not the only goal of the program. Thus it must be done with as little interference as possible with the attainment of the other goals. To accomplish this, it must be possible to gauge the separate contributions to welfare of various levels of such subsidization, as well as benefits to be derived from the attainment of the other goals. But such a separation of benefits cannot be performed if decision making is based on the principle of maximum subsidized benefit. It is preferable to adopt the broader perspective advocated above and *through that perspective* to evaluate city subsidization as simply one of several types of benefit. This approach is feasible because at least some of the benefits that stem from city subsidization are amenable to welfare analysis. Something other than simply a redistribution is discernible.

Benefits will be evaluated here, therefore, from the perspective of the entire metropolitan community. From this point of view the welfare significance of city (including city government) subsidization will be estimated, as well as the fulfillment of other program goals. This will furnish a consistent and unbiased frame of reference for welfare analysis.

## Contrast of Evaluative Foci

The procedure formulated above implies criteria different from those presumably used by federal and local administrators of the urban renewal program. While that procedure is not seriously irrelevant to the problems faced by these administrators, it does differ in certain respects from what is understood to be the evaluative process of government policy makers and administrators. The different approaches should not be considered as necessarily incompatible, however. They stem from perspectives based on radically different operational roles. This distinction will be sketched briefly.

The crucial fact is that administrators are operating programs that are limited in form by specific legislation. They may, for example, be limited by the terms of the program to relate their aims to a special population as clients. Positive or negative effects for individuals other than these clients are disregarded. Or, they may be trying to effect changes in a particular field for a given population (as, for example, transportation) and will disregard the effects of their actions on other fields. Evaluations based on such perspectives will of course be partial in both senses of the term.

In addition to this, their evaluations are likely to be absolute instead of relative. Administrators may believe that there are alternative ways of bringing about some of the achievements of the present program (for example, by modified versions of the program), but they are likely to deprecate the possibility of obtaining such alternatives as deliberate substitutes for the present program. Thus, they feel bound by the present program, not only in terms of its limitation of scope in labeling relevant beneficiaries and types of benefits (and costs), but also in terms of the existence of feasible alternative ways of achieving these particular types of benefits for these particular beneficiaries. These benefits will be obtained from the present policy, or they will not be obtained at all. Thus, they are inclined to underestimate the social opportunity cost of achieving certain ends under the given program—to make judgments about absolute achievements rather than about the program's achievements relative to those attainable by alternative programs.

In contrast, an outside evaluator need not be bound by the particular constraints of the given program. An explicit treatment of the total relevant population and of all dimensions of effect can be given. And various alternatives to the given program can be explicitly considered, so that the true social opportunity costs, or social *net* benefits, can be computed, instead of only *gross* benefits. An example of the latter difference is in the treatment of new construction in the redevelopment site, which will be discussed below. Administrators tend to treat any such construction as a total benefit produced by the program, failing to deduct the value of the output that would have been produced by the same resources if they were released for other uses.

It is not intended to suggest that the administrator's attitude is dishonest or even, from his point of view, wrong. The point being made is that the evaluative schema proposed here is not formulated from the administrator's point of view. It is based on an outsider's overall welfare focus, though it is not irrelevant to the problems of public policy. It is intended to be relevant to the role of the broad policy maker—in this case, the Congress of the United States. Thus, since the program is a federal one and the population of net beneficiaries is broader than that serviced by the local operative jurisdiction, impacts on the metropolitan population may usefully be studied. Any suboptimalities that may arise because of a cleavage between the population whose interests are *represented* in local projects and those actually *affected* by the projects may also usefully be pointed out. Such information is relevant to the broad federal political decision as to what character a federal urban renewal program should take. Admittedly again, it *is* less relevant to how local officials should select projects when subject to only minor constraints by the RAA.

CHAPTER III

# Elimination of Blight and Slums

As THE DISCUSSION so far has indicated, this study seeks to trace the positive and negative effects of urban renewal on the well-being of all involved individuals. No amendment need be made to this for the treatment of so-called "social goods."[1] This study is not a manipulation of theory for its own sake, however. It seeks to fashion a technique that will facilitate empirical measurement, and thus the need to deal with "social goods" will require some modification.

Urban renewal projects do not simply change the amount and quality of some goods and services; they may bring about extensive changes in the whole pattern of urban living activities. As has long been recognized, human-environmental interactions may be changed. Indeed, the possibilities of such profound and subtle changes rank high among the reasons for which urban renewal has been championed by its advocates.[2] Many of these effects can be

[1] The term "social goods" is used in the spirit of Paul A. Samuelson's "public goods," but is somewhat broader, as will be indicated briefly below. For an explanation of Samuelson's concept, see his, "The Pure Theory of Public Expenditure," *Review of Economics and Statistics,* Vol. 36 (November 1954).

[2] Much of the theoretical and empirical work in this area is in the sociological and social psychological literature. It is a large and controversial field. A list of some publications in the field is presented in the appendix to this chapter.

only vaguely delineated. Quantitative distinctions will be rudimentary. Furthermore, for some of these and even for other kinds of consequences that are more capable of being delineated, their action is so diffuse that it is difficult to separate the affected from the unaffected portions of the population. The influence on urban architecture, for example, is probably of this sort. Finally, some portions of the population who may not themselves be directly affected by the project nevertheless have strong preferences about how others fare under it—for example, the concern in the general population about how impoverished or racial minority groups are treated. Urban renewal involves "social goods" in this double sense of extensive, subtle external interactions and a broad concerned audience.[3]

These social-good effects are considered not only extensive but also very important foci of the urban renewal program. They may prove ultimately to be either measurable but trivial, or entirely intractable; but at the outset the kinds of effects that are likely to be involved must be examined, as well as their order of magnitude and the methods by which they can be measured. The complexity of some of these interactions has been mentioned above. An implication of this complexity is that since the environment of an individual cannot be controlled in order to measure his state of well-being, it is not a priori obvious which indices should be looked at to find the consequences of renewal activity. A desideratum of the procedure being formulated is operational feasibility. The admonition to observe everything fails this test.

A short-cut way to seek at least some of the directions of significant influence is to consider the purposes of the urban renewal program. The more significant of the many purposes—both explicit and tacit—that have been ascribed to it are: (1) elimination of blight and slums, (2) mitigation of poverty, (3) provision of decent, safe, and sanitary housing in a suitable environment for all, (4) re-

---

[3] The term "collective goods" also relates to highly diffused externalities, but not where these externalities are distributed with notable inequalities. Moreover, the externalities subsumed are of physical effects, and not of interdependence in the utility functions of individuals whereby one individual's well-being is a function of another's well-being, not of the other's particular consumption pattern. These are the major differences between "public goods" and "social goods" as used here.

vival of downtown business areas of the central cities, (5) maintenance and/or expansion of universities and hospitals, (6) achievement and/or maintenance of an adequate middle-income household component in the central city, (7) attraction of additional
"clean" industry into the central city, and (8) enhancement of the
financial strength of the central city government.

The redevelopment portion of urban renewal has been deemed
to have all of these same purposes; and all but numbers 4, 5, and 7
have been variously ascribed to residential redevelopment. Rehabilitation and "community renewal," two other renewal approaches
under the overall program, have had the same list ascribed to them.
Each item in the list will be examined in turn to discover its relationship with urban renewal and the nature of the benefits thereby generated.

## The Nature of Blight and Slums

What is the purpose of the federal urban renewal program?
Possibly the major target of the program is to eliminate "blight and
slums." There are at least two ambiguities in this objective, one associated with the meaning of "blight" and "slum," the other with
the purpose to be achieved by their elimination.

"Blight" and "slum" are not rigorously defined in the federal
statutes, nor in most discussions of the subject. The conventional
meanings are in terms of the physical characteristics of dwellings in
relation to their occupancy. The closest to an official definition is
found in the Housing Act of 1937: " 'Slum' means 'any area
where dwellings predominate which, by reason of dilapidation,
over-crowding, faulty arrangement or design, lack of ventilation,
light, or sanitation facilities, or any combination of these factors, are
detrimental to safety, health or morals.' "[4] To use more recent termi-
nology, the dwellings do not provide housing that is "decent, safe,
and sanitary." Slum dwellings are usually filthy and vermin infested
and are fire hazards. "Dilapidation," in the above definition, has
been given content by the Census Bureau in the 1950 Census as
follows: "A dwelling unit should be reported as dilapidated if, be-

[4] Sections 2 and 3. Cited in Jay Rumney, "The Social Costs of Slums," *Journal of Social Issues*, Vol. VII, Nos. 1-2, 1951, p. 69.

cause of either deterioration or inadequate original construction, it is below the generally accepted minimum standard for housing and should be torn down, extensively repaired or rebuilt."[5] This usage would certainly seem to be ambiguous for measurement purposes; yet the Census Bureau has apparently used it successfully.[6]

"Blight" is not ordinarily sharply distinguished from "slum." It often refers simply to the process, stage, or state that characterizes a slum but is more general in that it can apply to single structures as well as to clusters. It is more frequently applied to nonresidential structures than is the term "slum." Another difference is that "blight" sometimes is used to indicate the process by which property becomes substandard. So property may exhibit different degrees of blight, whereas the cluster of structures in a slum exhibits well-advanced stages of blight.

These definitions are based essentially on conventional judgment—judgment about what kind of housing is decent or safe or sanitary. Sometimes this is supplemented by a criterion that is more operational, the criterion of "standard" versus "substandard" housing. This criterion was formulated by the Census Bureau for the 1940 Census. A dwelling unit is defined as "substandard" if "it is in need of major repairs, or lack[s] a private bath, or private indoor toilet, or running water."[7] The first part of this definition is highly judgmental (as it turns out, more variably so than the later-defined "dilapidated"), and the remainder has been characterized as a criterion of architectural obsolescence rather than of disrepair.[8] Houses that are hampered today because they are of older architectural fashion and standards may in all other respects be in good condition.

Ambiguity about the definition of slums is bothersome but not decisive. Slums do exist, and most observers would agree on the classification of areas into slums and non-slums. Ambiguity introduces slippage into the consensus and makes fuzzy the enumeration of the critical dimensions of the problem.

[5] U.S. Bureau of the Census, *The 1950 Enumerator's Manual.* Cited in Rumney, *op. cit.,* pp. 75-76.

[6] *Ibid.*

[7] *Ibid.,* p. 75.

[8] Scott Greer, *Urban Renewal and American Cities: the Dilemma of Democratic Intervention* (Bobbs-Merrill, 1965).

## Slums and Resource Allocation

Under the definitions so far, slum and blight refer to poor housing—housing of low quality.[9] In addition, overcrowding means that the per capita accommodations are small. In this sense they refer also to housing of low quantity. It is not surprising that slums are typically inhabited by poor families.

### The "Demand" for Slums

What if these low-income families, given their poverty, want low-quality, low-quantity housing as part of a utility-maximizing pattern of expenditure? What if, given such a demand and considering the conditions of supply for housing, the continued existence of a stock of low-grade housing is part of an optimal overall use of resources? Then a policy goal of eliminating low-grade housing can yield benefits only if some further goal will thereby be facilitated.

Slum removal in itself can yield social benefits only if at least one of the following is true: low-income groups do not demand low-grade housing because of their small budgets; or demand and supply conditions together do not make low-grade housing an efficient resource use; or slums are something more than simply low-grade housing—that is, either they are themselves something more, or they have unintended consequences not easily controlled by consumers and others. Therefore the question must be raised whether slums can be said to be part of an optimal (given an assumed pattern of poverty) equilibrium situation. This must be investigated in some detail to put into better perspective the arguments of those who, on the one hand, assert that the housing market can in effect "do everything" if left undisturbed and those who, on the other, say that it can in effect "do nothing" unless radically disturbed.

If there is poverty, this means that some people are living a "substandard" way of life. Such a way of life must necessarily contain some "substandard" elements—perhaps inadequate food, or clothing, or recreation, or shelter, or various combinations of these. Poor housing may easily be seen as an effective way to economize

[9] The discussion at this point is confined to residential renewal. Some of the analysis will be relevant to nonresidential blight as well.

desperately scarce purchasing power. Moreover, it may be the easiest sacrifice to make. Hunger and cold are immediate pains and are barriers against holding gainful employment in a way that dirty, old, overcrowded living quarters are not. The "decency" of housing rests on conventional value premises that vary widely among groups with different economic, ethnic, and urban-rural backgrounds, and with differences in other dimensions of culture. Urban slums are occupied disproportionately by first-generation immigrant families; many of these migrated away from housing conditions so bad that the urban slum represented an improvement.

Thus, on the demand side it is conceivable that low-grade occupancy is part of the preferred expenditure pattern for many impoverished families. If these families nonetheless dislike such occupancy, and if the general public dislikes it for them as well, then the problem here is not slums but poverty. Subject to what determines the supply response of the housing industry (discussed below), one could argue that the eradication of poverty would eradicate slum occupancy, and indeed that "artificially" destroying particular slums without making an attack on poverty would not eradicate slum occupancy, since other slums would be created elsewhere. But the eradication of slum occupancy by dealing with poverty would be simply a symptom or a by-product of the improvement in the overall standard of living of poor people. The overall improvement is accounted as the benefit of the program. The slum elimination should not be accorded any additional benefits.[10]

## Factors Affecting Supply

The supply function for housing is influenced heavily by the durability of residential structures and the relative ease with which quality changes in either direction can be incorporated in existing structures. At any one time the marginal cost of providing some conventional unit of given quality of housing service during the next accounting period from the existing stock of housing is typically considerably less than from a newly built structure. Further, the difference in expected present value of net returns between an existing structure in tolerably good condition and a comparable new structure almost always favors the former—considering relative

[10] Later analysis in this book suggests that this is not the whole story. (See pp. 39 ff.)

quality of service and its value, the cost of incorporating quality changes, remaining expected lifetime, and expected maintenance cost, and counting acquisition cost as zero for the former. It rarely pays to build new housing explicitly to replace parts of the existing housing stock that are in at least fairly good condition.[11] New construction usually functions to expand the size of the overall stock. Where dwelling units are retired from the existing stock to offset the effect of new construction on size of stock, this retirement does not occur in the same part of the market that is primarily affected by the new construction. Rather, retirements come mostly from the low end of the stock—the dilapidated, lowest-quality structures. In any one year new construction forms only a small percentage of the total stock and is typically fashioned to the housing demands of middle-income and upper middle-income consumers. Public housing is a well-known exception, but of course it is not part of the private market response; even as an exception, moreover, it is a very small part of new construction.

Housing accommodations for lower-income households are typically made available by converting dwellings from use by higher-income households. This is known as "filtering."[12] Sometimes, the conversion requires more or less extensive physical alteration of the structure—as, for example, the installation of new partitions and walls and additional plumbing and electrical wiring if more occupants are to inhabit the same area. Sometimes conversion requires no physical change at all, but involves the amount and kinds of services that the property owner provides his tenants. Where conversion consists simply in a transfer of home ownership, no change in capital or services is involved at all. Since mobility within the housing market is apt to be greater at higher levels of income than at lower levels,[13] filtering is initiated largely by middle-income and

[11] Housing in tolerably good condition is likely to be directly replaced only if dramatic changes in land use are involved—for example, if a few single family dwellings are to be replaced by a large high-rise structure.

[12] This discussion depends heavily on William G. Grigsby, *Housing Markets and Public Policy* (University of Pennsylvania Press, 1963), Chaps. 2-3. The concept of "filtering" is controversial. For an extensive analysis, see *ibid.*

[13] It should be noted, however, that the wealthiest families are probably more fixed in domicile than any other group, including the poorest. The probability is a function of upward social mobility and dissatisfaction, as well as of wealth and insecurity; so there is a mixture of motives operating on any income class.

higher-income groups releasing their present accommodation in favor of newly constructed dwellings. Conversion occurs via changes in vacancy rates and relative prices. Thus, the housing stock gradually passes downward from one income group to a lower one. The private housing industry has generally not found it profitable to construct new dwellings for the lower-income groups in competition with the existing stock filtering down.

Thus a stock of typically old, worn housing, cut up in the process of downward conversion in order to decrease the size of the dwelling unit, is the type of accommodation that the housing industry provides to the poor. Unless one can show that such housing is still above the slum level, or that, while at slum level, the supply response reflects externalities that are not heeded in the market, one is led to the position that inferior housing for the poor may well be an equilibrium situation representing optimal resource use. In such a case, a policy devoted to direct eradication of slums produces no benefits on that score at all. It does so only if other goals are simultaneously met in the program.

## Suboptimality of Slum Housing: Market Externalities

In the analysis so far, slums and blight have been treated as though they referred simply to housing in a late stage of filtering— an orderly equilibrium market response to normal demand and supply forces. But *is* this what was described above as blight and slums? Low quality, low quantity is one problem; dilapidation, filth, and unsafe and unsanitary conditions may well be another. There are a number of reasons for believing that slums are not an optimizing response to normal market forces.

There are at least three respects in which slums may represent suboptimal resource use: (1) There are important "neighborhood effect" externalities in land use. These are likely to be especially significant in slum areas. (2) The profitability incentives to produce the particular type of low-quality housing that characterizes slums rest upon market biases that are either ethically disapproved or are the inadvertent result of public policies. (3) The functioning of slums entails the creation of important social costs that are externalities to the people involved.

## Neighborhood Effects

There are important externalities in the nature of housing services and hence in the value of the property that provides them.[14] The housing consumed by a household consists not only in occupancy of a specific dwelling but also in the location of the dwelling and its neighborhood. The neighborhood consists of other residential dwellings, of commercial and industrial establishments, of public services like schools, street lighting, and police protection, of recreational and cultural amenities, and, perhaps most of all, of people. Consider the simple model presented in Davis and Whinston.[15] The quality of the housing services associated with a particular dwelling depends on the character of the dwelling and the amount of maintenance and repair devoted to it; also on the character of dwellings in the neighborhood, together with their state of maintenance-repair. For each of the $n$ pieces of property comprising the neighborhood, the owner obtains the highest return if his property is undermaintained while all or most others are well maintained. He gets a smaller return if his, as well as all or most of the others, is well maintained, less if his and all or most others are poorly maintained, and least if his is well maintained while all or most others are poorly maintained. This is the payoff matrix of the "Prisoner's Dilemma" type of strategic game. Each owner has an incentive to let his property be undermaintained while others maintain their property well. But the very generality of this incentive means that it cannot be realized. All property will tend to be undermaintained. Yet this outcome is less satisfactory to all owners than the only other attainable outcome, namely high maintenance for all. The latter could not be attained by atomistic behavior, since each owner singly would shy away from high maintenance. But it is an outcome that all could agree to bring about simultaneously. That is, each could agree to it contingent on everyone else's agreeing to it.

[14] This contention is widespread and has been current for some time. Two recent works make this the cornerstone of a theory of urban renewal: Otto A. Davis, "A Pure Theory of Urban Renewal," *Land Economics* (May 1960), pp. 220-26; Otto A. Davis and Andrew B. Whinston, "The Economics of Urban Renewal," *Law and Contemporary Problems,* Vol. 26 (Winter 1961), pp. 105-17.

[15] *Op. cit.,* pp. 106-12.

*Private Response to Externalities*

The private market could achieve an optimal response in the face of these externalities by either of two means: (1) by voluntary agreements among property owners to coordinate their behavior so as to achieve mutually satisfactory results; (2) by an integration of resource decisions over neighborhoods through large-scale private assembly of land. Both means are likely to be inadequately used, however. Voluntary agreements of the sort envisaged are difficult to bring into being and even more difficult to maintain successfully. Often quite a large number of property owners is involved in any externality. It is an extremely onerous task to get voluntary agreement from enough of them to make a difference in the market. More important though, in order for such an agreement to be successful, some enforcement mechanism is needed, since without it each individual has an incentive to pretend to be abiding by the agreement in order to induce compliance by others and then to violate it by undermaintaining his property. Widespread violations are likely to result.

The integration of resource decisions through land assembly also faces obstacles. The large number of property owners who must be dealt with imposes very costly bargaining burdens on a would-be private assembler. The process of assembly is a sequence of bilateral monopoly confrontations, with each potential seller eager to squeeze out the full amount of profit to be obtained from the assembler's integrated decision making. The result for the latter is a very high cost in both time and money—a formidable obstacle when the number of necessary transactions is large.

Thus, the important externality of neighborhood means that the outcome arrived at by atomistic choice will typically be suboptimal, in the sense that nonatomistic coordinated choice would make all owners better off than when they are acting atomistically.

The notion of this type of externality is deemed so important by Davis and Whinston that they base their entire analysis of urban renewal on it and indeed redefine "blight" in terms of it. "Blight is said to exist whenever (1) strictly individual action does not result in redevelopment, (2) the coordination of decision making via some means would result in redevelopment, and (3) the sum of benefits from renewal could exceed the sum of costs."[16] Moreover, blight is sharply distinguished from slums. Slums are characterized by physical attributes, blight is a process of suboptimal land use. Under their analysis some slums need not reflect blight—they may represent optimal resource use. On the other hand, areas that are not slums may be blighted. To eradicate slums that are not blighted produces no benefits in terms of aggregate national product.

This analysis substantially complicates the discussion up to now. The immediate policy goal of the urban renewal program being the elimination of blight and slums, the two have been dealt with as near synonyms and in recognizably physical terms. If blight is the evil to be tackled and it bears no particular relation to slums, why are slums relevant at all? The problem of blight under this conception stems from the existence of externalities (in production and consumption)—the influence of the neighborhood. But this is a very general kind of influence and may be supposed to affect property in all areas. Moreover, neighborhood effects may not everywhere be such that low maintenance is suboptimal. There may well be situations where high maintenance is suboptimal. Is the market any better able to adjust land uses to the complicated pattern of such externalities in upper-income areas than it is in lower-income areas? At first glance, it would seem that one would have to be willing to say that suboptimal land use can occur anywhere, at any level, in any direction, and to any extent, depending only on accident; and that one would apply the term "blight" to only those areas whose misallocation could be corrected at smaller "redevelopment" cost than the degree of misallocation.

It should be made clear that land misuse can take many forms: undermaintenance or overmaintenance; or the very character of the housing services, such as single versus multiple occupancy dwellings, high-rise versus walkup apartment buildings, attached versus detached structures, etc.; or even the residential-commercial-industrial use mix. The very diversity of these misuse patterns seems to push residential slums further into the background.

[16] *Op. cit.,* pp. 111-12.

## Social Action and Slums

Yet there is a special correlation between this type of market suboptimality and slum areas. Neighborhood effects are generally recognized, and special social mechanisms have been devised to minimize their adverse consequences. Building codes, health codes, and zoning are examples of measures that seek to moderate some of the worst effects of land-use externalities. They set lower limits on housing quality to avoid the sheer physical dangers of fire and disease; they forbid a degree of heterogeneity of use that would have significant nuisance value; and through residential zoning, they stipulate quality and quantity minima above that of avoiding physical inconvenience to preserve a desired homogeneity of social status. It should be noted that most of these involve setting lower limits but never upper limits. Overmaintenance and "inappropriate" upward conversion are not controlled by zoning and building codes.[17] Undermaintenance and downward conversion are the objects of control.

While the scope and enforcement of these control instruments vary widely, there is much in the planning and renewal literature that suggests that zoning and building codes are less effective for low-quality areas than for high-quality areas.[18] There are a number of reasons for this. First, slum homeowners are likely to have low incomes. But depreciation on their old dwellings makes necessary substantial maintenance expenses, sometimes major repairs. Their own resources are likely to be too meager, and their efforts to borrow from private sources are almost invariably frustrated. Loans through conventional channels are very nearly unobtainable. When they can be obtained, interest rates are likely to be quite high,[19] thus

[17] However, it is argued below that such upward conversion, while by assumption a more expensive use of the land than is warranted, may well mean significant external economies to the rest of the community—that is, heterogeneity introduced through selective upward conversion can result in community benefits that heterogeneity through selective downward conversion may not.

[18] See, for example, Charles S. Rhyne, "The Workable Program—A Challenge for Community Improvement," *Law and Contemporary Problems,* Vol. 25 (Autumn 1960), pp. 685-704.

[19] Jane Jacobs, *The Death and Life of Great American Cities* (Random House, 1961), Chap. 16.

cutting down the demand. The credit available for housing in these areas is typically undercover financing at very high interest rates for dealers in speculative housing. This encourages not maintenance but conversion of dwellings to slum use.[20]

Second, the situation is somewhat the same for landlords. Low-income rentals often involve tenants who have only slight stakes in the community, often recently migrated from rural, culturally different societies, with little appreciation of the necessary disciplines involved in urban living. Their occupancy is very likely to accelerate markedly the depreciation of their dwelling units. Again adequate maintenance is likely to be very expensive, and, when major repairs are needed, it is likely to be thwarted by the unavailability of credit. Thus, the rapid, even accelerated, depreciation of property makes upkeep onerous. This is enough to induce some homeowners to skimp on maintenance and to risk code violations. For landlords it provides a temptation to skimp; but this temptation is not enough to provoke violation, if to do so would mean weakening their market position *vis-à-vis* tenants. But tenants in these poor areas are likely to have very low bargaining power in the market. They have little wealth, little mobility, highly inadequate knowledge of alternatives, and—as is disproportionately true in slums—they are discriminated against in housing as in employment, education, and political influence. Their alternatives are meager. Finally, they have often migrated to the urban area from an even poorer environment, so that the building code standards are apt to seem to them like high standards and not absolute minima. In short, they do not often either notice, or complain of, or take effective action against poor maintenance and code violations.[21] The uneven political as well as economic contest between landlord and tenant makes code enforcement politically unpopular. In addition, it is unusually expensive in a high-density area, where improvement can be forced legally in many instances only by the costly, cumbersome process of the city taking over property from impecunious or dishonest owners,

---

[20] *Ibid.*

[21] Of course, what may be tolerable housing, from the point of view of both individual and group, in rural areas may be intolerable in a city, because it creates externalities. The individual does not see its effects on third parties who have no power to affect the terms of the transaction. This is discussed at considerable length below.

sometimes evicting poor tenants in the process. The frequent result is widespread lack of code enforcement.

Thus, the kind of misallocation of resources dealt with by Davis and Whinston *is* likely to have unusually heavy incidence in slum areas. Slums are likely to represent suboptimal land use.

## Biases in the Profitability of Slum Creation

Slums do not simply happen. They represent a pattern of resource use that is man made. They are produced because they are profitable. It is argued here that this profitability stems partly from a kind of market situation that is not "normally approved" but rather generally desired by the electorate to be publicly rectified. It also stems partly from certain existing public policies, which are also capable of correction. Thus, the profitability of slums is not inevitable, nor does it rest on market forces that are ethically neutral. In a special sense it can be said that it is "socially inadvertent."

Slums are produced both intensively and extensively. Intensive production means converting property to lower and lower use and then, for lowest uses, to lower and lower quality levels of service. Extensive production means extending the spatial boundaries of slum concentrations. The two often go hand in hand. The most important kinds of intensive production are to convert dwellings to increasingly overcrowded occupancy and to allow the state of the property to deteriorate progressively.

To say that slums are profitable to produce is not to say that all property owners get excess returns. It means rather that high rewards are available to "innovators," and, initiative having already been taken, it pays others to follow suit, sometimes against their personal preferences. Profitable opportunities exist, and the dynamics of contagion through neighborhood effects magnifies the drift. There are profitable opportunities because of the characteristics of the demand for inferior housing and because of legal and financial policies.

### The Effect of Demand

On the demand side urban slums have historically been occupied by those who are in the lowest income groups. As was argued above, they have typically been recent immigrants into the area and members of what were at that time minority groups. They have often come to the area in large, concentrated numbers and have been poor. They have been seriously uninformed about housing alternatives and too poor to seek such information. They have been self-conscious about their differences from the rest of the urban community and have therefore been anxious to live in close proximity with members of their own group. They have been largely ignorant of their civil rights, of their rights as tenants, and of the housing code and other aspects of the law.

Such groups would have poor economic leverage on these grounds alone. On top of these bargaining disabilities, however, the rest of the community has often imposed the artificial disability of discrimination. This has become especially onerous in the present generation, when the Negro is preponderantly the slum dweller. The problem of slums is not at present solely a problem of race, but the fact that the Negro disproportionately inhabits the slums aggravates the problem. Discrimination against Negroes in employment and housing has been especially severe. In housing it takes the form of segregation.[22] Large areas of the city are effectively closed to Negro occupants, even when they are able and willing to pay the stipulated rents or acquisition costs.

As a result of all this, there is, especially under tight housing conditions, a strong uninformed, highly inelastic[23] demand for low-quality housing in concentrated areas. Expansion of the quantity supplied most profitably comes from conversion to overcrowding. Moreover, the owners, instead of making up the higher cost of accelerated depreciation by increasing rents, make it up in a less noticeable way by neglecting to maintain the property up to legally required standards. Thus, conversion to slum use often increases revenues without increasing costs and may even actually decrease costs. It is not at all unusual for property to be run down profitably to a state where the cost of bringing the structure up to the legally

---

[22] Interestingly, there has been more housing segregation in northern than in southern cities. This does not imply that there has been more prejudice in the North. In the North, segregation by housing has been the only way that social, political, and educational segregation could be maintained. In the South, segregation was long maintained by custom and by law.

[23] Inelastic because of a paucity of known, feasible alternatives.

required minimum level exceeds the value of the property. The property in this sense has *negative* social value.[24]

Slum profitability stemming from these demand characteristics is a dynamic phenomenon. It does not represent a permanent source of surplus. The supply of housing is quite competitive, and the relative shortages that especially favor slum creation tend gradually to be made up. But the high durability of structures, the substantial lead time required for new construction, and discrimination combine to keep the relevant housing stock limited for significant periods of time, although conversions of existing stock down to slum use do partly offset this. A gradually decreasing profitability of slum ownership as the supply increases relative to demand tends to diminish further downward conversions. Besides, longer-run trends in population and construction can moderate slum creation over time.

But such moderation is not equivalent to reversal. It is easier to create dwellings suitable to slum occupancy than to "uncreate" them. One reason is an asymmetry in the functioning of neighborhood effects. The existence of spots of low-quality occupancy in an otherwise higher-quality neighborhood is more likely to depress occupancy levels downward than is the existence of high-quality occupancy spots in an otherwise low-quality area to raise levels. This is because the minority spots are a nuisance calling for majority adjustment in the former situation but not in the latter. Thus, any incentive on the part of property owners to enhance the competitive attractiveness of their slum units when the market loosens tends to take the form of price cuts rather than extensive physical upgrading or outright replacement. Moreover, the attempt to offset these neighborhood effects by elaborate private redevelopment and large-scale simultaneous replacement tends to be discouraged by the very heavy transaction and bargaining costs of large-scale land assembly. Thus, overcrowding often takes place in periods of tight housing,

---

[24] Irvin Dagen and Edward C. Cody, "Property, *et al.* v. Nuisance, *et al.*," *Law and Contemporary Problems,* Vol, 26 (Winter 1961), pp. 70-84. Compare this with other treatments of the profitability of slums: Chester Rapkin, *The Real Estate Market in an Urban Renewal Area* (New York City Planning Commission, 1959), p. 120; Metropolitan Housing and Planning Council of Chicago, *The Road Back—The Slums* (Chicago, 1954); August Nakagawa, "Profitability of Slums," *Synthesis* (April 1957), p. 45.

especially when substantial in-migration of minority groups is taking place. Subsequently, in periods when housing is much looser, higher-quality housing options come from other areas (predominantly through filtering), and the slum area experiences not an upgrading but simply a higher vacancy rate and lower rental levels. Slum occupancy decreases, but slum property remains (except where vacancy becomes so great as to warrant abandonment). In sum, while slum-creating forces are sporadic, their effects are asymmetric: once formed, slum structures tend to persist. Indeed, there are additional forces, to be mentioned below, that help induce slum owners to keep their property in existence longer than the age and condition of the property would ordinarily warrant.

This dynamic impetus to slum creation may be likened to the profitability from fraud and adulteration in ordinary markets, since both depend to some extent on consumer ignorance and other disabilities. In the latter kind of situation the market response is not considered to be the product of "normally approved" market forces. The consumer is considered to be "unfairly" disadvantaged, and government action is typically called upon to offset the disadvantage. To the extent that such protection is not yet forthcoming, the market outcome is "socially inadvertent." And slum creation too has this element of "social inadvertency."

## Supply Effects

On the supply side the profitability of slum production is significantly enhanced by a number of "artificial" factors—artificial in the sense that they are inadvertent consequences of certain public policies rather than inherent characteristics of the market. They are remediable. Federal and local tax systems are important factors of this kind.

INCOME AND CAPITAL GAINS TAXES. The federal income and capital gains tax system plays an important role here. A landlord can report accelerated depreciation on his property, thereby obtaining a substantial deduction from taxable income. This depreciation is not offset by maintenance outlays. When the property has been completely depreciated for tax purposes, it is still habitable, despite a lack of physical maintenance of the property, with little impairment of its competitive market position relative to the rest of the neighborhood, due to the neighborhood effects and the bargaining disabilities characteristic of the tenants. The property can then profitably be sold, because the new purchaser can subsequently take depreciation on the property anew, while failing to maintain it, and can in turn resell it profitably. The same property, many times dilapidated, is pressed into lower and lower occupancy use while continuing to be depreciated for tax purposes. Thus, where market conditions permit undermaintenance of property—as occurs in slums due to the characteristics of demand and the absence of code enforcement by government—the income tax provides an incentive to keep the property in existence longer and at a much lower level of quality than its age would warrant in the absence of the tax. This does not mean that the tax makes slum property (or indeed any old property) more profitable than non-slum (or new) property. It means simply that property already in existence is *no less profitable, regardless of its age,* than new property, so long as its owner is not forced to maintain it well (the increasingly onerous costs of upkeep being a principal reason for the replacement of old by new housing).

Where transactions can be carried out on a large scale, it is often the capital gains advantage that predominates. Speculators are led to initiate a sizable amount of deliberate conversion of non-slum structures to slum use. They buy non-slum dwellings relatively inexpensively and refashion them for the overcrowding that increases revenues and sets the stage for faster deterioration. Then they sell them. The prospects for high income flows from slum property and subsequent capital gains enable them to realize large present capital gains, which are subject to the advantageous capital gains tax rates.[25]

There is another pattern in which primary attention to income flows through depreciation allowances induces each owner to hold onto a given piece of property for only a few years before selling it and buying another property. The rapid turnover is encouraged by the fact that depreciation allowances are greatest in the early years of ownership. The same property does continue in existence under

[25] David Laidler, "The Effects of Federal Income Taxation on Owner-Occupied Dwellings" (Unpublished Ph.D. thesis, University of Chicago, 1964); Alvin L. Schorr, *Slums and Social Insecurity* (U.S. Department of Health, Education, and Welfare, 1963), p. 91.

different owners, as above. Even with this structure of depreciation, however, primary attention to capital gains will induce each
owner to hold a property for a longer period when no reconver-
sion is involved.[26] Here again the property is allowed to deteriorate
badly. As with the pattern noted above, both these procedures
stem from the fact that gains—whether income flows or captial
gains—do not depend on adequate maintenance of the property.
On the contrary, systematic neglect of maintenance increases the
amount of net gains.[27]

REAL ESTATE TAXES. The local property tax under existing appraisal
practices also encourages slum use and discourages elimination of
slums. Tax assessments do not take into account the (partly illegal)
profitability of slum use; but assessments *would* be raised for
conversion upward. Assume, for example, that property in slum
use earns profits of $x$. Now suppose that, despite the neighborhood
effects dragging down the quality of property use, additional investment in maintenance and renovation would succeed in increasing profits to $x + a$. But the higher value of the improved property
would result in higher property tax assessments, thereby reducing
total profits to some $x + a - b$, where $b$ is the additional tax; and
the additional tax ($b$) may be greater or less than the additional
profits ($a$). This asymmetric assessment response acts as a drag on
capital expenditures to improve the quality of both slum and non-
slum property. Thus, even in the especially favorable case assumed
here, the property tax biases resource use toward less capital-
intensive uses of land. Of two land uses that, aside from the property tax, would yield equal returns, there is an incentive to choose
the less capital-intensive use—lower-maintenance, lower-quality
use.[28]

[26] Before 1964, owners were able to treat sales prices in excess of the depreciated value of most real property as capital gains. The Revenue Act of 1964,
however, restricted this practice. Under present law, the taxpayer is required to
treat as ordinary income a percentage of the excess of depreciation actually taken
over straight-line depreciation. The percentage declines gradually from 100 percent on property held two years or less to zero on property held over ten years.
[27] Schorr, *loc. cit.*
[28] George W. Mitchell, "The Financial and Fiscal Implications of Urban
Growth," *Urban Land* (July-August 1959), pp. 1-6; Mabel Walker, "Tax Responsibility for the Slum," *Tax Policy* (October 1959); Mary Rawson, *Property Taxation and Urban Development,* Research Monograph 4 (Urban Land Institute,
1961); Schorr, *op. cit.*

CREDIT PROBLEMS. Capital rationing to slum and near-slum areas has an even stronger effect. The essential unavailability of credit for remodeling and repairs[29] discourages speculators from attempting to upgrade the neighborhood as a whole and also discourages homeowners from attempting to maintain quality or remove slums. Credit sources apparently base their judgments on marginal considerations: each single effort on its own is likely to fail to offset downward neighborhood pressure. They fail to allow for the effect of the pattern that would be created if all applications for credit were approved as part of an explicit policy.[30] The credit freeze contributes to the production of slums in yet another way; the inability to upgrade dwellings in declining but non-slum areas means that homeowners can usually obtain higher-quality or even comparably well-maintained dwellings only in other—usually outlying—areas. This tends to increase the supply of dwellings for cheap, and often quick, sale in the declining areas. The purchasers for such bargains are more than likely to be speculators who buy for the purpose of converting large numbers of dwellings to slum use. Their efforts are abetted by the fact, noted above, that the neighborhood effects work asymmetrically. Low-income minority groups are undesirables to higher-income "majority" groups, but not vice versa. Speculative provision to admit the former is nearly unbeatable, since the former can drive out the latter just by their presence; speculative attempts to do the opposite *could* succeed, but strong enough attractions would have to be provided to offset the often-considerable antipathy to the presence of the indigenous group.

PREJUDICE. Ethnic prejudice encourages slum creation in two ways. The first, which has already been mentioned, involves the disabilities, the immobility, and the poverty of groups that can be herded into concentrated ghetto areas and constrained to remain

[29] Jacobs, *op. cit.*, Chaps. 15-16.

[30] It is admittedly difficult to demarcate empirically what is here referred to as an *imperfection* in the capital market, and the tighter credit conditions that can reasonably be expected in view of the poorer risk or greater uncertainty situation of many property owners in slums. I am indebted to Richard Muth for emphasizing this point. On the other hand, in the case of poor risk and uncertainty, a perfect capital market would respond in terms of higher interest rates on available loans. The actual response is simply to make loans unavailable at any rate of interest. See *ibid.*

there. The second is that the expected result of such concentration pressure is differentially higher housing costs for given quality within the segregated area. There is generally a pent-up demand for better quality and less expensive housing. This demand occasionally presses into "majority" areas when the prejudice of sellers is offset by the prospect of profits due to the weak bargaining power of minority group members. But a single successful incursion often results in panic flight by the indigenous majority, followed by a large-scale migration of the minority group into the area. The pent-up demand pressure of the minority group is often so great that, whatever the original character of the area was, it becomes profitable to convert dwellings to slum use. Initial panic sales create bargains for speculators, even though ultimately prices are likely to rise at least to previous levels.[31] Rapid turnover of property favors slum creation, since it destroys the stable neighborhood expectations that could anchor land-use patterns to the previous style.

This last factor concerns the extensive rather than intensive production of slums—its spatial spread rather than its effect on worsening quality in any one area. The profitability of spread stems from the same factors that favor its intensive production. Spread takes place because of higher real prices for housing of given quality within the slum area than outside, which create incentives to increase the supply of housing available to slum dwellers.[32] The greater the facility with which this is accomplished, the less is the profit obtainable from the intensive production of slums. On the other hand, constraints on external spread, such as from segregation, enhance the profitability of intensive production. In this process one must distinguish between the spatial spread of minority groups and the spatial spread of slums. The former predisposes to the latter, but they are not identical.

Underlying this discussion of the profitability of slum creation has been the assumption that the overall housing supply is tight. Some differential pressure on the supply between slum and non-slum is to be expected even in the absence of such tightness, just

[31] Luigi Laurenti, *Property Values and Race* (University of California Press, 1960); Anthony Downs, "An Economic Analysis of Property Values and Race," *Land Economics* (May 1960), pp. 181-88.

[32] For an example of an explicit model of this type, see Martin Bailey, "Note on the Economics of Residential Zoning and Urban Renewal," *Land Economics* (August 1959), pp. 288-92.

because of the tendency toward segregation. But an overall buyer's market in housing, or even a relative paucity of demand in the slum sector, can substantially reduce the production of slums. Filtering may proceed faster, the degree of overcrowding may lessen, dwellings may be retired from the stock sooner. The effect will be an improvement in the average quality of housing; some slums will be eliminated. Thus, the discussion above should not be taken to mean that slums are constantly and relentlessly being produced, regardless of the state of the supply and demand for housing. There are dynamics in the creation of slums such that the process tends to feed on itself and to have asymmetric features; but a reduction in slum occupancy can be brought about by important changes in the tightness of the market.

If a period of relative oversupply does occur, one consequence is likely to be a spatial spread in minority group housing. Here the spread of minority housing would not be tantamount to a spread of slums, unlike what was described above as the "typical" situation.

There is some indication that the general tightness of housing of the 1940's through the late 1950's accompanied by substantial interregional migration (especially from rural to urban areas), a situation which favored production of slums, is gradually being reduced. Some diminution in the intensity and extent of new slum creation can be expected while such a trend continues; and there may possibly even be some "natural" decrease in its overall reach.

To summarize, slums are not simply low-quality housing. There are forces on the demand side other than mere poverty (ignorance, minority status, concentrated migration, etc.), forces on the supply side (tax bias, capital market imperfections, ethnic prejudice, etc.), and more general market forces (neighborhood externalities) that together raise the real prices of low-quality housing in concentrated areas relative to those outside. These higher real prices systematically result from a quality level lower than legal minima, whether or not quality depreciation is accompanied by higher money prices as well (the case of exploitation). In other words, *within the stock of low-quality housing,* there are forces that tend to produce a clustering toward the lowest end of the quality scale without tending to increase comparably the overall stock of low-quality housing.

In cases where there is no exploitation, a reduction in quality and an increase in money prices are alternative forms that higher real prices may take. It might be supposed that in these cases it makes no real difference which form they take. But this is not so. If housing price pressure in this part of the market takes the form of overcrowding and dilapidation—that is, slums—this may have great social significance, for it has been strongly argued that the mere physical existence of slums involves substantial social costs. These are costs imposed both on slum dwellers themselves and on outsiders. Both types result from externalities and are therefore inadvertent in that they were not taken into account in the market transactions that determined patterns of housing occupancy and use. To the extent that the existence of such costs can be substantiated, they establish the suboptimality of slums in overall resource allocation. This social cost of slums will be considered below.

The point to be made here is that, among the market forces that are responsible for creating slums, there are some situations that either are socially disapproved or are the inadvertent result of remediable public policies. There are, for example, a serious lack of information, low mobility, prejudice, systematic tax biases, and capital market imperfections. With respect to the first three, our society has shown a willingness to overrule consumer sovereignty when the exercise of self-choice imposes considerable damage either to the choosers themselves, to market partners, or to third parties. As for the last two, capital market imperfections and public policy biases are by no means believed to be exempt from public scrutiny. They are not typically considered to be necessarily desirable or ineradicable. In short, slums are not natural; they are not inevitable; and they may not be desirable.

## The Social Costs of Slums

It was indicated above that the existence of slums and hence their eradication could well have far-reaching effects on living patterns in the city. For many years the existence of slums has been alleged to generate important social evils:[33] physical, psychological, and health hazards to inhabitants and passers-by; and heavy

[33] A partial bibliography will be found at the end of this chapter. As a counter to some of this literature, see John Seeley, "The Slum: Its Nature, Use and Users," *Journal of American Institute of Planners* (1959).

resource costs to inhabitants of the rest of the city. These ills are believed to be due not only to the low quality of each dwelling in the slum, but perhaps more to the heavy clustering of a relatively homogeneous poor population in poor housing. The concentration generates serious enough external diseconomies to produce the alleged ills. The diagnosis in much of this literature is as follows:

1. Slum dwellings are likely to be fire traps, significantly increasing the likelihood and extent of fire damage.

2. Given overcrowding, filth, and inadequate sanitary facilities, slum areas arc likely to be a health menace, increasing the frequency and severity of illness for both inhabitants and outsiders (through contagion). Insofar as slum dwellers receive subsidized medical care, moreover, some of these costs are borne by the general taxpayer. Additional costs are borne at large through the effect of illness on the overall productivity of the economic system.

3. Slums breed crime. Admittedly, crime stems partly from poverty. But slum living itself adds to the incidence of crime. Overcrowding and lack of privacy—especially in the context of general economic deprivation—tend to generate lack of respect for the individual and frustration over the constant obtrusion of others. Human teeming aggravates many kinds of externalities. This is amplified because the individual is surrounded by a pattern of life and values in the slums that contrasts greatly with the dominant values of the broader culture. Opportunities for crime and recruitment into criminal subcultures are aided by the closeness and swarming of life.

4. Slums generate personality difficulties. For example, beyond poverty, slums can create subcultures of despair, or bitterness, or violence, because the degree of overcrowding makes it possible to obtain a critical mass for many such movements. Many of these groupings of mutual dependency result in vicious circles: the surrounding examples provoke and support a collapse of socially functional aspiration levels, the outside culture with its achievement orientation is too far away. Recent social science emphasizes the effect of the environment of culture on the socialization of the individual. Inevitably the ethos of the slum becomes a significant part of personality development and hinders many in their attempts in later life to join the dominant culture of the society.

These are examples of the costs alleged to stem from slums,

though their existence is by no means generally agreed upon. Chapter X considers how to evaluate these claims and how to measure their magnitude.

For the present, it must be emphasized that these claims are not contravened by evidence that the housing is actually chosen by its residents or that the behavior giving rise to the alleged "social costs" is deliberately engaged in. For example, the causative patterns that are said to be operating are often extremely subtle and difficult for direct participants to observe. For another, many of the processes involve significant external effects. Each individual may or may not be disadvantaged by his own action; but it imposes disturbances on others considerably greater than any disturbance to himself. This general type of relationship can be seen in the following example. An additional motorist entering a congested highway adds to the total congestion. He thus inconveniences himself slightly by his own action. But the sum of the discomfort he adds to all others is a large multiple of this. Similarly, most of the discomfort he feels is the result of the action of others. So it is also in slum living.

A final pattern involved here is that the individual is caught in a dynamic circle of interaction with others—a vicious circle. At each step he takes what seems to be the best possible action for him, given admittedly poor circumstances. The similar choices of each under the same circumstances in fact worsen the circumstances and thus call for further action on the part of each. This carries the progressive deterioration of the living environment further and further. Each is trapped into a marginal response that assumes the environment to be beyond his own power to change. No one can break the pattern as a whole. Thus, the overall pattern is unwanted by all or most, yet the marginal response which unalterably contributes to this pattern is deliberately chosen. The situation is suboptimal.

## Summary

A major purpose of the urban redevelopment program, it has been indicated, is to eliminate blight and slums. To a degree, slums provide a type of commodity that is desired by poor households— low-quality, low-quantity housing. As a first approximation, slums represent an economically efficient way to produce this commodity. Elimination of slums by large-scale demolition would interfere with this warranted response of the market. It would generate not benefits, but costs on balance, even if none of the costs of elimination are considered.

Slum elimination can be considered to produce gross benefits only if slums represent an inefficient market response. It has been argued here that substantial externalities and "artificial," socially questionable incentives in the housing market tend to bring about the particular type of land use known as a slum in contradistinction to simply low-cost housing. Therefore, the slum may not be an efficient market response after all. Moreover, the existence of a slum, however brought about, may engender important social costs to society at large. For these reasons the elimination of slums could well produce gross benefits. The desirability of eliminating them is measured, of course, by comparing these benefits with the real costs of bringing them about. The redevelopment type of project under the urban renewal program is one way of eliminating slums. One of the fruits of this long analysis, however, has been to cast light on the reasons why slum elimination might bring benefits, and therefore on the sources of suboptimality in slum land use. The advantage of this procedure is that it helps to specify an alternative, or set of alternatives, to redevelopment for eliminating the sources of inefficiency in slums. Such alternative policies would either prevent slums from forming, or help them to be transformed, or aid in mitigating whatever social ills they generate. Thus, rehabilitation, spot clearance, code enforcement, credit and tax policies, and income supplements to the poor, may also contribute in producing benefits of this sort.

# APPENDIX TO CHAPTER III

## Selected Bibliography on the Effects of Slums and Upgrading

Advisory Commission on Intergovernmental Relations, *Impact of Federal Urban Development Programs on Local Government Organization and Planning.* Washington: U.S. Government Printing Office, 1964.

Barer, Naomi, "A Note on Tuberculosis Among Residents of a Housing Project," *Public Housing,* August 1945.

————, "Delinquency Before, After Admission to New Haven Housing Development," *Journal of Housing,* December 1945-January 1946.

Bebout, John E., and Harry C. Biedemeier, "American Cities and Social Systems," *Journal of the American Institute of Planners,* Vol. 29, May 1963, pp. 64-76.

Burgess, Ernest W., and Donald J. Bogue, eds., *Contributions to Urban Sociology.* Chicago: University of Chicago Press, 1964.

Chapin, F. Stuart, "An Experiment in the Social Effects of Good Housing," *American Sociological Review,* Vol. 5, December 1940.

Dean, John P., "The Myths of Housing Reform," *American Sociological Review,* Vol. 14, April 1949.

Fagin, Henry, "Planning for Future Urban Growth," *Law and Contemporary Problems,* Vol. 30, Winter 1965, pp. 9-25.

Faris, R. E. L., and H. W. Dunham, *Mental Disorders in Urban Areas.* Chicago: University of Chicago Press, 1939.

Federal Emergency Administration of Public Works, Housing Division,

*The Relationship Between Housing and Delinquency.* Research Bulletin No. 1, Washington, D. C., 1936.

Federation of Social Agencies of Pittsburgh and Allegheny County, Bureau of Social Research, *Juvenile Delinquency in Public Housing,* 1944.

Ford, James, *et al., Slums and Housing.* Cambridge: Harvard University Press, 1936.

Fried, Marc, and Peggy Gleicher, "Some Sources of Residential Satisfaction in an Urban Slum," *Journal of the American Institute of Planners,* Vol. 27, November 1961, pp. 305-15.

Goldfeld, Abraham, "Substandard Housing as a Potential Factor in Juvenile Delinquency in a Local Area in New York City," unpublished doctoral thesis, New York University, 1937.

Hawley, Amos H., "Community Power and Urban Renewal Success," *American Journal of Sociology,* Vol. 68, January 1963.

Hole, Vera, "Social Effects of Planned Rehousing," *The Town Planning Review,* Vol. 30, July 1959, pp. 161-73.

Jackson, William S., "Housing as a Factor in Public Growth and Development," unpublished doctoral thesis, New York University, 1954.

Jacobs, Jane, *The Death and Life of Great American Cities.* New York: Random House, 1961.

Knittel, Robert E., "The Effect of Urban Redevelopment on Community Development," *American Journal of Public Health,* January 1963.

Lander, Bernard, *Towards an Understanding of Juvenile Delinquency.* New York: Columbia University Press, 1954.

Lee, T. H., "Demand for Housing: A Cross-Section Analysis," *Review of Economics and Statistics,* Vol. 45, May 1963, pp. 190-96.

Millspaugh, Martin, "Problems and Opportunities of Relocation," *Law and Contemporary Problems,* Vol. 26, Winter 1961.

Mogey, John M., *Family and Neighbourhood.* New York: Oxford University Press, 1956.

Morris, Peter, "The Social Implications of Urban Redevelopment," *Journal of the American Institute of Planners,* August 1962.

Mowrer, E. R. *Disorganization, Personal and Social.* Philadelphia: J. B. Lippincott and Company, 1942.

Perloff, Harvey S., Book Review, "The Federal Bulldozer—A Critical Analysis of Urban Renewal, 1949-1962," by Martin Anderson, *American Economic Review,* Vol. 55, June 1965, pp. 628-30.

Pond, M. Allen, "The Influence of Housing on Health," *Marriage and Family Living,* Vol. 19, May 1957.

President's Advisory Committee on Government Housing Policies and Programs, *A Report to the President of the United States, Recom-*

*mendations on Government Housing Policies and Programs,* Appendix 2, Report of the Subcommittee on Urban Redevelopment, Rehabilitation, and Conservation. Washington: U.S. Government Printing Office, 1953, pp. 109, 151-54.

Rumney, Jay, "The Social Costs of Slums," *Journal of Social Issues,* Vol. VII, Nos. 1-2, 1951.

Rumney, Jay, and Sara Shuman, *The Social Effects of Public Housing.* Newark: Housing Authority of the City of Newark, N.J., 1944.

——— ———. *Cost of Slums.* Housing Authority of the City of Newark, N.J., 1946.

Schorr, Alvin L., *Slums and Social Insecurity,* U.S. Department of Health, Education, and Welfare, 1963.

Shaw, C. R., and H. D. McKay, *Juvenile Delinquency and Urban Areas.* Chicago: University of Chicago Press, 1942.

Walker, Mabel, "Economic Costs of Slums and Blighted Areas," *Urban Blight: Papers Presented at Thirteenth Conference of the Government Research Association,* 1942.

Weaver, Robert C., *The Urban Complex: Human Values in Urban Life.* New York: Doubleday, 1964.

Wilner, Daniel, Rosabelle Walkley, and Matthew Tayback, "How Does the Quality of Housing Affect Health and Family Adjustment?," *American Journal of Public Health,* Vol. 46, June 1956, pp. 736-44.

———, *The Housing Environment and Family Life: A Longitudinal Study of the Effects of Housing on Morbidity and Mental Health.* Baltimore: The Johns Hopkins Press, 1962.

Winger, A. R., "An Approach to Measuring Potential Upgrading Demand in the Housing Market," *Review of Economics and Statistics,* Vol. 45, August 1963, pp. 239-44.

# Other Goals of Urban Renewal

So FAR IN THE DISCUSSION of blight and slum elimination, only what is to be removed or destroyed has been considered—not what is to be added or constructed. The urban renewal program has concrete goals concerning what is to be substituted for slum and blighted areas. These must be examined as well for indications as to the benefits and costs that are likely to be engendered. Here too, as in the case of slum elimination, such an examination will serve the second purpose of suggesting what methods other than redevelopment could be used to accomplish the same purposes.

The following are the important goals associated with urban renewal that were listed in Chapter III, numbers 2 to 8 being the "constructive" goals: (1) elimination of blight and slums; (2) mitigation of poverty; (3) provision of decent, safe, and sanitary housing in a suitable environment for all; (4) revival of downtown business areas of the central cities; (5) maintenance and/or expansion of universities and hospitals; (6) achievement and/or maintenance of an adequate middle-income household component in the central city; (7) attraction of additional "clean" industry into the central city; and (8) enhancement of the financial strength of the central city government.

On the whole, slum removal differs appreciably from the other goals. It can in principle involve almost exclusively the real incomes of the present slum landlords and their tenants—for example, by policies directed toward internalizing the externalities in the housing market. This is true of both redevelopment *and* nonredevelopment approaches to slum removal. Whatever income-redistribution, as opposed to aggregate, effects are involved concern primarily slum landlord–slum tenant relationships. But the other goals involve distribution to a far greater extent; and the redistribution often extends considerably beyond the parties to slum transactions. In general, slum clearance aims at correcting market distortions; the others aim at subsidizing particular land and/or consumption uses of particular groups.

The distinction is not hard and fast, however. On the one hand, there is reason to believe that slum clearance does sometimes involve large income-distribution effects relative to its aggregate effects. On the other hand, subsidization can, in a dynamic setting, have aggregate effects; and these several goals differ in their ratio of aggregate to distribution effects. In any case, one should avoid making too great a methodological distinction between the level of income and its distribution. Granted that it is easier in a benefit-cost analysis to compute and add up aggregate effects than distributional effects, this does not mean that the latter cannot involve net benefits. Where income transfers are intrinsic to the giving of subsidies to achieve "public goals," such transfers and the concomitant goal achievement (the goal might be just those transfers themselves) do engender net benefits. The benefit-cost procedure used here cannot deal with the evaluation of such benefits; but at least their existence must be pointed out. The ultimate decision makers must weight them as components of the overall packages represented by alternative public policies.

The study thus concentrates on goals that have a high ratio of aggregate income effects to redistribution effects. Both the aggregate and the redistribution effects of realizing such goals are treated. Less attention is given to other goals; but the nature of the aggregate income component in each is indicated, as well as the chief form of subsidization involved. Some of the subsidies have a high social value; some do not. It is not for the present study to indicate which is which, but simply to present them as a way of facilitating their orderly evaluation by the ultimate decision makers.

The goal of eliminating blight and slums was discussed in Chapter III. The other seven goals will be examined below.

## Mitigation of Poverty

It has been argued that urban renewal is an attempt to mitigate the evils of poverty. Slum inhabitants are poor. Their slum housing represents extremely low-quality occupancy. If such housing is made unavailable, then those households will obtain higher-level housing. The poor will have been helped.

The argument in this form is fallacious. Consider the housing stock as a linked array of different commodities that are imperfect substitutes for one another, both in consumption and in production, the degree of substitutability varying from item to item. The well-to-do buy housing at one end of this array, the poor largely at the other. The relative prices in the array depend on the relative demands (which stem from the distribution of tastes and incomes) and on the relative supplies (which stem from the costs of conversion to respective occupancy levels and the results of past construction and conversion decisions). Given these forces, an equilibrium of sorts can be assumed to result. Suppose now that a considerable number of low-quality dwellings are demolished and that their place is taken by the newly constructed, high-quality dwellings. The relative supply of the former having declined and that of the latter increased, the price of low-quality housing will rise, and that of high-quality housing will fall. Consumers of low-quality housing—those dislocated from the demolished dwellings as well as others inhabiting close substitutes—will be induced to shift to higher-quality dwellings and to additions to the lowest quality via downward conversions (doubling up, etc.) that occur because of higher prices. Despite the new conversions—which occur all the way down the line from the level of the new construction (filtering)—the above relative price shift remains, because consumption and production substitutability are less than perfect. It costs something to move or to convert.

Thus inhabitants of dwellings at or near the quality level where the stock is increased are benefitted. The inhabitants of lowest-quality dwellings are worse off than before—all to some extent, and those dislocated from the redevelopment site most of all, since, in addition to the decrease in rentals available, they are the only ones *forced* to move by other than relative price considerations. At best, they can obtain only second-choice housing. Moreover, the elimination of one slum area will be offset to some extent by the creation of new slums elsewhere (because of the higher profitability of downward conversion to the lowest quality). Even so, the net elimination of slums may on balance help *some* of those who shift to higher-quality housing against their original wishes—whether by outright dislocation or a change in budgetary allocation after the relative rise in the price of lowest-quality housing. This would be due chiefly to "inadvertently" moving out of the "cesspool of external costs" allegedly associated with slums. But considering the opposing and qualifying forces listed above, this is likely to be only a partial offset to the loss of real income by slum dwellers and near-slum dwellers as a whole as a result of the redevelopment. In sum, the poorest as a group lose most; those who are better off gain most.

A project of this sort clearly does not mitigate poverty. To do so, it must be modified and/or supplemented. The obvious modification is to use the redevelopment site for construction of low-cost housing instead of additions to stock at a higher-quality level. Since private construction of such housing tends to be discouraged by present building codes, consumer tastes, and the quality characteristics of the existing stock, among other things, new low-cost units usually come from subsidized public housing. Thus, in the absence of radical changes in the housing industry—for example, important technological and building code changes—the necessary modification is to replace the demolished slum largely with public housing, with no net reduction but an actual increase in dwelling units at the low end of the quality level. This is usually done by increasing housing density (more units per acre) but decreasing overcrowding (fewer dwellers per unit). The result is a subsidized upgrading of the quality of housing for the poor, with little or no increase in rents, and an improvement of the living environment to eliminate various alleged social evils.

Redevelopment may ameliorate poverty, even without emphasis on public housing, if the project is supplemented by a provision for subsidies. The slum may be replaced by somewhat higher-quality housing out of reach of the erstwhile slum dwellers; but if the latter are given housing allowances that enable them to buy higher-quality housing than they could previously, their position will be improved. This method changes the relative quantities of high-level, middle-level, and low-level units in the housing stock while public housing does not (to a first approximation). Therefore, it tends to change relative prices adversely for the poor (this is offset for those who are subsidized, but not for those who are not) and beneficially for higher income-level groups, while the public housing approach does not. A second difference is that, while the allowance approach probably raises the average quality level in the housing stock higher than does the public housing approach, it does not impair the profit incentive for producing slums as much as does the latter.

Both methods are similar in that they involve subsidies to the poor. Under the public housing method the subsidy consists of any explicit rent reduction relative to housing costs plus the equivalent of local property tax and normal profit, *and* the difference between the site value under the alternative use and that under public housing.[1] Under the housing allowance, the subsidy is simply the amount of the allowance. Parenthetically for purposes of this study —but of course of central significance for a major empirical study —redevelopment projects in the first fourteen years of the program's existence did not partake of either of these modifications. For the 106 projects completed as of June 30, 1963, almost twice as many dwelling units were demolished as were proposed to replace them; and most of the replacement units that were built were at quality levels considerably higher than those removed by the redevelopment. Only 8 percent of these replacement units were in public housing.[2] Furthermore, no program of housing allow-

---

[1] The local public agency (LPA) disposes of the site by a "sale" transaction, whether it is to be used for public housing, some outright public use, or private development when disposed of to a private developer. Thus, a site value is established. If absence of arms' length bargaining in the first two cases establishes too low a price, this affects the distribution of the total subsidy between its two components but not necessarily its total size. Too low a price increases the opportunity cost loss of the land-use component, and equivalently decreases the rent reduction *vis-à-vis* the cost component. A higher price for the site would reverse the two.

[2] Figures provided by Sylvan Kamm of the Urban Renewal Administration, U.S. Housing and Home Finance Agency, in letters to the author, June and Octo-

ances to the dislocated has been in effect during this period. Cash payments have been made to offset some of the costs of moving, but no more; and formalized relocation aid—even where given—has not generally secured housing bargains for those being relocated.[3] But the paucity or absence of aid to the dislocated is not a necessary feature of the program. The 1964 Housing Act established the principle of temporary rent supplements to relocated households, and further legislative proposals seek to extend such allowances even to poor families that are not dislocated from redevelopment sites.

The method of housing allowances raises a more general question. Both methods try to mitigate poverty by improving the level of housing consumption by the poor without otherwise changing their overall budgetary constraint. The public housing approach offers a subsidy in the form of housing; the allowance approach offers the subsidy for the purpose of housing. But except for the inadvertent costs entailed in living in a slum—which have been considered elsewhere—what special leverage is there in attacking poverty through housing? It is not at all clear that there is any. One can make a case for subsidies that distort budgetary allocations contrary to private tastes in fields like medical care and education, where very important externalities are involved in the decisions to be made. But private decisions about the budgetary share for housing, except where they are related to quality in the sense of externality-created social costs of slum living, do not entail externalities on a comparable scale.

Housing subsidies involve a cost, and where they are present in a particular project, the benefit-cost analysis must be modified accordingly. The procedure used here is to include as part of an alternative to redevelopment the equivalent purchasing power given as a

---

ber 1964. The public housing figure is low partly because of a complicated financial disincentive to associate public housing with renewal projects that was in the legislation until 1959. The disincentive was dropped at that time, and in the 1964 law a positive incentive was created. The percentage will probably rise in the future.

Data on demolitions and planned replacements for all 185 projects on which land disposition had been completed as of 1964 (but with redevelopment not necessarily completed) show a much smaller disparity, with some figures suggesting a ratio as low as 5:4. But the quality discrepancy, although somewhat smaller for some recent and proposed projects, remains high.

[3] Martin Millspaugh, "Problems and Opportunities of Relocation," *Law and Contemporary Problems,* Vol. 26 (Winter 1961), pp. 6-36.

general subsidy to the poor. The pattern of uses to which they would be put would depend on individual household tastes. Except in special cases—particularly where externalities are involved (either to others or to oneself at later periods of one's life)[4]—traditional welfare analysis concludes that the general subsidies have greater enhancement capability than do special subsidies.

In sum, redevelopment is intrinsically neither particularly suited nor particularly unsuited to the mitigation of poverty. Its impact on poverty depends on the individual features of each project. Since any features designed specifically to mitigate poverty are likely to involve a separable marginal cost, a proper evaluation of the program from the point of view of this goal must ask whether resources comparable to this marginal cost could have at least as much impact on poverty if applied in some other way than on redevelopment.

It is instructive to compare the impact of redevelopment on poverty with that of another approach under the renewal program —rehabilitation. Rehabilitation consists in mobilizing private incentives, augmented by code enforcement and liberal credit availability, to upgrade existing dwellings so that they conform to at least minimum standards. Under this approach there is considerably less decrease in the size of the housing stock[5] than under redevelopment and a much more modest disparity between original and final quality levels. Both differences mean that rehabilitation has a smaller adverse effect on the structure of the housing stock from the point of view of poor households. It requires a smaller ancillary rental allowance to the affected poor to offset their losses than does redevelopment. On the other hand, as will be pointed out in Chapter XIII, rehabilitation is not likely to succeed in transforming as many slum units, and thus may account for a smaller decrease in the social costs associated with slum living. All in all, rehabilitation is likely to have a less regressive impact on real income distribution than the kind of redevelopment projects that were most important during the first fourteen years of the urban renewal program.

---

[4] It is in these terms that exceptions for medical care and education could be justified.

[5] Whatever decrease occurs takes the form largely of a reduction in the number of units within any given structure so as to increase the spaciousness of units.

## Decent, Safe, and Sanitary Housing

The goal of providing decent, safe, and sanitary housing in a suitable environment for all looks superficially like a simple statement of the long-run objective of the urban renewal program. Wherever there are large pockets of unsuitable housing and neighborhoods, the program tries to improve the situation. Surely the effect of such a program must be finally to give every household adequate housing. The rate at which the goal can be realized must be limited only by the size of the program.

But some factors may considerably qualify such optimism. The reasoning would be correct if the quality of the housing stock were static and independent of use. If it were, finding dilapidated dwellings and keeping new construction ahead of the rate of deterioration would suffice to solve the problem. But blight is not a passive function of age; it depends on the kind of use to which the property is subject. It was noted above that if a slum is replaced by upper-income housing, those dislocated are likely to find housing in areas that have an incentive to become more slumlike to accommodate them. New slum conditions are created as old ones are rectified. The higher overcrowding in these secondary areas accelerates physical deterioration and the dilapidation that come with low-quality usage. Furthermore, insofar as filth and violence depend on the mores and condition of people as well as on the condition of structures, these will simply shift sites along with the dislocated households.

The conclusion from this is not that the quality of the housing stock can never be raised, nor that the lowest level effectively in use can never be raised above some socially desired minimum. These objectives *can* be achieved if the amount of new construction is large enough to accelerate filtering and hasten retirements from the housing stock. But the incentives for over-use and over-extending the lifetimes of buildings continue to exist, so new construction must be great enough to cause a substantial "oversupply" of housing in order to achieve the goal. Furthermore, the "slumlike behavior" lag can be expected to keep housing-use standards low for an interim period, even when there is such an overbuilding program. And the more redevelopment projects replace slum housing with housing of a *considerably* higher quality, the greater the overbuilding that is necessary to eliminate effectively all unsatisfactory housing use. The redevelopment pattern so far observed in practice may therefore have advanced the goal under consideration only very modestly.

A final point should be noted. Achievement of the goal under discussion would require a large commitment of resources to housing. One must ask again, why is housing so important? Would the equivalent resources applied to other fields, or perhaps applied less preponderantly to housing, have a comparable impact on social well-being? The case for disproportionate public attention to the general housing field is not now easy to make, except for the problem of slums. The story was quite different in the early post-World War II years, when there was a substantial housing shortage. But this has now been essentially made up. Indeed, in certain markets there are signs of an oversupply.[6] Consequently, it will be assumed that general investments in housing that are either directly public or induced by public subsidies do not bring about net benefits. The opportunity costs are at least as great as the gross benefits. This constitutes the value judgment that general subsidization of housing is a public purpose of low priority under present circumstances. Admittedly this position is open to debate.

There are signs that this view may be held by public decision makers as well. In recent years local planners have been shifting the emphasis in urban renewal away from housing needs toward commercial, industrial, institutional, or an overall mix of needs. This suggests, among other things, that no top-priority urgency is felt for purely housing goals.

## Revival of Downtown Business Areas of Central City

The original 1949 Housing Act envisaged redevelopment as primarily a matter of demolishing residential slums and replacing them with higher-quality residential structures. That is, the program was conceived of as essentially one of residential housing. In subsequent amendments the concept of "community improvement" has

---

[6] It has been argued that oversupply is a means of gradually eliminating slums, which is tentatively assumed to engender benefits. But in this discussion slum removal as a policy goal is separated from the goal of adequate housing for all.

become more important, and projects are giving increased attention to nonresidential forms of renewal.[7]

One of the most popular goals under the community improvement concept is the revival of the downtown business areas of the central cities. Downtown commercial areas have typically suffered in recent years from two related developments. One is that middle-income and upper-income consumers have been moving farther away from downtown and have become increasingly attracted to decentralized suburban shopping centers. Their place has been taken in large part by lower-income groups. Furthermore, in addition to the loss of customers, the downtown areas have become surrounded, and sometimes themselves invaded, by blight. Blight further decreases the competitive status of these areas.

Two kinds of redevelopment patterns have been devised to help the commerce of the downtown area. One concerns project areas adjacent to and near downtown. It involves replacing existing structures with upper middle-income and upper-income residential structures. This is designed to reverse the adverse population shift. The second concerns downtown areas themselves and land immediately adjacent to them. This involves large-scale construction of new—usually radically new—forms of commercial, cultural, and residential facilities. These packages are likely to be large and complicated, and frequently involve radical architectural innovations, tending to give the various components the character of inseparability. As a result, one would expect these projects to include in the redevelopment site many structures that are not themselves blighted. A redevelopment site can legally include areas occupied by structures of which as few as 20 percent are blighted. Since the purpose of these projects is to change the neighborhood as a whole, otherwise unobjectionable buildings must often be demolished to give redevelopment the necessary scope and configuration.

It is evident that redevelopment (and other techniques of renewal) can affect markedly the commercial vigor of the downtown area. And again, the specific character of each project determines its impact. But the critical issue here is, what is the justification for such a goal? There is clearly an important subsidy component in this. Benefit to the central city's downtown area comes at the expense of

[7] Ashley A. Foard and Hilbert Fefferman, "Federal Urban Renewal Legislation," *Law and Contemporary Problems*, Vol. 25 (Autumn 1960), pp. 662-72.

alternative decentralized commercial areas. It is easy to see why such benefits are considered *net* benefits by the urban renewal planners in the central city. Commercial cost to suburban shopping centers and Main Streets can be simply—and totally—neglected. They are outside the legal responsibilities of the planners. Are there any nontransfer components to the goal, in the sense of a public purpose?

In the literature on the theory of the city, elements are stressed that might help to justify downtown revival on other grounds than subsidizing special interests.[8] A large city is something more than a comparable sum of towns. The key differences are in density, diversity, and size. Cities have diverse populations and diverse usages, and the density and overall size of the city is great enough to make it feasible to cater to a number of these diversities. This makes possible the existence of cultural facilities, such as museums, galleries, orchestras, opera companies, and zoos, as well as highly specialized commercial enterprises, which would not be feasible in smaller communities, or even in groups of smaller communities, no matter how wealthy the communities were.

For these distinctive fruits of urban concentration to be forthcoming and maintainable the city must contain a population that cares and a revenue capacity that together make them feasible. The decentralizing, suburbanization trend, which has hurt the downtown areas, has also eroded both of these requirements for a rich cultural offering. The pattern of population shift and the change in tax base envisaged in projects to revitalize downtown areas conform with what is required to protect or amplify the fruits of urban concentration. Thus, enhancement of some kinds of centripetal force can bring benefits to the metropolitan area over and above the simple shift of competitive market advantage from one group of businessmen to another.

The magnitude of these benefits or, indeed, the way in which they can be measured, is another problem. For the present, two factors can be mentioned. On the one hand, renewal projects are not very large relative to the size of the whole central city. No radical

[8] For example, Robert Redfield, *The Primitive World and Its Transformations* (Cornell University Press, 1953); Lewis Mumford, *The Culture of Cities* (Harcourt, Brace, 1938); also his *The City in History* (Harcourt, Brace, and World, 1961); Jane Jacobs, *The Death and Life of Great American Cities* (Random House, 1961).

changes in population composition, or tax base, or even "civic pride" can be expected to result. On the other hand, the benefits considered are critical mass phenomena. They involve thresholds. Even small changes at the margin can have disproportionate effects by exceeding thresholds that would otherwise be unreached. Indeed, these benefit impacts may be intrinsically nonlinear. Short of critical thresholds, benefits may be negligible; at thresholds, they may suddenly be very substantial; but beyon the thresholds, negligible again.

Achievement of the present goal is the first one to be considered in this study that engenders significant financial gains and losses to local governmental jurisdictions. Downtown revitalization means higher assessed valuations of commercial and residential property. It also means a greater value of retail sales. Both enhance tax revenues for the central city government and diminish—or at least slow the rate of growth of—tax revenues for suburban governments. Moreover, these land uses do not involve very high governmental costs, relative to the cost of utilities and services for large-family, low-income households. The result is a "profit" for the central city governments at the expense of outlying governmental units.

"Profits" for governmental bodies are not generally benefits in the framework of this study. Governments are not themselves consuming units; they are coordinating units representing the interests of the electroate. Their financial balance has relevance per se to these interests. But, as will be argued in Chapter V, such "profits" (as subsidies to governmental decision-making structures) can in some circumstances produce aggregate benefits. Since this kind of effect is involved in the remaining goals also, evaluation of them in the specific context of the urban renewal program will be reserved until the last category.

A final point should be made. The present goal is strongly competitive with that of mitigating poverty and partly competitive with that of adequate housing for all. Displacement of lower-income families and provision of additional opportunities for higher-income families, are very nearly essential ingredients of this kind of program, and these tend to worsen the situation of the poor—worsen or at least fail to improve their housing levels. Much the same conclusion can be made about some of the other goals still to be discussed. The result is that the seven goals listed here for the urban renewal program do not form a consistent set. Enhanced achievement in one direction means reduced achievement in another. A balance must be struck; where, depends on the relative weights placed by the community on different configurations of accomplishment.

## Expansion of Universities and Hospitals

The objective of maintaining and/or expanding universities and hospitals faces two problems that have been increasing over the last decade or so. First, such institutions, located in various sections of a central city, have found themselves increasingly surrounded by slums. The area of blight surrounds them more and more tightly, and the degree of blight worsens. Second, with population and income increases over time, the demand for the services of both kinds of institutions increases substantially. There are strong incentives to expand operations by expanding scale. But this expansion is hampered by the need to assemble sizable areas of land out of numerous small parcels owned by a multitude of surrounding property interests. Thus, renewal is wanted in the first case in order to eliminate blight and slums. In the second, slum elimination is incidental to the real purpose, which concerns the character of the new structures wanted for the affected area.[9] (Since radical transformation of land use is sought for a considerable area, the preferred renewal technique is redevelopment.) The distinction between slum elimination and specialized replacement makes a different type of analysis pertinent to the two goals, even though in actual practice a single project often includes both elements. Each element should be evaluated separately.

Under the first, public redevelopment clears away the slum and substitutes any of a variety of non-slum uses. The benefits of such a project are simply those of slum elimination, which have been

[9] Universities and hospitals are not the only institutions for which this analysis is pertinent. But they have been explicitly mentioned in the legislation and are probably the most important of the relevant institutions in terms of actual renewal activity.

treated above and will be explained more fully below. Universities and hospitals gain, but as the beneficiaries of aggregate, not simply distributional, effects. The existence of slums in their immediate vicinity exerts a negative neighborhood effect on their services. As for universities, the slum decreases the quality—and therefore the social value—of their services by providing an unhealthy, dangerous, and uncongenial environment for the students. The slum also increases the cost of university services in the offsets necessary to attract and hold a desirable faculty and staff despite these disadvantages. These factors may operate for hospitals as well, but to a far lesser degree, since they are inherently weaker; and they may be largely offset by a locational *advantage* in such a situation. The hospital's clients may come largely from slum areas. The quality of care may be significantly *enhanced* by the ability to treat emergencies earlier. Elimination of the slum enhances the quality and decreases the cost of the university's and probably the hospital's services. This is a real, not simply a pecuniary, externality. The spillover effect is an aggregate income benefit. This will be discussed at greater length below. The point to be made here is that it falls under the earlier category of goals—the elimination of slums—and therefore warrants no further general analysis at this time.

The relationship between redevelopment and institutional expansion is quite different. In projects where expansion is involved, part or all of the prepared redevelopment site is sold to the institution[10] at a "fair market price." This price takes account of the land's value as a base for subsequent institutional use; but it does not include the cost of assembling the land, demolishing the structures, and preparing the site—the net project cost. Thus the use by government of the power of eminent domain to decrease acquisition cost substantially, as well as the resource cost of operations on the site prior to disposition (together comprising the so-called "land writedown"), are donated to the institution free. The institution achieves its needed land for expansion by bypassing the

---

[10] Some of the land would typically have been owned by the institution in question prior to redevelopment. The value of any such land assembled for redevelopment is treated as part of the local government's one-third contribution to the net project cost. The interests of the institution and of the local government are thus identified closely in the federal legislation.

market and saves considerable expense. So this kind of redevelopment project represents a direct subsidy to the institution involved.

Once again one may ask whether this really involves something other than simply a necessary byproduct of slum elimination. Under slum elimination the cleared land is disposed of to redevelopers. They too pay a "fair market price" that reflects the land's subsequent usefulness but not the resource cost of assembling and preparing it ("land writedown"). In this sense a subsidy is involved for them too. But it has not been considered necessary to ascribe additional benefits to this. There is an important difference between the two situations, however. In the case of institutional expansion, a certain type of resource use is being subsidized; in the case of general residential redevelopment, not a type, but only a certain location of resource use is being subsidized.

A residential redeveloper is not constrained by previous capital commitments to any particular location for subsequent residential construction. Indeed, even the amount of resources available for such subsequent resource use is not so constrained. The redeveloper must be given the inducement of a price for land that is not saddled with a high acquisition and preparation cost if he is not to avoid locating on such sites. Thus, residential construction resources, and construction resources generally, are mobile. To attract their flow into land that is subject to competitive disabilities, they must be given inducements. Thus, the so-called "land writedown" does not subsidize construction itself but only construction on the desired site. In its absence the same construction resources would be used elsewhere.[11]

Subsidization of a certain location does have a public purpose, and therefore it does render social benefits. But the purpose is nothing other than slum elimination; and the benefits are simply those that come from slum elimination. To accord additional benefits to the subsidization would be double counting.

The case of institutional expansion is different. It is a specific, already established institution that is interested in bringing con-

---

[11] A very slight overall encouragement to construction may be involved, since an index of land-use costs would decline slightly because of the subsidy on project land.

struction resources to a specific location. The desirability of the location results from the constraint of large-scale capital commitment of the present establishment. While the institution wants to expand, it may well prove too expensive for it to assemble the requisite land parcel by parcel, subject to the delay and hard bargaining that is necessary for such a painfully sequential operation. Less expensive acquisition elsewhere might, on the other hand, require a duplication of certain types of overhead capital already in use in the established location. The result may well be a decision not to expand. The subsidy to the institution by means of land writedown triggers the expansion: it subsidizes an expansion of this particular type of land use by this particular institution.

The subsidy therefore has two combined effects. To some extent it encourages location rather than type of use when it encourages expansion of the same type of use next to an existing establishment instead of elsewhere (expansion either by the existing establishment or under different auspices). To some extent it encourages a net increase in this type of use when less or no such expansion would occur in the absence of the subsidy. The two situations have different benefit implications. The locational subsidy will bring aggregate net social benefits if it helps save resource costs in the process of institutional expansion. If there are substantial economies of scale—as indeed there are—in university and hospital operation, adjacent expansion can save a great deal over nonadjacent expansion by making it unnecessary to duplicate overhead facilities like libraries and laboratories. The saving can be measured by the capitalized value of the difference in capital and operating costs minus the difference between net project cost for adjacent expansion and the comparable[12] cost for the private nonadjacent acquisition and preparation.[13]

[12] Comparability requires an adjustment for the government's bargaining advantage under eminent domain.

[13] The situation is actually more complicated than this. There is an alternative to both adjacent and nonadjacent expansion by the institution in question, namely, expansion by an institution offering services that are a substitute for those of the institution in question. This factor introduces important complications because the substitute services are not likely to be identical with those of the institution in question, and it is therefore difficult to measure relative costs of comparable "outputs." Frequently the institution in question is a facility of exceptionally high

Not every locational subsidy effects a real cost saving. The pecuniary amount of the subsidy may be large enough to trigger adjacent expansion even where the disadvantage of nonadjacent expansion is less than the size of the true social cost of the subsidy. So the existence and size of the benefit has to be explicitly calculated for each project.

The net expansion component has a different sort of benefit. Since full employment of resources in a sense to be discussed below is assumed, it is not assumed that the resources embedded in the new construction represent a net social gain. Rather, the gain results only because resources are induced to shift to a different balance of uses. The gain results because expansion of this particular use of resources is being subsidized at the expense of other uses. The benefit, therefore, is the social value of subsidizing this resource shift. The evaluation of such a benefit is beyond the scope of this study, as has been noted above. It is for the body politic to place the appropriate value when comparing alternative policy packages.

Finally, both the locational and the expansionary aspects of institutional expansion are practically, but not logically, closely related to slums. Land acquisition barriers are greater when the institution is surrounded by a plush residential area than when it is surrounded by slums. But the social value of institutional expansion is not inordinately high. The government would not in fact step in to subsidize the destruction of valuable dwellings at public expense. Since the value of dwellings acquired for demolition is included in net project costs, the potential benefits from redevelopment would be swamped by its costs. The practical affinity of institutional expansion for slum removal derives from the fact that when account is

---

quality, with only very imperfect substitutes within the relevant area—as, for example, in Chicago, the University of Chicago and Michael Reese Hospital. Often it is the very uniqueness of the institution that enables it to qualify for a redevelopment project. Where this is so, the social benefits of the project may be simplified to fit the formula in the text, without much analytic loss, but with considerable computational advantage, by assuming implicitly that expansion of alternative facilities compares unfavorably with expansion of the institution in question. (It is assumed in all this that current market conditions make the latter wish to expand, but not the former. Expansion of the former would become market-indicated only gradually as the latter continued to fail to expand.)

taken of the social cost of slums, the social value of the dwellings that must be demolished is deemed to be far less than its market value—approaching zero or even some negative number. Thus, the social value of institutional expansion is linked to the benefits from slum elimination, not in any logically necessary way but as a matter of practical politics.

In sum, institutional maintenance requires no special treatment of benefits. Institutional expansion does, and the treatment must separate the locational from the net expansion components. However, the latter of these requires social valuation by ultimate decision makers, and the former requires explicit project-by-project treatment. In the chapters to follow, this study reverts to the abstract residential project, and therefore does not give further explicit attention to this source of benefits. In the real world, where the features of a particular project warrant, further examination must, of course, be made.

## Middle-Income Households in the Central City

To achieve and/or maintain an adequate middle-income household component in the central city usually means attracting middle-income families back to the central city from the suburbs to which they have moved, or inducing those about to move to remain. It is sometimes closely associated with the revival of downtown business areas, both as a goal and as an instrumentality of policy. It does, however, have an independent goal dimension, as well as technical independence in particular projects.

First, there is certainly an important component of subsidization—of middle-income families in this case. There is also, however, an element of general benefit. The population trends mentioned in the discussion of downtown revitalization sometimes have the effect of leaving larger and larger areas in the central city to low-income, often minority-group, families and to childless older couples. The political complexion of the city tends to become narrower. In this sort of situation, attracting middle-income families with dependent children is not desired for its own sake; it is rather an attempt to retrieve some balance for the overall population.

Such balance is important for commercial diversification, for more efficient use of public services (for example, improvement of the public school system), and for greater cultural and political vigor.

As with downtown revival, it is difficult to measure the magnitude of such benefits. "Civic balance" represents a quite amorphous set of externalities. It may be that the benefits are less discontinuous than under the previous category: the threshold phenomenon may not be quite so important here.

Also like downtown revival, the emphasis on attraction of the middle class decreases the ability of the project to mitigate poverty. It is the middle class to whom new opportunities—indeed, subsidized opportunities[14]—are provided; the lower class from whom opportunities are removed.

## Attraction of "Clean" Industry into the City

In addition to residential and commercial areas, industrial areas have also been involved in urban renewal. This is legally restricted to no more than 10 percent of renewal areas, but it has recently been attractive to localities. Replacing low-value industrial land use with higher-value industrial land use increases tax assessments for the central city while requiring very few public services. Industry is a highly profitable form of land use for local governments. This attractive force is sometimes great enough to give rise to projects where industrial development replaces not only low-value industries but also residential slums. This is not very common as yet.

Whatever the value of fiscal strengthening for the central city government, there are offsets typical of a subsidy program. If the central city succeeds in attracting some industry by providing through renewal an unusually desirable location with ample scope,

[14] At the least the projects involve "land writedown." In a few cases, some property tax abatement is allowed. See William L. Slayton, "State and Local Incentives and Techniques for Urban Renewal," *Law and Contemporary Problems* (Autumn 1960), pp. 793-812; Louis Winnick, "Economic Questions in Urban Redevelopment," *American Economic Review,* Vol. 51 (May 1961), pp. 292-95; also his "Facts and Fictions in Urban Renewal," in *Ends and Means of Urban Renewal,* Papers from the Philadelphia Housing Association's Fiftieth Anniversary Forum (Philadelphia Housing Association, 1961), pp. 23-46.

or an outright subsidy in the form of land writedown or tax abatement, this generally means that the industry locates here *instead of*
elsewhere—in some outlying area or some other central city. While
one can argue that the loss of middle-class families from the suburbs is overshadowed by the balance function that they play in central cities, the same argument does not hold for industry. It is
difficult to see the latter as anything but a pure transfer activity,
except that it relieves an alleged desperate plight of local government in the central city, which will be discussed in Chapter V.

Net benefits from differential location of industry can be established only if the pre-redevelopment land use was suboptimal as a
result of market externalities. But this type of benefit is not specific
to industrial relocation; it can occur with any type of land use.
While suboptimality can involve any quality or type of land use,
actually only low-quality uses—industrial, commercial, and residential—are likely to be superseded by industrial uses.[15] This generation of net benefits can be subsumed under the first goal—the
elimination of slums.

Finally, emphasis on industrial development minimizes the
achievement of all the goals concerning residential housing, whether for the poor or not. Any immediate decrease in the housing stock
increases the real cost of housing across the board, but mostly in
that part of the stock that experiences the biggest loss. If the presumption is correct that if residential uses are superseded it is likely
to be in the low-quality portions of the housing market, then the
brunt of the real income loss will be borne by the poor.

## Summary

The six goals other than slum elimination treated here (the sev-
enth, referring to city government finances, will be treated in the
next chapter) all contain important elements of subsidy involving
real income redistribution. Only one of these—institutional maintenance—*dependably* generates aggregate income benefits, and these
are simply benefits from slum elimination. Two other categories are

[15] A flamboyant exception is the bringing of crude petroleum drilling into the
very heart of some Southern California communities.

capable of generating aggregate benefits of a distinctive sort—downtown revival and attraction of the middle class. But these depend on specific circumstances, and their very existence must be established on a case-by-case basis. The nature of the benefits in each is very subtle. Measurement is extremely difficult if not impossible in principle.

Of the subsidy components, aid to education involves a salient public purpose, aid to downtown and city governments probably somewhat less, and support for population heterogeneity possibly still less. Aid to housing generally and attraction of industry to city locations probably today have least salience. Amelioration of poverty is of course the most important subsidy direction of all; it is omitted here because it involves a separable and nonessential part of redevelopment. Indeed, the typical character of the redevelopment project militates against poverty amelioration, and only explicit—but separable—adjuncts can partially or fully offset this. Any substantial adjunct of this sort is more appropriately evaluated marginally against alternative policies to aid the poor, rather than as a part of urban renewal.

In addition to these characteristics, analysis of the six goals suggests here, just as it did for slum elimination, the kinds of difficulties that renewal can help solve. It therefore suggests also what alternatives to redevelopment can solve some of these same problems. To promote the mitigation of poverty, for example, a simple alternative would be to make general grants to the poor with funds equal to the amount of the subsidy for the poor involved in any particular redevelopment project. This has been touched on above. As another example, for the goal of providing adequate housing to all, an alternative approach would be to enforce health and building codes more rigidly. This would lead to spot redevelopment, rehabilitation, and selective rent increases in the slum area. It would tend to displace some of the very poor, as usually happens under redevelopment projects, and would improve housing quality in the relevant areas. But since the quality improvement would be far less than in the typical redevelopment project, relative housing prices would not change so adversely in the low end of the housing stock, and no price declines would occur in the upper end. The resource cost of such a package would be considerably less than under redevelopment. On the other hand, there are substantial problems associated with such an approach. Some have been mentioned with respect to the differences in difficulty of enforcement between slum and non-slum areas. These and others, some of which will be touched on in Chapter XIII, may amount to a substantial barrier.[16]

---

[16] Problems of "political feasibility" must be excluded, however, if the analysis is to be comparable with that of redevelopment, since the latter is based on the assumption that political action can be tailored to the affected population—for example, the discussion of metropolitan government above. In fact, the basic methodological *raison d'être* of benefit-cost analysis is the Platonic motto, "To know the good is to do the good," where "good" is defined in terms of the dimensions of benefit and cost.

CHAPTER V

# Governmental Profits and Intergovernmental Subsidies

THERE ARE TWO QUITE DISTINCT perspectives within which changes in the fiscal balance of the planning government are interpreted as generating net benefits. One, which will be called the "prospective benefits" approach, postulates that any marginal budgetary surplus enhances the ability of the local government to carry out subsequent valuable social coordinating functions and therefore renders net social benefits to the community. The other, which will be called the "retrospective benefits" approach, claims that it is not the health and functioning of the local government that is at issue; rather a marginal budgetary surplus indicates that the renewal program instituted by the government created more market value than it used up; it therefore created net benefits. The difference between the two is fundamental. The retrospective approach measures the values already created; the prospective approach measures the ability to create new values in the future. Since no important new issues are raised by the retrospective approach, it will be dealt with briefly first.

The retrospective approach treats governmental "profit" simply as an index of the kinds of benefits and costs that have already been considered. The production of a marginal budgetary surplus has nothing to do with benefits to the government (unlike in the prospective approach). This is only coincidental. It concerns the size of the costs incurred by the redevelopment project (public outlays) on the one hand, and the size of the value created at large by the project, as allegedly exemplified by changes in assessed valuation and thus by changes in public revenue, on the other. The value is enjoyed by redevelopers of the prepared site, but the government is assumed to exact a payment in the form of higher taxes equivalent to this created value. So what is involved here is not a kind of benefit different from those that have already been discussed, but only a special way of measuring slum clearance benefits. In Chapter VIII the adequacy of this method of measurement will be assessed.

The situation is quite different with regard to the prospective approach. Here the gains secured by government are the very essence of the alleged social benefits. There are three different arguments, and their differences are fundamental for a welfare analysis. The first, least subtle, and probably the most widely heard, is that an improvement in the budgetary balance of the decision-making governmental body that is achieved without resort to an increase in tax rates is good for that governmental body and is therefore good for the community.

This is a defective argument. A governmental body is not a collection of final consumers; it is only the organizational representation of a governmental jurisdiction—a mechanism for collective decision-making. Consequently, it cannot benefit or suffer like a household. It can have satisfactions only in the figurative, intermediate sense of providing satisfactions to its constituents. The government's gains and losses are only the gains and losses of the members of the community, whether government is the relevant decision-maker or not. Thus there is no special category of beneficiaries for government. A marginal budgetary surplus relates to aggregate (or even distributional) welfare only where it reflects benefits and losses to members of the community. Thus, the only interpretation under which this argument is not simply wrong refers back to the retrospective benefits approach.

## The Plight of City Government

The second argument does not maintain that *any* gains to *any* governmental body produce social benefits, but rather that some governmental jurisdictions have particular, serious financial problems and that the amelioration of their plight generates social benefits. The governmental jurisdictions involved are the governments of central cities within metropolitan areas. Three types of movement since 1945, all of substantial magnitude, have weakened the finances of such governments: the suburbanization of middle-income and upper-income groups, the suburbanization of industrial plants and commercial enterprises, and the influx into the central cities and differentially high birth rates, of low-income (often racial minority) groups. These have had the effect of adding to the city population units that require large amounts of government services—schools, police, fire, sewage, and health and welfare services—but that have too low an income to be liable to substantial taxes. At the same time they subtract from the population units that require much smaller amounts of government services but whose incomes or value of transactions would make them liable to very substantial taxes. The city governments therefore feel that they have to increase outlays while their tax bases have been decimated or at least prevented from increasing apace. To some extent, indeed, some of their loss of "desirable" inhabitants (including industrial concerns) has been due to the fact that such population units are unwilling to bear the resulting disproportionate part of the city's rising burden. In short, the process of differential movement, once begun, feeds on itself.

One of the consequences of these trends has probably been a progressive rise in tax rates, which has the effect of encouraging more shifting of units from the central city jurisdiction to other jurisdictions. Another is probably a relative paralysis of government operation. In fear of provoking more such "jurisdictional mobility," the government fails to appropriate enough to furnish "adequate" service levels to meet the "needs" of the population—especially the poorer groups. The result, then, is government that is suboptimal because it is not neutral toward the location of economic activities and induces wasteful movement of resources, or because it is unresponsive to the needs of its constituents. Therefore, a marginal improvement in the city government's budget position tends to improve the efficiency of government since it weakens the forces making for waste. An improvement in the efficiency of decision making by any unit—in this case the collective decision-making apparatus of the whole community—constitutes presumptive evidence of improved resource allocation and therefore an aggregate income benefit.

This argument must be examined carefully. Essentially it concerns what are desirable and what undesirable compositions of population in the central city. Greater heterogeneity is considered desirable, since the argument is not that the poorer groups should stop immigrating or reproducing, but that the richer should stop running away. This will make for better decision making, but not because heterogeneity makes possible more responsible, or more deliberate, representation. It is because the presence of a larger number of richer units makes possible a larger total subsidization of government services to the poorer by the richer through majority rule. What is wanted is a larger total imposition of "external diseconomies"[1] by the political majority onto the minority through the political system, or, in other words, a more progressive redistribution of income through government action.

It is important to understand that the compositional changes in population do not make it totally impossible for the majority to choose its preferred collective alternative. Considering only the terms of the present argument, the migrations change the absolute and relative prices associated with the different service programs. The "impoverished" government is not necessarily acting unrepresentatively when it adopts low service levels or, indeed, when—with a full understanding of its probable effects on jurisdictional mobility—it raises tax rates to provide higher service levels. Since the welfare analysis used here does not seek to judge the values of decision makers, but only to gauge the extent to which they have been realized in choice, it accepts majority rule as the criterion that generates the legitimate content of collective decision-making prefer-

---

[1] To borrow the political analogy used by James M. Buchanan and Gordon Tullock in their analysis of the normative basis of constitutional government, *The Calculus of Consent, Logical Foundations of Constitutional Democracy* (University of Michigan Press, 1962).

ences, regardless of the identity of the majority and the minority. Thus, this analysis does not point to the conclusion that the financial pinch of the central city government represents a suboptimal situation or, therefore, that a budgetary improvement (without changes in tax rates) represents an aggregate benefit.

But this too must not be misunderstood. The argument is basically one about income redistribution. Migration trends have had an untoward effect on the possibility of progressive income redistribution through central city government action. They have sometimes made income distribution worse. This is decried. A loosening of the financial pinch on the city government is deemed to make it possible to improve distribution. Because the analysis in this study cannot grant that this kind of effect is an aggregate improvement does not mean that the argument is unimportant. Since it is implicitly an argument about the optimal pattern of local government representation in metropolitan areas, it is persuasive for many, but its substance belongs with the other distribution effects treated here, not with the effects on income level.

## Inefficiency of Public Decision Making: A Model of Local Government

The third "prospective benefit" argument, unlike the other two, does establish a category for income-level effects. For one explication it is necessary to complete the model of local government from which the analysis of the preceding argument was drawn. If, in the spirit of welfare analysis, local government is thought of as a welfare-enhancing instrumentality to improve decision making, then both the composition of constituencies (including the definition of jurisdictional boundaries) and the specification of legitimate action, are variables. Under majority rule a majority group can impose costs on an opposing minority group.[2] Where the composition of majority and minority groups changes from issue to issue, persistent

[2] Despite Buchanan and Tullock's term (*op. cit.*), these are not really *external* costs since the minority group is party to the decision making. Notwithstanding the unfavorable character of a given legislative decision, the presence of the minority—or more precisely, of a spectrum of interests—will have made a difference in arriving at that decision and not some other. If "the minority" in question were absent, the outcome might have been worse for them.

displeasure with the existing jurisdictional composition is not likely to arise. But where the same dominating and dominated line-ups appear on an important cluster of issues, there will be some incentive for the persistent minority to establish their own political jurisdiction. Thus, majority rule leads to incentives for homogenizing jurisdictions, an important form of which is "home rule." The greater the homogeneity of each jurisdiction, the smaller the degree of redistribution is likely to be that will be sought by public policy.

Home rule incentives have the effect of fractionizing government jurisdictions into small, relatively homogeneous units. But they are to some extent offset by an agglomerative incentive. The smaller the boundaries of political jurisdictions are, the greater the volume of economic and social transactions that occur *across* boundaries is likely to be, and therefore the more public policy in one jurisdiction is likely to affect members of other jurisdictions. Whatever the extent of *economic* externalities across boundaries, substantial *political* externalities are created. Members of one jurisdiction find themselves seriously affected—and without representative recourse—by public actions in another jurisdiction; or they find that they are prevented from accomplishing a certain public purpose in their own jurisdiction without securing explicitly coordinated (or integrated) behavior from the members of the other jurisdiction. That is, they cannot automatically guarantee themselves comparable collective action in that jurisdiction. Thus, for example, a small jurisdiction cannot hope to impose a sales tax on cigarettes successfully if its geographically adjacent jurisdictions do not.

The existence of these externalities means that political decision making among a collection of neighboring jurisdictions will be inefficient. Insofar as public decisions affect resource use, resources will tend to be poorly allocated. This source of inefficiency can be overcome by internalizing the externalities within a single decision-making apparatus: that is, by political coalescence. Thus, local jurisdictions tend to become larger in order to avoid generating externalities across boundaries, and tend to become smaller in order to avoid generating externalities among majority and minority groups within the government. Actual jurisdictional boundaries are likely to reflect a compromise between these two forces.

Metropolitan areas are especially replete with political externalities. Suburbanization has been impelled not only by the availability of land on the outskirts but by the opportunity to achieve specialized zoning, specialized educational systems, and specialized population homogeneity. This last is to avoid politically-inspired income redistributions, to meet, for example, the need of poorer groups for heavy public services and also to avoid, as a matter of taste, living near these other groups. So the spread of density has been accompanied by a proliferation of political jurisdictions in areas crisscrossed by very substantial economic and social transactions. Resolution of the political decision-making suboptimalities that result from the existence of substantial externalities generally calls for some integration of decision making to internalize the externalities. Remedies more partial than this, such as sets of subsidies and taxes, would require detailed examination of specific biases. No general pattern of such interventions could be established without close examination. But one broad tendency may be discerned that appears more or less markedly in metropolitan areas and that makes possible an alternative panacea, a panacea to which the budget balance of local governments is relevant.

## Jurisdictional Mobility and Metropolitan Externalities

The tendency in question concerns a combination of jurisdictional mobility and certain asymmetrical externalities. Either without the other would not suffice to establish the particular remedy to which governmental "profits" are relevant. Consider a simplified version of the suburbanization story.[3] Households choose between living in the central city and in the suburbs on the basis of two main factors: (1) a composite of "taste" elements concerning location of occupation, style of life, aesthetic elements, attractiveness of neighbors, pattern of public services, etc.; and (2) the real cost of public services.

Assume now that some households have moved to the suburbs, but that any corresponding decentralizing shift of recreational, cultural, commercial, and industrial facilities has been less than proportional because of the greater importance of scale economies in locating the latter than the former. Consequently, the suburbanites

[3] A more precise, mathematical version of this model is given in the appendix to this chapter.

—members of a different local political jurisdiction—continue to use the central city for a number of purposes: employment, transportation, recreation, shopping. Because of the presence of these suburbanites in the streets, the shops, the trains and buses, and the offices, of the central city, the central city government must, in providing its own constituents with public services, provide them jointly to these suburbanites as well. A policeman cannot refrain from apprehending a criminal because his victim is a suburbanite; his colleague cannot selectively direct only traffic represented by city automobiles, refusing to control automobiles driven by commuters. This means that in order to provide central city dwellers with a level of public services adequate *for them,* the government must employ enough resources to meet the *joint* consumption of many of these services by suburbanites as well. The level of resources needed therefore depends on the amount of usage there will be by nonresidents as well as by residents.

In this account critical use is made of the distinction between the level of government services provided (that is, the level of *output* of public goods) and the resources needed to produce this level of services (the level of *inputs*). The level of inputs necessary for the central city government to produce a given output level of public goods desired on behalf of its constituents is greater with commuters present than it would be without them. Thus, from the viewpoint of city dwellers, suburbanites impose on them external diseconomies, because the commuters generate the extra costs, but the city dwellers have to pay at least part of them. It is assumed that no perfectly *quid pro quo* financing is available to the city government. But there is no such effect in the suburbs. The daily flow of central city dwellers to the suburbs is assumed to be very small and to generate negligible external costs. So the resource cost of the desired level of suburban government output is a function of the suburban population alone.

This asymmetrical externality makes the resource cost of desired public goods output in the city higher than the comparable cost in the suburbs. This has the effect of increasing the incentives of households to move from the city to the suburbs. It also increases the incentives of industry and commerce to make the same shift, but it is assumed for now that the attraction of a centralized location is harder to offset for these establishments than for households, since some consumers are already predisposed toward such movements.[4] Thus, an initial shift to the suburbs tends to induce more shifts in consecutive rounds. An equilibrium is reached only when the marginal impact on differential government resource costs of a further unit population shift is no longer greater than the now-marginal taste *antipathy* against moving of the next most eager (or really next least hostile) household remaining[5] (a magnitude that has been rising as less and less eager households have been persuaded to shift).

As the scale of suburbanization increases, the total of external diseconomies imposed on the central city increases. This is offset only by a decreasing unit rate of diseconomy as business establishments are increasingly persuaded to decentralize or shift entirely to the suburbs and therefore progressively decrease suburban use of the central city. But it is assumed that this falls behind the rate of household shift. Thus the social cost of providing public goods for a given population is greater with substantial suburban decentralization than with a heavy concentration in the central city. This represents social waste to the extent that the decentralization stems from tax differentials rather than from taste factors. Moreover, the central city government makes resource decisions that are affected by the actions of individuals who are significantly outside their taxing jurisdiction. The cost of many prospective programs is artificially inflated relative to their benefits, thereby systematically inducing an underutilization of resources for local public purposes. This represents inefficient decision making—suboptimal allocation of resources.

Here the relevance of the government budget balance can be established. Suppose some higher level of government, whose exercise of its taxing powers does not influence the jurisdictional mobility in question (that is, its level is high enough to internalize the present externalities), makes a grant to the central city government, allowing the proceeds to be used at the recipient's discretion. Then this increase in the city's general funds will reduce the amount of

[4] These simplifying assumptions are made just to indicate the conditions that must be met for the argument to hold. The empirically problematic status of these assumptions will be indicated below.

[5] This antipathy includes, and in some cases may be dominated by, the sheer costs of moving.

money that has to be raised by taxes from the city constituents for each level of total governmental outlay on services. It will decrease the city population's real cost of financing each level of service and thus decrease the city-suburb cost differential. Thus there will be a smaller total incentive for suburbanization, and therefore a smaller suburban population. This will decrease the total resource waste due to external diseconomies and lessen the externality-promoted inefficiency of city government decision making. An intergovernmental grant will thus improve the allocation of resources. It will produce aggregate social benefits.

The urban renewal program operates as an indirect mechanism for transmitting intergovernmental grants. The federal government pays roughly two-thirds of the net project costs of redevelopment. By this means the central city government is able to recoup net "profits" from its participation, since the increased tax base resulting from productivity improvements in the site land, from new construction on the site, and from the enhanced value of neighborhood spillover property, generates tax revenues often substantially greater than the city's one-third contribution to net project costs.[6] These "profits" are likely to be less than the federal contribution— that is, they would be negative in the absence of federal participation—and hence they would not generally be undertaken by the city alone. The federal subsidy is restricted as to the manner in which it must be obtained (acting as a trigger to specific investment), but not as to the manner in which it may subsequently be used. So it fulfills the character of the intergovernmental grant that can generate aggregate social benefits.[7]

[6] Indeed, various nonresidential projects are more "profitable" in this sense than is the typical residential project. This may be a reason for greater recent emphasis on such projects and pressure on Congress to change the law to permit even more.

[7] In a more pragmatic vein, there is a related respect in which the federal subsidy tends to offset alleged inefficiencies in the decision making of the central city government. Under the urban renewal program, federal subsidies to the locality are conditional upon the local government's formulation of a comprehensive plan for meeting community land-use problems. It is sometimes argued that two forms of inefficiency at the local government level are inertia—an unwillingness either to learn about or to solve real problems—and piecemeal expediency—an unwillingness to face large complicated and ramifying problems except in piecemeal fashion. Insofar as local governments are induced to under-

## Government Profits as an Aggregate Benefit

This is a subtle but potentially dangerous argument. The key to the generation of benefits is the ability to produce "profits" without increasing the real cost of public services to the city dwellers. Why cannot this principle be generalized: that it is desirable for the central city government, even on its own initiative and without the stimulus of intergovernmental aid, to undertake new programs and reformulate existing ones so as to make profits, so long as this does not increase the real cost of public goods?

Acceptance of such a principle would seriously distort the role of government, since in the kind of society of which we are speaking that role is to perform functions that should not be left to profit-seeking actions of the private market. Many such things are not susceptible to *quid pro quo* pricing, and a profitability criterion is entirely inappropriate to them. Under this criterion, therefore, the government role would be significantly abdicated.

If it were accepted as a general doctrine, this principle would have radical effects upon the nature of government. One may therefore wish to interpret it marginally instead in somewhat the following form: the present assumption of responsibilities by local government should be accepted on the basis of traditional governmental function. This status quo results in systematic underfinancing due to interjurisdictional externalities. Only new activities should be selected with "profitability" in mind; and the total of "profits" sought should be equal to the amount of the underfinancing. This proposal is defective too. The welfare impact of these new "profit-making" activities, with existing programs held constant, might be far worse than would be a modification of certain existing programs to enhance their profitability (subject to the important qualification). Except for political inertia, there is no

---

take comprehensive studies of, and to form integrated solutions to, large problem clusters as a cost of obtaining federal subsidy, overall decision making is improved. This can be interpreted as the federal government's *buying* greater local responsiveness to local problems. In cases where political unresponsiveness to change has been marked, this stimulus to community introspection can be very important. Thus, here too aggregate income effects can be generated.

analytic reason for wishing to restrict profitability considerations to a set of new programs while keeping older programs untainted. If then the whole repertoire of governmental activities is to be open to modification, yet in a more conservative manner than would be implied by acceptance of profitability as a general (and predominant) criterion, this is tantamount to asking the government to be aware of the budget-balance impact of each program relative to the incentives for jurisdictional mobility. In other words, the government is asked to take explicit account of the existence of independent external constraints on expenditure needs and revenues. But this is presumably what the government does take into account. And because of its awareness of this problem, its overall operations imperfectly reflect the public's wants. Thus, to insist on partitioning activities beforehand between those that must be and those that must not be tainted by the virtual "capital-rationing" constraint is inferior to opening the overall budget "conservatively" to the same constraint. But the latter procedure is not obviously different from, and may be identical to, the existing practice.

A third interpretation of the position is that while profitability should not become the predominant criterion of government action, if a program is being considered on other grounds, then any profitability inhering in it that is not associated with an increase in the real cost of public goods should be accounted a benefit. Profitability should be one of a number of criteria considered. Even this position, which appears reasonable, involves many of the same problems. If the several criteria are considered substitutable in any significant way, then policies shaped to emphasize profitability at the expense of other goals could well be judged preferable to policies aimed at more traditional goals. Thus the role of government could be shifted substantially toward profitability (although not as radically as under the first interpretation, given certain sets of policy alternatives).

Such a shift in the role of government prompts a deeper look at profitability as a criterion. It is advanced as a "second best" solution to a problem of unrepresentative government. But is not a better solution available? If so, reliance on the profitability criterion could preclude basic improvement by serving as a comfortable crutch.

Insofar as the main problem stems from the presence of metropolitan-wide impacts without metropolitan-wide political jurisdiction, the "best" solution would be to establish a metropolitan government. This is difficult to achieve, for just the reasons that produce the problem in the first place.[8] But its advent will not be aided unless the need for it is spelled out in each context in which that need is clear. Assuming, however, that metropolitan government cannot realistically be considered a feasible present alternative to urban renewal, more feasible alternatives do exist. For example, the tax system may be changed. The local property tax may accentuate jurisdictional mobility, but a city income tax,[9] or a shared federal-state-local income tax, would do far less. Besides, fees can be imposed that approximate the marginal cost of providing public services, thereby tending to tailor needs to revenues. Finally, while full metropolitan government is most difficult to bring about, limited specific forms of cooperation across local jurisdictions may be easier to achieve. These too improve government responsiveness directly. Thus, there are partial and total solutions within the political process itself. To introduce profitability as a criterion of public action would further distort the responsiveness of public decision making, although it would ease the budget problem. As a makeshift device, it tends to weaken the incentive to make more appropriate structural changes.

Since adherence to the profitability criterion is competitive with structural change, the same accounting procedure may be used that was used for separable components of urban renewal. Instead of the *gross* benefits for such components, only the excess of such benefits over those of the best alternative—that is, its *net* benefits—are listed. So only the extent to which its improvement of public decision making exceeds that of the structural changes that it makes less likely is ascribed to the governmental profitability of redevelopment. It is suggested that the former may be inferior to the latter, depending on the degree of suboptimality and the feasibility of structural change. Which is preferable must be determined by the specific circumstances of each case.

The foregoing criticism of profitability as a benefit category as-

---

[8] A combination of motivation for home rule and free rider status.

[9] This assumes that residence decentralization is easier to promote than employment decentralization because of the important scale economies in locating commerce and industry.

sumed that the case for the kind of suboptimality circumstances that made profitability relevant was in fact established. But this is by no means certain. The two empirical cornerstones of the analysis are that households are influenced to an important extent in their location by the real cost of public goods (jurisdictional mobility), and that residential decentralization outpaces commercial-industrial-cultural decentralization so that there is a significant asymmetry in the generation of interjurisdictional externalities. There are doubtless circumstances where both of these are true. But there are probably also situations where property tax rates are not high enough absolutely to make city-suburban differentials important in determining location. Moreover, decentralization of non-residential activities has been very important in some areas, and one can expect this to increase with time. It may well be great enough to diminish total externalities substantially and to eradicate asymmetries in the ones that remain.

Consequently each case must be examined on its own merits. It must first be determined whether the conditions producing asymmetrical externalities of the relevant kind exist. If so, government profitability is at least *potentially* productive of aggregate benefits (that is, *gross* benefits are produced); otherwise it is not. It must then be determined whether the special circumstances make profitability competitive with feasible structural change and how feasible the direct alternatives are. Only if redevelopment profitability is empirically relevant and uniquely attainable and does not serve as a pernicious precedent toward generalizing the profitability principle, can it be considered a source of aggregate net benefits. These are not easy conditions to meet. Probably in the majority of cases no net benefits are generated. Either the model does not apply, or structural changes can better meet the problem. But in some specific cases genuine net benefits may result. Each of these cases must be established separately.[10]

[10] Compare this treatment of government profitability with that of Max R. Bloom, "Fiscal Productivity and the Pure Theory of Urban Renewal," *Land Economics,* Vol. 38 (May 1962).

# APPENDIX TO CHAPTER V

# A Model of Metropolitan Suboptimality

Let:

$N$ = the total population of the metropolitan area.
$N_1$ = the number of residents in the central city.
$N_2$ = the number of residents in the suburbs.

Then:

$$N_1 + N_2 = N.$$

$N_1$ and $N_2$ are subject to different political jurisdictions. Two models will be considered: Model I with jurisdictional mobility but no interjurisdictional externalities; Model II with jurisdictional mobility and asymmetrical interjurisdictional externalities.

## The Demand for Public Goods in the Metropolitan Area

Let:

$G$ = the demand for public goods.

Then:

(5.1) $G = G(N) = G(N_1 + N_2).$

This demand does not depend on the distribution of $N$ between $N_1$ and $N_2$. It is assumed that the supply always equals demand; excess demand is zero.

## Resource Cost of Public Goods

Resource cost is an input measure; the level of public goods is an output measure. The two are distinct.

*In the suburbs, Model I:*

(5.2a)  $S_2 = S_2(N_2) = P_2 N_2,$

> where $S_2$ is the inputs needed to produce the demanded public goods in the suburbs having a population of $N_2$, and $P_2$ is a constant, the average resource cost of public goods to $N_2$. $S_2$ is a function of $N_2$ alone. The presence of $N_1$ does not affect the cost of public goods in the suburbs.

In the present simple model a linear cost function is assumed (no scale economies or diseconomies).

*In the suburbs, Model II:*

(5.2b)  $S_2 = S_2(N_2) = P_2 N_2.$

The equation is the same in both models, since there are no externalities in the suburbs.

*In the central city, Model I:*

(5.2c)  $S_1 = S_1(N_1) = P_1 N_1 = P_2 N_1,$

> where $S_1$ is the inputs needed to produce the demanded public goods for the city population $N_1$ in the presence of the suburban population $N_2$. Then $P_1$ is $S_1/N_1$, average cost of $S_1$ for population $N_1$. Under Model I, with no interjurisdictional externalities, $P_1 = P_2$.

*In the central city, Model II:*

(5.2d)  $S_1 = S_1(N_1,N_2) = P_2 N_1 + E(P_2,N_2) = P_1(N_1,N_2)N_1 = P_1 N_1.$
> $E$, the externality cost function, is a positive function, and $E(0) = 0$.

As households shift from $N_1$ to $N_2$ the city government provides a lower level of public goods. But in the act of providing $N_1$ with its desired level of public *output* (for example, a certain *degree* of police *protection,* not a certain number of policeman hours; adequate transportation for the desired level of commerce, etc.), the city government must also provide some of this jointly to $N_2$. The level of *inputs* necessary to give $N_1$ its desired level of *outputs* depends on the amount of joint usage by $N_2$—a function of the size of $N_2$.

These one-way externalities produced by $N_2$ raise the resource costs of a given level of public goods desired by $N_1$. The tax liability for $N_1$ would not rise above $P_2$, despite this, if the central city government could tax $N_2$ for the increased costs. (Integrating both city and suburban governments would also erase $N_2$'s advantage, but would distribute the higher total resource cost of $G$ due to suburbanization to $N_1$ and $N_2$ equally.) Such a tax is assumed to be either totally or partly unavailable. So $N_1$'s tax rate rises above $P_2$ because, while $N_2$ incur the extra costs, $N_1$ are forced to pay at least part of it; $N_2$, moreover, are not forced to bear the full burden of their choice of suburban location.

## Jurisdictional Mobility

To simplify the exposition, only residential location decisions will be explicitly treated, not commercial or industrial. However, the latter will be included indirectly, since they influence the former.

It is assumed that households locate within the metropolitan area to achieve access to amenities, commercial activities, and places of employment, and to minimize their tax liability for the resource cost of desired public goods. (Differential rental levels are assumed to be strictly the *result* of locational decisions in this long-run equilibrium model, and so are excluded). So the overall distribution of $N$ between $N_1$ and $N_2$ is given by the household location function:

(5.3) $N_1 = L(N,A,C,T_2/T_1)$,

>where $A$ is the spatial distribution of amenities over the metropolitan area, $C$ is the spatial distribution of commercial and industrial activities over the metropolitan area, and $T_1$ and $T_2$ are the tax liabilities on $N_1$ and $N_2$ to finance $P_1N_1$ and $P_2N_2$, respectively.

Consider Model I. With no externalities, $P_2 = P_1$, and so $T_2 = T_1$. Then the chosen distribution of $N$ is:

(5.4) $N_{1I} = L(N,A,C|T_2/T_1 = 1)$.

Under Model II, $P_2 \leqq P_1$, and, depending on the tax system, $T_2 \gtreqless T_1$. Then the influence of the externalities on the spatial distribution of the population can be expressed:

(5.5) $N_1 = N_{1I}[1 - M\{(1 - T_2/T_1),A,C\}]$,

where $M$ is the function expressing households' residential mobility responses to tax differentials.

$M(0,A,C) = 0;\quad 0 \le M(d > 0,A,C) \le 1;\quad (1 - N/N_{1f}) \ge M(d < 0,A,C) \le 0$,

where $d \equiv (1 - T_2/T_1)$ and $\partial M/\partial(T_2/T_1) < 0$; that is, an increase in the central city tax rate relative to that of the suburbs decreases $N_1$ relative to $N_2$.

## The Problem of Distributional Optimality

Find the level of suburbanization that minimizes the total resource costs of supplying $G$ to $N$ subject to fulfilling households' *informed* locational preferences.

(5.6)   $\min.\ S = S_1 + S_2 = P_1 N_1 + P_2 N_2$,

$$\text{subject to: } N_1 = L\left( N, A, C, \frac{T_2}{T_1}\right)$$

$$= \left[ \frac{\partial S}{\partial S_1} \frac{\partial S_1}{\partial N_2} + \frac{\partial S}{\partial S_2} \frac{\partial S_2}{\partial N_2} \right] \div \frac{dS_1}{dN_1} \right).$$

*Model I.* In the absence of externalities, $P_1 = P_2 = T_1 = T_2$ for all degrees of suburbanization. So the optimal distribution given by the constraint in (5.6) is also the actual distribution given by (5.3). And $S$ is the overall minimum possible for population $N$, since any suburbanization arising from (5.3) has no effect on total resource cost: suburbanization by choice is costless.

*Model II.* The optimal distribution between $N_1$ and $N_2$ is obtained where a perfectly adaptable tax system exists by which the central city government imposes charges on $N_2$ for the marginal cost of suburbanization on $S_1$, denoted by $\partial S_1/\partial N_2$ (the impact on $S_2$ is met by suburban taxation). But this impact is the result of externalities too diffuse and difficult to calculate for any system of charges directly linked to specific activities. And the limited jurisdiction possessed over $N_2$ by the central city government (as income earners, shoppers, motorists) is, realistically, often inadequate to permit sufficient taxation. As an empirical generalization, central city charges on $N_2$ fall significantly short of $\partial S_1/\partial N_2$. In the present model it is assumed for simplicity that none of this impact is recaptured from $N_2$. So $T_1$ fully reflects all of $S_1$, and $T_2$ reflects only $S_2$. Thus $T_2/T_1 < \partial S/\partial N_2 \div \partial S/\partial N_1$, since in (5.2d) $E(P_2,N_2) > 0$ for any $N_2 > 0$.

Suppose $\hat{N}_1$ is determined by tastes for suburbanization as given by the constraint of (5.6). Since the resulting $\hat{N}_2 > 0$, $T_2/T_1 < 1$. Moreover, as a result of imperfect taxation $T_2/T_1 < \partial S/\partial N_2 \div \partial S/\partial N_1$. Because

$T_2/T_1 < 1$, some households nearly indifferent between city and suburb at $T_2/T_1 = 1$ will move to the suburbs, increasing $N_2$. But:

$$\partial E(P_1, H_2)/\partial N_2 > 0, \quad \text{and so} \quad \partial\left(\frac{T_2}{T_1}\right)\Big/ \partial N_2 < 0.$$

Thus, $T_1$ rises again relative to $T_2$, and a second group, nearly indifferent in the previous round, now moves to the suburbs. Each increase in $N_2$ brings about conditions for a further increase by increasing the tax differential more and more adversely for city dwellers.

This cumulative process of suburbanization beyond the optimal level specified in (5.6) may often be self-limiting. First, the successive households that must be affected by tax differentials for additional moves to occur have increasingly strong preferences for city over suburb, so only increasing differentials will be effective. Second, the rate of increase of the differential is a declining function of the relative size of $N_2$, since commercial and industrial activities, and some amenities as well, will gradually follow population concentrations to the suburbs. The net creation of externalities by $N_2$ will be decreased, and a reverse flow of externalities will be initiated. (This will be slightly offset locationally by making preferences for accessibility less centered on the city.) An equilibrium will be attained if the declining $\partial E(P_2,N_2)/\partial N_2$ becomes just low enough to fail to offset the transfer antipathy of the next least opposed household, that is, if:

(5.7) $T_2/T_1 + [\partial(T_2/T_1)/\partial N_2]dN_2 = (MRS)_{N_{20} + dN_2}$,

where $(MRS)_{N_{20} + dN_2}$ is the marginal rate of substitution in tax differential terms between city and suburban location for the household(s) whose transfer to the suburbs would raise the latter population from $N_{20}$ to $N_{20} + dN_2$. This condition corresponds to:

(5.8) $\partial M/\partial N_2 = 0$.

Thus, the externality results in suboptimal resource use. Three aspects are important. First, suburbanization is carried too far. Second, this incurs a total resource cost $S$ in excess of both the situation without externality—the excess measured by $E(P_2,N_2)$; and that with externality completely internalized by marginal taxation (the optimum defined by [5.6])—the excess measured by $E(P_2,\bar{N}_2) - E(P_2,\hat{N}_2)$, where $\bar{N}_2$ is the equilibrium level and $\hat{N}_2$ the optimum level of $N_2$. ($E[P_2,\hat{N}_2]$ measures the social cost which the population is *willing to pay* for the optimum level of suburbanization.) Third, while this has been excluded from the present model, a slight enrichment of the model would make the level of public goods demanded be a function of the price of public goods. Then the central city government, faced with suboptimally high price (that is, $T_1 > T_2$), will choose to provide a lower level than in the suburbs, either in the form of a smaller quantity or a lower quality. In such a model, this response will influence further locational shifts to the suburbs.

It may be objected that $E(P_2,\overline{N}_2) - E(P_2,\hat{N}_2)$ overstates the social waste because the extra inputs used in the public sector under suburbanization really produce extra public output—more transportation, police protection, etc. Whether or not the present model's assumption about zero extra output is accepted, $E(P_2,\overline{N}_2) - E(P_2,\hat{N}_2)$ does measure the extent of the systematic distortion of suburbanization and public service decisions.[11]

## Intergovernmental Grants

An intergovernmental grant to the central city, unencumbered as to use, decreases $P_1$, since $P_1$ denotes expenses that must be financed by the city population and the grant pays for part of total outlays. The decrease in $P_1$ decreases $P_2/P_1$ and therefore tends to decrease the equilibrium degree of suburbanization—that is, $\overline{N}_2$. Thus, the size of $E(P_2,\overline{N}_2)$ is decreased and with it, social waste and/or the degree of inefficient decision making. So the grant is a partial substitute for structural change to internalize decision making between city and suburban governments.

[11] Greater realism is attainable by assuming that residential use "requires" more public goods than does industrial and commercial use. This distinction does not affect the argument about suboptimal resource allocation, or even the earlier argument about income redistribution through local government. Again an optimal spatial distribution of land uses is defined in terms of desired locations when all marginal public goods costs are paid for by whoever incurs them. This distribution depends on the initial distribution of residential and nonresidential uses. High central concentration of the latter will lower $T_1$ relative to $T_2$; at the optimal distribution, conceivably $T_1 < T_2$. But an imperfect system of public charges will again permit asymmetric externalities favoring the suburbs. Now the size of per unit externalities, depending on the location of nonresidential uses, is endogenous, decreasing with nonresidential suburbanization. Since it is assumed that residential uses respond more sensitively than nonresidential to $T_2 - T_1$ differentials, marginal locational decisions by the former and thereafter by the latter will be affected, thereby generating a cumulative excess of suburbanization for both (even though $T_2 > T_1$). The resulting suboptimality will be less than in the simpler model because of induced nonresidential dispersion, but the ability to use the central city government for income redistribution will be more adversely affected.

CHAPTER VI

# Structure of Benefit-Cost Comparisons

THE FRAMEWORK WITHIN which the measurement of costs and benefits will be made must now be specified more precisely. The task is to measure the net gains (positive or negative) from urban redevelopment under the federal program (call this Alternative R). But this means net gains relative to some alternative or alternatives. One such alternative is appropriately a status quo alternative (call this Alternative S). In this study another alternative is also introduced. This, as has been noted previously, is a package comprising several policy measures designed to attack the various problems on which redevelopment has a beneficial impact—that is, a set of policies for the alternative realization of goals by which redevelopment generates benefits over the existing situation (call this Alternative M). Some of the possible components of this alternative may be other techniques within the urban renewal program. Redevelopment and this nonredevelopment modification package are both evaluated against the status quo and then are evaluated with respect to one another.

While it is beyond the scope of this study to specify any exact

Alternative $M$, some examples can be given. First, it is important to note that there is a very large family of such packages that could be used, since there are many alternative ways of meeting any particular problem. For some purposes a unique choice is necessary, for others only the choice of a subset of $M$'s. The latter would be the case when one seeks to know only whether redevelopment is the best policy available. For this purpose a negative answer can be obtained so long as one can find any $M$ preferable to $R$. If $R$ is persistently favored, then the *best* $M$ must probably be sought as an alternative to $R$. If one is interested in determining which are the best possible modifications to make in redevelopment policy, one generally has to compare successive $R$'s with the best available $M$.

Inclusions in $M$ are suggested by the previous analysis of the goals of the urban renewal program. To combat slum formation, reform of property tax assessment procedures may be considered, as well as provision of mortgage credit for dwellings in blighted and nearly blighted areas, more rigid enforcement of health and building codes, spot demolition, and rehabilitation of individual dwellings. To combat poverty and intra-family problems, general-purpose monetary grants would be effective, or informational services, or programs for special education (like Operation Headstart), or additional social work services. Other inclusions might be better garbage disposal services and police protection, and open-occupancy programs to combat the segregation pressure that adds to the profitability of slum creation.

As will already have been noticed, a slight modification of this procedure was introduced in the discussion of nonessential, separable elements of urban redevelopment. These are components that can be added or subtracted at will without affecting the fundamentals of redevelopment. One such component that has been mentioned is a variety of measures designed to ease the negative impact on the poor. These are "elective" elements, having easily calculable marginal costs. Since the choice among "electives" is very wide and none affects the character of redevelopment itself, no chosen set of these is evaluated here as part of the indissoluble bundle of redevelopment. Rather, for convenience, these elements are considered separately. More precisely, the question is weighed whether alternative policies designed to accomplish the same goal are more efficient than the elements in question. Only if the latter exceed all the former are additional benefits ascribed to redevelopment by adjoining the elements in question. Thus, the separable *net* benefits of these elements relative to the *best* of other alternatives are calculated as well as the benefits for redevelopment proper, which are net only with respect to the status quo. This modification is not a matter of substance.

## The Life-span of the Housing Stock

In comparing benefits among *S, R,* and *M,* differences in impact not only immediately but also in the future must be specified. This is highly important. As has been indicated, slum creation is closely associated with a normal adaptation of durable capital stock in the housing market. There is a "life cycle" through which items in the housing stock pass. Housing on present slum sites will gradually be retired on private initiative, the rate of retirement and nature of the replacement depending on supply and demand conditions in the market. Moreover, a reduction in slums (significant uncrowding and structure rehabilitation) does occur voluntarily, and often on a considerable scale.[1] Thus the status quo policy with respect to a particular site does not imply a permanent commitment to slum use.

In the same vein, redevelopment does not imply a permanent commitment to non-slum use on the site in question. Indeed, there are reports that certain types of redevelopment—with or without public housing—may accelerate the process of slum formation, not only by pushing slums elsewhere in response to the demands of those who have been dislocated, but by decreasing the non-slum lifetime of new structures.[2] It is alleged that these types of redevelopment encourage high crime rates and behavior that leads to

[1] For an expression of this position, see Jane Jacobs, *The Death and Life of Great American Cities* (Random House, 1961), Chap. 15. She argues that forces making for such a reduction in slums are substantial but are hampered by "artificial barriers," consisting largely of public policies.

Figures from the *National Housing Inventory* and the *1950 Census of Housing* indicate that the number of substandard occupied dwelling units declined by 4,567,000 or 31 percent between 1950 and 1956 and that 60 percent of this decrease (2,750,000 net units) resulted from improvements in the quality of given dwellings (occupied in both years). Cited in William G. Grigsby, *Housing Markets and Public Policy* (University of Pennsylvania Press, 1963), pp. 258, 265.

[2] Harrison E. Salisbury, *The Shook-Up Generation* (Harper, 1958); Jacobs, *op. cit.*

depreciation of property in neighborhoods where the property is still new. Thus, some of the behavioral phenomena associated with slums may occur in environments dissociated from old, obsolescent structures.

These allegations must, of course, be scrutinized carefully. Their effect is to draw attention to an important and sometimes neglected dimension in the evaluation of benefits and costs, namely, forces determining the *useful* lifetime of items in the housing stock —the length of time during which each item renders services no worse than a specified minimum acceptable quality level. Forces that shorten the useful lifetime thereby generate costs, those that prolong this lifetime thereby generate benefits. Distinction must be made, of course, between the two general processes that determine the useful lifetime of capital—depreciation and obsolescence. The procedure here refers only to depreciation.[3] Obsolescence, on the contrary, is not a capital-wasting but a capital-enhancing process, since it comes about as a result of technical improvement. It adds better—as well as newer—units to the housing stock without decreasing the quality of existing—older—units. Acceleration of obsolescence implies a more useful stock of capital; acceleration of depreciation, a less useful stock.

A second distinction must be made, between filtering and depreciation. Filtering means that items in the housing stock move to lower and lower use—but in the sense of being attainable by lower and lower-income households, not necessarily in the sense of becoming less and less fit for human habitation. Filtering occurs because newer, more desirable structures are added to the stock. Admittedly it is sometimes the depreciation of existing structures that makes their inhabitants willing to build or move into new structures or into better existing structures; but in this they would be frustrated if new units were not somewhere available, assuming a continuation of the upward trend of population in the United States. Thus, filtering almost always includes a component like obsolescence; and it sometimes also includes a component of depreciation. But the proportions depend on the particular situation. So an accelerated rate of filtering is not per se to be counted as generating either costs or benefits; but it may more often be part of an enhance-

---

[3] Depreciation refers not only to the physical character of a structure, but also to the pattern of its use—including the neighborhood.

ment of the housing stock's usefulness than the reverse. Specific judgment must be based on the particular situation involved.

## The Discount Rate

This raises the question of the time factor. The benefits deriving from redevelopment are not concentrated in a single time period. They occur as a flow over an extended time. Moreover, not only will alternatives other than $R$ also give rise to benefit flows over time (relative to $S$, of course), but these flows may have different time shapes than that of $R$. Thus, there arises the familiar problem of making time flows comparable.

The method for doing so in benefit-cost analysis is to convert all dated benefits and costs into present discounted values. A central question concerns the rate of discount to be used. The choice of a discount rate can affect the choice among projects, the optimal timing for any selected project, and the total amount of resources to be used in this area. The choice of a discount rate is an extremely complex and controversial question. Even fundamental issues have not been definitively resolved.[4] No full-scale assault on the problem will be made here. Rather an approach will be sketched briefly that appears reasonable in the present context on something less than profound analysis. The position taken is not fixed. It is open to reconsideration, but is presented here in order to complete the over-all procedure. Very little in the rest of the analysis depends on the exact character of the resolution here. As will be elaborated in Chapter VII, the benefits dealt with in the general model are the temporal effects of an improvement in the productivity of real estate occurring at a single point in time and a change in the flow of slum-generated social costs of human interaction. The benefits from alternative policies are of the same general structure. An appropriate

[4] For a discussion of this point, see, for example, Maynard M. Hufschmidt, John Krutilla, Julius Margolis, and Stephen A. Marglin, *Report of Panel of Consultants to the Bureau of the Budget on Standards and Criteria for Formulating and Evaluating Federal Water Resources Development* (June 30, 1961); Roland McKean, *Efficiency in Government Through Systems Analysis* (Wiley, 1958); Otto Eckstein, *Water-Resource Development; the Economics of Project Evaluation* (Harvard University Press, 1958); and Jack Hirshleifer, James De Haven, and Jerome Milliman, *Water Supply: Economics, Technology and Policy* (University of Chicago Press, 1960).

discount rate should reflect the true social opportunity costs and social time preference involved in intertemporal resource use for the resource packages actually involved.[5]

Neglecting for the moment the government financing of redevelopment, and considering only the benefit side, the flow of benefits from a change in real estate productivity would seem to be most appropriately discounted by the relevant market interest rate. In other words, the present value of the flow should be estimated as the change in capital value, or market value, of the property in question. This discount rate is suggested because the services rendered by the property in question are extremely close substitutes for those rendered by other property privately held. Admittedly some land is disposed of by the LPA (local public agency) to public agencies for "public uses," and some of the land sold to private redevelopers carries with it certain conditions designed to "protect the public interest" in subsequent redevelopment. These circumstances affect the market value of the site relative to disposition in the open market. But this effect on market value is not a reflection on the discounting of future returns into a present value. Rather it affects the size of the annual future pecuniary returns.[6] Any land similar in attributes could be similarly applied to a "public purpose," with the same effect on the money market price. Redevelopment does not interpose on the market a social judgment on the intertemporal structure of resource use so much as on the location of such use.[7]

Discounting of the flow of changes in slum-generated social costs of human interaction is somewhat more difficult to settle. These costs have both production and consumption components. Neither would seem to have significant public dimensions; that is, the enhancement of labor-power and of consumer satisfaction of the affected population is not earmarked to any particular public pur-

[5] If the amount of resources to be used is itself a variable, then so too is the relevant discount rate. It is determined simultaneously with optimal size of resource use as the equilibrium (optimal) discount rate.

[6] The true social value of the land is the money value it can command in a sale *plus* the nonmonetized social value of the "public purpose" being achieved by the disposition or the conditions on disposition.

[7] It has some effect on the intertemporal structure of resource use, of course, because it influences the age distribution of the housing stock.

pose. Moreover, there is no real change intended in the temporal structure of labor supply or consumer satisfaction. The whole level over time is intended to be raised. A market rate basis for discounting would seem to be appropriate here too.

In both cases the relevant market rate would be a long-term one, since the investment becomes embodied in real estate and personal lives for the lifetime of the respective resources. The risk components for the two types of benefit flow would typically differ, each depending on the relative riskiness of investment in that particular resource. But any component in a market rate that reflects the administrative cost of processing small loans, as well as the imperfect ability to pledge labor productivity and consumption improvement as collateral, would be omitted as irrelevant.[8] This factor affects the interaction benefits much more than the real estate benefits. Market price capitalization serves as a good approximation to the latter.

A rate of discount has three related functions to perform in this area: to compare alternative government programs, especially those aimed at the same goals; to compare the desirability of different timing for any given program; to compare governmental with nongovernmental use of resources. In principle the discount rate chosen should express the real opportunity cost in each type of comparison. If all decision makers were in equilibrium, a single rate, abstracting from risk considerations, would be applicable to all. It is doubtful whether anything like full equilibrium exists in the relevant markets. Therefore, a procedure that used different rates for different comparisons would not be intolerable per se.

The argument so far is incomplete with respect to all three types of comparisons. It has been argued simply that redevelopment produces outputs highly competitive with private outputs, without imposing any significant change in the intertemporal structure of input-output flows. Since society typically does not interpose a standard of intertemporal comparisons different from that of the market in this general sector,[9] the intertemporally-neutral character of its

---

[8] The latter because while a borrower can renege in a *private* transaction despite benefiting from the loan, in the hypothetical *social* transaction it is the benefit that represents "repayment."

[9] Allowance is made for the federal government's role in the mortgage market.

own similar operations here offers little justification for interposition when evaluating redevelopment. With this the argument may be extended to cover the governmental-nongovernmental resource use comparison. Redevelopment is financed by both federal and local levels of government. But the respective borrowing rates do not reflect real differences in the social opportunity costs of the resources provided by each level (whether or not they are actually raised by borrowing). Their levels are strongly influenced by liquidity and tax considerations and by risks specific not to the project but to the general repaying ability of the government. Since the service flows in question are so closely substitutable for privately produced services, it seems best to treat the opportunity cost of the resources as the market rates relative to such private flows, with the adjustments noted above. In other words, the earlier analysis does cover the comparison between public and private resource use.

The comparison between redevelopment and other forms of renewal (or, more broadly, other programs designed to achieve the same goals) is much the same. Even more than with the status quo alternative, redevelopment is likely to be competitive with and have an intertemporal structure very similar to that of various packages under $M$. The appropriateness of the market discount rate for $R$ would seem to apply to $M$ as well.

One implication of the close similarity of intertemporal structure is that the choice of a discount rate will have little effect on choices between redevelopment and alternative renewal policies. Preference for one or the other will depend far more on absolute levels of impact relative to cost than on the time pattern of inputs and outputs (for example, the use of long-lived versus short-lived capital, high versus low capital-output ratios). Thus, if there is a public commitment for a relatively fixed amount of resources to be used for urban renewal and the only real question is how to spend them, then the problem of which discount rate to use becomes nearly trivial. One may be selected arbitrarily, or for convenience it may be dispensed with entirely. If, however, the question of how many resources government *should* commit to this work is relevant, or if the timing of different projects becomes an issue, then the selection of a proper discount rate—with all its complexities and as yet unresolved problems—is more serious.

## Summary

To summarize, the benefit-cost measuring procedures will compare three alternatives, *R, S,* and *M*—the federal program, policies that maintain a status quo condition, and a combination of policy measures that attack the problems underlying redevelopment, respectively. The choice of *M* may or may not be unique, depending on the particular purpose of the overall analysis. The three will be compared in terms of a present value of the flow of expected outcomes over some considerable planning period. In such a flow, retardation or acceleration of the rate of depreciation of the housing stock is a dimension of benefit or cost. The rate of filtering does not correspond with the rate of depreciation. It may on balance reflect an opposite effect on the usefulness of the housing stock.

PART TWO

*The Measurement of Benefits*

CHAPTER VII

# A Model of Redevelopment Impact

As was indicated at the start, the portion of urban renewal to which major attention is given in this study is residential redevelopment. In this chapter an analysis is presented of the impact of residential redevelopment in terms of the kinds of benefit that have been mentioned. This analysis forms the basis for a comparison of redevelopment with other renewal techniques. To facilitate analysis the housing stock is grouped tentatively into two classes: low-quality housing units $(H_1)$[1] and others $(H_2)$. The first is further divided into low substandard $(H_{11})$ and low standard units $(H_{12})$. Using capital letters to identify the set and lower case letters to identify the number of elements from the set, a redevelopment project destroys $h_{11}$ units of $H_{11}$—the redevelopment site—and substitutes for it $h_{12}$ units of $H_{12}$ and $h_2$ units of $H_2$.[2] In addition to residential

[1] A housing unit is officially defined as housing accommodation designed for the residence of a single household. This is somewhat ambiguous. More than one "household" in the sense of "family" often live in a single unit. Moreover, the size of a unit is not standardized. Thus, the "unit" is by no means a standard *quantity* of housing.

[2] For simplicity any standard units demolished in the redevelopment site are ignored, on the pretense—contrary to fact—that only substandard dwellings are

115

units, commercial (*C*) and industrial (*I*) units may be involved in either the demolition or the replacement.

In this model three types of impact are assumed:[3] (1) more efficient resource use as a result of internalizing market externalities; (2) differential real income effects according to location, income level, owner-tenant status, and functional classification of property, as a result of changes in numbers and location of housing units and commercial and industrial property; and (3) changes in slum-generated social costs as a result of the destruction of slum property. The first and third of these are aggregate effects on the level of real income; the second is chiefly an effect on the distribution of real income.

## Externalities and Land Use

The first arises out of the neighborhood effects, which have such an important influence on the quality of housing services. It has been noted that the existence of such externalities typically results in a divergence between private benefits and costs and the corresponding social magnitudes, which produces a suboptimal situation. The difficulty is that within an area large enough to impart a dominant character to property within it (a neighborhood), the property has many different owners. In the case of a slum neighborhood, a hypothetical example was examined above where each property owner had most to gain if he could undermaintain his property while all others were maintaining theirs well. But the very generality of the motivation meant that it was not a stable possibility. Therefore, only the general undermaintenance options were attainable. Of these, the attraction of *differential* undermaintenance would lead to behavior that would result in *general* undermaintenance, de-

---

demolished. For the replacement units, $h_{12}$ or $h_2$ may be zero. Indeed, the homogeneity of many projects is such that it might be more typical to speak of replacement by $H_{12}$ or $H_2$, but not both.

[3] Any aggregate benefits that stem from such accomplishments as invigorating downtown areas, obtaining a better population balance in the central city, and beautifying architecture and land-use configuration are omitted. Any such benefits are highly diffuse and not susceptible to detailed measurement. They represent output packages whose existence should be called to the attention of the electorate. It is for the electorate implicitly to call out a valuation for these packages through their relative support for different policies.

spite the fact that property owners by assumption found general high maintenance more profitable than general undermaintenance. The actual situation may not be of this specific type, but it will have the same basic properties for purposes of this analysis.

The suboptimality stems from the fact that, without coordination, the property owners are individually led toward the inferior overall situation. By supposition, if they could coordinate their choice, they would presumably choose the set of individual actions that would give the preferred overall situation. But coordination is costly to achieve. Information must be collected from the group; the preferred total action must be formulated out of this information; the analysis must be conveyed back to the group with the respective individual action assignments; and conformity with assigned actions must be enforced. At each stage the needs of coordination are potentially thwarted by the higher gains to be won by each individual in tricking the group into taking the group action while he himself reneges (the "free-rider" problem).

The need for enforcement especially foredooms most attempts at coordination that do not rest at least in part on formal contracts. For slum land, a coordinated floor to property maintenance can be obtained through government action—by means of strict code and zoning enforcement. But concerted private action does not have this option. Aside from *appealing* to government for strict enforcement, in order to remain legal the requisite formal contractual quality is likely to be forthcoming only through common ownership, although some forms of voluntary association may occasionally succeed as well. Common ownership is far more likely than any voluntary means to produce any desired level of overall maintenance instead of simply a minimum acceptable level.

To broaden the type of externality, assume that in a certain area there are a large number of small land ownership parcels and on each a small structure. Suppose now that application to this area of a technological change in construction methods would increase the total profits to land and improvements (and also the profit rate on improvements) by replacing the several structures with a single large structure. Suppose that in this large structure the same number and quality of dwelling units could be provided much more efficiently. Here it is actually *group integrated* action, not simply coordinated individual action, that is needed to realize the economy.

Even government regulation would not suffice. For the kind of integrated action needed, common ownership is a requisite.

Thus, land assembly is either uniquely required or simply most appropriate to internalize many externalities, depending on the precise nature of the externalities. But land assembly is expensive. The more individual parcels there are to purchase, the more difficult is the task. Besides, the more knowledge there is about the plans for large-scale assembly, the stronger and more obstructive becomes the bargaining power of the property owners who must be bought out. The bargaining losses and delays that must be accepted in land assembly can easily dissuade private entrepreneurs from undertaking the project.

Government redevelopment substantially cuts the cost of land assembly through use of the right of eminent domain. This bypasses any potential bargaining power that property owners might gain because of the sequential nature of the assembly process. No holdout can block assembly by setting outrageous terms. Thus, assembly by eminent domain enables land in the redevelopment site to be used in large enough units to internalize neighborhood externalities —either for coordination only or for integrated use.

Herein lies the first major type of benefit from redevelopment projects. Under fragmented tenure, land use is suboptimal because coordination or integration across tenure plots is unavailable. The land itself has lower productivity than it might have because the barrier of fragmented ownership forces it to be used in units that are too small. Government assembly for redevelopment incurs all the costs of assembly, demolition, clearance, and site preparation in order to create what is in effect a new type of land input—land that can be used in units large enough to internalize neighborhood externalities.[4] It is as if a technical innovation were made, transforming all units of a certain input to ones with higher productivity. This virtual input transformation is the source of the externality benefits. It represents net social gain in terms of national income.

It should be noted that it is the large-scale assembly of land, made possible by eminent domain, that creates the internalized decision making, not demolition and site preparation. Yet the latter

[4] One way of looking at the phenomenon—although this is not quite accurate—is as an example of increasing returns to scale.

two are responsible for much of the real costs involved in the project. This distinction is of some practical importance. Chapter XIII considers a proposal to modify renewal policy by retaining assembly while dispensing with demolition and site preparation. Government action would be called upon solely to bypass the costliness of private land assembly. It is important, therefore, to be clear as to the role played by demolition and site preparation in renewal policy.

Land acquired by government under eminent domain could simply be sold "as is" in large parcels to private interests. It is assumed that some change in land usage would result, since by assumption the new internalized decision making would lead to the availability of more profitable options than before. But the new land use need not involve eliminating slum occupancy completely in the area. For government, on the other hand, not only pecuniary gains but also the social costs associated with slum living must be considered in deciding on the most desirable change in usage. Government responsibility for demolition and preparation is explained at least partly by the desire to guarantee that slum elimination will form part of the process of transformed land use. So the benefits associated with slum elimination are intimately connected with the demolition and site preparation components of redevelopment projects.

A result of the internalization of decision making is that higher land use becomes economically feasible. When redevelopment has brought about such use, the "improvement" in this neighborhood increases the attractiveness of real estate in the adjoining neighborhoods, thereby increasing their value. Since the quality of housing services stems in part from the neighborhood, this spillover effect is a true nonpecuniary (real) external effect. The increase in value then is a kind of productivity effect and counts as an increase in aggregate income.

The effect on the redevelopment site of this virtual transformation of the land input, other things being equal, is an increase in the land's value. But redevelopment involves as well the replacement of $h_{11}$ by $h_{12}$ and $h_2$. Whether these affect the enhanced value of land in the development site must be considered. Analysis of this extends through the second, or redistributional, impact of redevelopment. It is assumed as a good first approximation that redevelopment does not affect the total demand function for housing in the metropolitan area or the separate total demands for low-quality and other housing:

1. Zero effect on overall community income is assumed.[5]

2. While slight effects on the distribution of money income may occur, the impact on overall housing demand is likely to be negligible; the larger redistribution occurs through income effects fully reflected in a given demand function.

3. Replacement construction of $H_{12}$ and/or $H_2$ on the redevelopment site may have a demonstration effect on housing tastes, especially if attractive new features are embodied in these structures. This might increase the overall demand for housing. Such an effect cannot be counted on for most projects, however. To carry out the analysis of a typical project, it is assumed that such taste changes are absent or negligible.

The project itself demolishes $h_{11}$ units. Two cases must be treated: (1) where $h_{12} = h_{11}$ and (2) where $h_{12} < h_{11}$. Of the two, the latter is by far the more realistic. Indeed, the first is treated more as a point of comparison than as a real possibility.

## Effects on the Structure of the Housing Stock

Case I: $h_{12} = h_{11}$ and, $h_2 = 0$. *Low-quality dwelling units exactly replace demolished units.*

There is no net change in the size or composition of the housing stock between $H_1$ and $H_2$. The size of the low-quality stock is unchanged, but more units meet minimum standards, while the number of "housing services" is decreased, since quarters that were previously legally overcrowded are now less crowded.[6] (See Figure 1

[5] The reason for this assumption will be discussed at length in Chap. VIII.

[6] When doubling-up occurs in a certain housing unit, it is reasonable to say that the same unit is now providing more "housing services" than previously. The two "households," or "families," share certain overhead facilities of the unit, so each obtains more than—say—half of the preceding quantity of services. The total is increased.

The decrease in supply of services is more marked if one allows for the fact that a slum "unit" is often larger than a "unit" in a newer dwelling. The replacement, it is assumed, may well reduce total dwelling space as well as housing "services." But this does not affect the basic analysis, and this treatment is, in effect, given in terms of an exact replacement of dwelling space instead of "units" by tacitly assuming that new and old units reflect equal space.

**FIGURE 1**

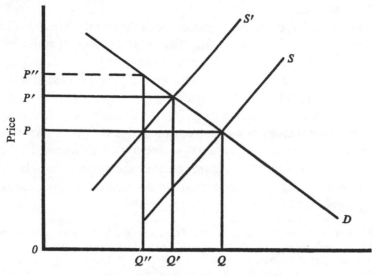

Quantity of $H_1$ "housing services"

The supply decreases from $S$ to $S'$. The first response is to decrease the quantity to $Q''$, whereupon price rises to $P''$. The supply elasticity greater than zero is due to the fact that when inferior dwellings are highly profitable—as a result of rising prices, for example—property owners find it advantageous to convert their dwellings to inferior use—preponderantly to slum use. The elasticity is not infinitely great because of the imperfect substitution in different parts of the stock and the sometimes substantial costs of conversion. In the present case, the amount supplied increases, and the new equilibrium is at $P'$, $Q'$. The price is higher, the quantity lower.

The conversion to inferior—probably slum and near-slum—use from $Q''$ to $Q'$ does not affect the demand for land. As was noted earlier, the housing market typically meets entrepreneurial factor demand for $H_1$ through filtering rather than through new construction. So property owners who want to convert simply refashion their own existing structures to the desired use. No land transactions are involved. Thus, land prices—and so land rentals—do not change except for the original impact on redevelopment site land.[7]

---

[7] A small amount of the filtered housing may come from $H_2$, reflected as an

Case 2: $h_{12} < h_{11}$. *Replacement is less than demolition of low-quality units.*

This is the typical case under redevelopment: $h_{12} < h_{11}$, and $H_2$ increases; but $h_{12} + h_2 < h_{11}$. The total number of units in the overall stock decreases.[8] (See Figures 2a and 2b.)

The supply of $H_1$ declines and that of $H_2$ increases, with no change in demands. $H_2$ prices decline; $H_1$ prices rise.[9] Thus, there is an incentive for conversion from $H_2$ to $H_1$. This is accomplished by filtering rather than by new construction and is shown by movements along the respective supply curves: from $Q_2''$ downward to $Q_2'$; from $Q_1''$ upward to $Q_1'$.[10] Again, neither the original supply shifts nor the subsequent conversions involve differential bidding for land. So aggregate land prices are again untouched.[11]

---

inward shift of the supply curve of $H_2$. Thus, a slight intermarket reverberation between $H_1$ and $H_2$ may occur, even in this case. Most of the elasticity of $S_1$ is probably accounted for by filtering within the $H_1$ stock. For whatever intermarket reverberation occurs, there may be an even slighter increase in the demand for extra-marginal land to be drawn into the provision of housing services and with it, a very slight upward effect on land prices.

[8] As was indicated earlier, Renewal Assistance Administration figures place the ratio as approximately four units demolished (mostly in $H_1$) to each three units of planned replacement (mostly in $H_2$). Planned public housing replacement ($h_{12}$) is put at 8 percent of total planned replacements. As was noted above, in the simplified model it was assumed that all demolitions were from $H_{11}$, although this is not in fact true. Within the redevelopment site there are typically many $H_{12}$ units. A site need not have anything like 100 percent blight to qualify for redevelopment.

[9] Supply curves $S_1'$ and $S_2'$ represent conditions after intermarket reverberations have worked themselves out. They are, in effect, the supply conditions compatible with a new multi-market equilibrium. Thus curve $S_1'$ is slightly more elastic than $S_1$ because it reflects the lower price of $H_2$ services. With the increase in the stock of $H_2$ houses and the decrease in the stock of $H_1$ houses the price differential between them decreases. Therefore, owners of $H_2$ units are more likely to convert their property to $H_1$ units for each subsequent upward movement in $H_1$ prices.

[10] As was indicated in note 7 to this chapter, the positive supply elasticity of $S_1$ partly reflects substitutability between $H_1$ and $H_2$. The movement from $Q_2''$ to $Q_1'$ may be accompanied by a slight decrease in $S_2$. The positive elasticity of $S_2$ is less likely to be associated with $H_1 - H_2$ substitutability, since upward conversion is probably more difficult than downward conversion.

[11] An aggregate effect on land prices is again possible, but likely here to be even smaller than before. As was indicated above, a conceivable result of the net decrease in housing units is to substitute for filtering new construction on low-density land, especially in suburbs. But suburban expansion is a substitute for $H_2$ units, and these have risen here. So any such land price effect will be treated as negligible.

**FIGURE 2a**

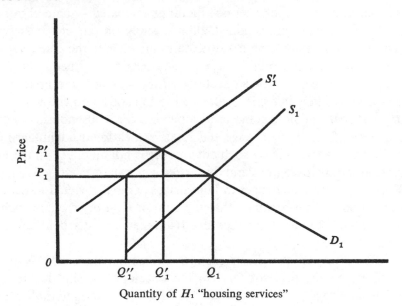

Quantity of $H_1$ "housing services"

**FIGURE 2b**

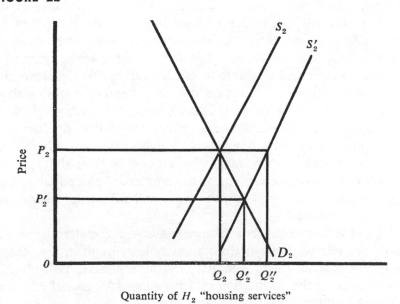

Quantity of $H_2$ "housing services"

There are factors under Case 2 that may affect the prices of some land. Along with residential units there are likely to be commercial units and public service facilities relocated—some eliminated from the site, others added, both directly on the site and adjacent to it. This relocation may substantially change the character of the commercial and public service adjuncts to the neighborhood and, if extensive, to broader sections of the metropolitan area. This is especially likely in projects attempting to revamp downtown areas or to attract middle-income and upper-income households. A consequence of this is to change the relative locational advantages of different areas. Changing such advantages is not an effect on the aggregate productivity of land but only on relative attractiveness. Thus, only relative changes in land prices can be expected to occur. For simplicity it is assumed that the sum of land price changes due to a redistribution of locational advantages and disadvantages is equal to zero.

To summarize the effects of redevelopment so far: there is, first, an effect on the price of land in the development site due to the greater leverage possible with land in this form—the internalization of externalities. This generally leads as well to spillover gains in the attractiveness of neighboring land and improvements. There are, second, differential effects on the size of different portions of the housing stock. These influence the relative prices of different accommodations and therefore hurt tenants whose dwelling units have become more expensive while helping those whose units have become cheaper and available in greater variety. At the same time they have the opposite effect on dwelling owners, benefiting those whose property has appreciated and hurting those whose property has depreciated. These differential effects in relative supplies leave land values essentially untouched. Land values are affected by changes in locational advantages brought on by these shifts and by their influences on the movement of commercial and public service facilities. Such locational influences are redistributional rather than aggregate, however.

Land values on the redevelopment site will, therefore, generally show two effects: one a net productivity improvement, the other a relative locational effect. The first is of interest here. To isolate it, use is made of the assumption that the sum of locational effects in the metropolitan area is zero and that these effects are the only sources of land price changes elsewhere. It can easily be shown algebraically that the land price changes on the redevelopment site ascribable to internalization of externalities can be measured as the sum of land price changes in the metropolitan area, including the redevelopment site (assuming that all other influences on land prices are unchanged).[12]

Let:

$\Delta P_s$ = the total land price change in the redevelopment site.

$\Delta P_{sE}$ = the land price change in the redevelopment site due to internalization of externalities.

$\Delta P_{\bar{s}}$. = the total land price change elsewhere in the metropolitan area (assumed due only to changes in locational advantages).

Then:

(7.1) $$\Delta P_{sE} = \Delta P_s + \Delta P_{\bar{s}}.$$

## Social Costs of Slum Living

Next to be discussed is the third type of benefit—the social effects of eliminating slum property. From the model it may be seen that conversion of dwellings to low-quality use takes place in both Case 1 and Case 2, but more extensively in Case 2, since relative prices are affected more strongly. This means that three types of effect on slums can be expected. First is the actual elimination of slum property in the redevelopment site. Second is the movement of dislocated slum dwellers into already overcrowded slum units, thereby increasing the degree of overcrowding. An increase in housing costs to these people induces them to purchase even smaller quantities of housing than previously (and this applies as well to slum dwellers elsewhere who are not dislocated but whose own accommodations rise in price because of the new competition from those who are dislocated).[13] Third is the conversion of property down to slum level

---

[12] See the appendix to this chapter for the derivation.

[13] Relocatees may move not to more overcrowded but rather to less overcrowded quarters if they allow themselves to be persuaded to do this by a forceful government relocation program. If so, their housing costs will rise further. However, an increase in crowding will occur for households at and below the level of the housing now more vigorously competed for by the relocatees.

use for the first time—the spread of slums. The net effect, therefore, is a consolidation of elimination, worsening, and spread. On balance, a smaller physical area, and probably fewer total units, are likely to be at slum level, but this effect will be smaller than the area and number of units demolished for redevelopment; and some worsening of conditions in existing slums is likely to have occurred.

Whatever the extent of the reduction in slums, this can be expected to bear on the intensity of the social problems allegedly generated by the existence of slums. The size and character of the impact should probably be expected to depend on the particular composite of effects listed in the preceding paragraph. For example, the influence on fire hazard probably depends on what has happened to the geographical extent and the degree of overcrowding of slums. Health hazards probably depend more on the degree of overcrowding than on the geographical area covered. Personality problems are likely to be affected by the size of the adverse income effect on poor families and the amount of household rotation that takes place before the reverberations of dislocation work themselves out. Unfortunately, little of a general nature can be adduced to predict particular patterns in the "typical" redevelopment project.

One aspect of the last factor should be commented on, since it can affect the extent of slum usage *both* in actual slums *and* in the redevelopment site itself or in newly constructed dwellings designed to house dislocated families. It has been persuasively argued[14] that characteristics of community functioning that are usually attributed to slums—crime, violence, filth, property abuse, and social irresponsibility—stem not so much from the physical characteristics of dwellings, or from population density, as from social rootlessness, the sense of living in a transitional or temporary situation to which one does not really belong and to which one therefore feels no commitment. Stability of neighborhood and the encouragement of diversity of opportunity, it is claimed, enhance responsible behavior—whatever the socio-income level. On the other hand, a rapid

[14] See Bernard Lander, *Towards an Understanding of Juvenile Delinquency* (Columbia University Press, 1954), p. 79; Alvin L. Schorr, *Slums and Social Insecurity* (U.S. Department of Health, Education, and Welfare, 1963), pp. 142-43; Jane Jacobs, *The Death and Life of Great American Cities* (Random House, 1961), Part I and Chap. 15; Harrison E. Salisbury, *The Shook-Up Generation* (Harper, 1958).

turnover of inhabitants represents an eating up of social capital, a destruction of the reciprocal social expectations to which individuals could assume responsibility. Similarly, excessive homogeneity of situation and opportunity discourages the assumption of specialized community roles, which builds a network of social support and sanctions.

Certain types of redevelopment, by moving many people *en masse,* tear up intricate supportive social interrelationships and give them little in return. This problem might be only transitional—albeit a difficult one—if redevelopment did not sometimes set other stages for repetition of the same phenomena. Slum-by-slum redevelopment may sometimes be a repeated chase to catch blight spread from previous projects. Moreover, an emphasis on extreme homogeneity of accommodation in many projects prepares the ground for subsequent successive waves of immigration into and out of such areas, thereby depriving them of the materials important for stabilizing them as neighborhoods. This is a type of neighborhood utilization that can accelerate the depreciation of property in the manner discussed earlier in this book.

Thus, the third type of benefit (and cost) from redevelopment is highly complicated. Some benefits are likely to be produced; but there are possibilities for substituting one kind of social disutility for another. The fact that one or both kinds may prove difficult to measure does not excuse planners and outside observers from giving them attention. They will be considered more fully below.

# APPENDIX TO CHAPTER VII

# Calculation of Land-Use Externality Benefits

This appendix isolates the effect of internalizing land-use externalities from other influences on land prices. The following notation is used:

Let:

$\Delta P_s$ = land price changes in the redevelopment site.

$\Delta P_{sE}$ = land price changes in the redevelopment site due to internalization of externalities.

$\Delta P_{sL}$ = land price changes in the redevelopment site due to changes in locational advantages.

$\Delta P_{\bar{s}}$ = land price changes elsewhere than in the redevelopment site (but within the metropolitan area).

$\Delta P_{\bar{s}L}$ = land price changes elsewhere than in the redevelopment site (but within the metropolitan area) due to changes in locational advantages.

$\Delta P_s$ and $\Delta P_{\bar{s}}$ are observables, but $\Delta P_{sE}$, $\Delta P_{sL}$, and $\Delta P_{\bar{s}L}$ are not. Assuming that the sum of locational effects in the metropolitan area is zero, and that these effects are the only sources of land price changes in the area, then:

(7.1a) $$\Delta P_s = \Delta P_{sE} + \Delta P_{sL},{}^{\text{a}}$$
(7.1b) $$\Delta P_{sL} + \Delta P_{\bar{s}L} = 0,$$
(7.1c) $$\Delta P_{\bar{s}} = \Delta P_{\bar{s}L};$$

so:

(7.1d) $$\Delta P_s = \Delta P_{sE} - \Delta P_{\bar{s}}$$

or

(7.1e) $$\Delta P_{sE} = \Delta P_s + \Delta P_{\bar{s}}.$$

Notice that equation (7.1e) derives the desired nonobservable as a function of observables only.

<hr>

[a] For simplicity, it is assumed that there are no property taxes on land. The question of tax capitalization as it appears in land prices will be treated in Chap. VIII.

128

# CHAPTER VIII

# Internalization of Externalities

As HAS BEEN SEEN from the model of redevelopment impact, benefits from the internalization of externalities are measured by the value of increased productivity of the land on the redevelopment site and any resulting spillover enhancement of attractiveness of neighboring real estate, both land and structures. For measurement purposes an effort will be made to obtain the magnitude of the first by observing the difference between the highest price at which the local public agency (LPA) can sell the prepared site under competitive bidding and the price that it paid to acquire the site. As has been seen, such a change in land price is likely to include effects of changing locational advantages. Therefore the adjustment indicated in equation (7.1e) in the appendix to Chapter VII must be made in order to solve for $\Delta P_{sE}$.

Another theoretical modification is necessary if $\Delta P_{sE}$ is to be measured. The selling price of land in a competitive market reflects the net productivity of the land, that is, its productivity less any tax liabilities that must be paid on its value or use. Since the site land will be subject to the local—and perhaps state—real property tax, the price that a private redeveloper is willing to pay is less than its productivity by the capitalized value of the expected tax liabilities on the land. A distinction must therefore be made between the "productivity value" of the land and its selling price.

Let: $V_E$ = the productivity value of the redevelopment site land attributable to nonlocational factors (the factors that are subject to the externalities that the project internalizes).

$t(P_E)$ = the capitalized value of anticipated taxes, assuming that these taxes depend chiefly on market value.

Then it can be shown that:[1]

(8.1) $$P_E = V_E - t(P_E)$$

and

(8.2) $$\Delta V_E = (\Delta P_s + \Delta P_{\bar{s}}) + t(\Delta P_s + \Delta P_{\bar{s}}).$$

## Selling Price as an Estimate of Social Value

Thus, to calculate the relevant change in value one must know the change in land prices for the site and for the rest of the metropolitan area and the change in capitalized value of taxes for both. This is subject to a number of pitfalls:

1. The price at which the LPA sells the prepared site may diverge substantially from the competitive market price. The LPA does not always ask for competitive bids. Furthermore, it often insists on disposing of the site to a single redeveloper, even though some fragmentation might yield a higher total selling price.[2] In asserting that assembly makes possible more efficient land utilization because of the larger unit of land-use decision making, the issue of how large a unit would be most efficient for the given situation was not prejudged. This question is essentially to be answered by the market. However, a public policy by the LPA that insists on disposal to a single redeveloper prevents the market from giving an answer. The danger of such a policy is that by requiring the purchaser to redevelop the entire site, the LPA is very likely to be imposing a substantial barrier to entry. Very few redevelopers have the organi-

---

[1] See the appendix to this chapter for derivations.

[2] See Lyman Brownfield, "The Disposition Problem in Urban Renewal," *Law and Contemporary Problems*, Vol. 25 (Autumn 1960), pp. 732-76; Eli Goldston, Allan O. Hunter, and Guido A. Rothrauff, Jr., "Urban Redevelopment—The Viewpoint of Counsel for a Private Redeveloper," *Law and Contemporary Problems*, Vol. 26 (Winter 1961), pp. 118-77.

zation and access to capital to enable them to bid. The result is oligopsonistic bidding at the very least—lower bids than could be expected if entry were easier.

There is another difficulty of this sort. The LPA redevelopment plans often call for rather special characteristics. The agency is not willing to sell to the highest bidder, irrespective of the redevelopment plans of the bidder. Certain types of bid are entirely disqualified, while others have to be modified in terms of the requirements of the LPA's conception of desirable redevelopment. This complicates greatly the problem of discovering the true new market value of the site. The difficulty is that the measuring procedure used here tacitly envisages only private gains as benefits of this first type. When the LPA plans place constraints on the configuration of redevelopment, consideration for social costs and gains intrudes on market transactions. It is hard to believe that the resulting thinness of the market can give price quotations tolerably close to the social valuation of the productivity of the land. The assumption is made, of course, that the social valuation of the desired pattern of redevelopment on the site must be at least as great as the private valuation of highest private market use, or the site would be released to private use. This tells something about the lower bound of value, but does not otherwise help the measurement problem much, since the price actually accepted by the LPA for approved redevelopment is not the private unconstrained valuation and gives no indication of the amount of subsidy involved in meeting the social constraints. A better approximation would require detailed information about the profitability of alternative unapproved types of redevelopment.

In a situation like this, the observer can try to discover whether bids for unconstrained "highest market use" were made to the LPA in the course of disposals. The highest of any such known bids, if it exceeds the bid actually accepted, can be taken as a lower limit to the new value of the land. In addition, estimates can be made of the additional profitability that might have accrued to the land if LPA planning constraints were not imposed and this addition capitalized. This can be aided by the derivation of demand and supply functions for housing, with quality transformed into quantity equivalents by means of regressions testing behavior substitutability in both demand and supply. The simplest hypothesis is that behavior is symmetric with respect to changes in value stemming from either quantity or quality.

2. A second difficulty in this formulation is that it is implicitly assumed that when the LPA buys property under eminent domain, it shifts the same capitalized tax liability backward to the seller that a private purchaser would.[3] Does the LPA in reality gauge the land's worth by acting as though it were itself to be subject to tax liability? This is not reasonable, but a stronger rationale is given by supposing that the LPA expects to lose out by the backward shifting capitalization of newly expected tax when *it* disposes of the land after site preparation. The land *is* worth less to the LPA by the expectation of this backward shifting at the time of disposal; it therefore will pay less when it purchases the land. This reasoning may not in fact reflect practice. If not, the procedure shown in equation (8.2) is incorrect. Rectification in such a case may not be difficult. Associated with most projects have been the legal suits brought by former property owners against the LPA contesting the adequacy of compensation under eminent domain.[4] Examination of the court's decision in a number of these cases would very likely indicate whether or not, or to what extent, the capitalized tax was subtracted. The appropriate correction could be made on this basis.

3. A third difficulty is less a problem of principle and more one of statistical practice. Land price changes for the redevelopment site are presumed to include the impact of changing relative locational advantages. These changes are to be eliminated by calculating their offset—changing land prices in the rest of the metropolitan area. The problem concerns the measurement of this last. Time series data would seem to be most appropriate for this. Yet such

[3] In deriving (8.2) and (8.1f), the latter of which is in the appendix to this chapter, it is implicitly assumed that:

(a) $$P_{E0} = V_{E0} - t(P_{E0}) \text{ and}$$
(b) $$P_{E1} = V_{E1} - t(P_{E1}),$$

where (a) refers to the LPA's valuation when it buys the land from private owners and (b) refers to the private purchaser's valuation when he buys the land from the LPA. The key assumption is that the capitalization function $t(P)$ is the same for both.

[4] David Berger, "Current Problems Affecting Costs of Condemnation," *Law and Contemporary Problems,* Vol. 26 (Winter 1961), pp. 85-104; see also Irvin Dagen and Edward C. Cody, "Property, *et al. v.* Nuisance, *et al.,*" *Law and Contemporary Problems,* Vol. 26 (Winter 1961), pp. 70-84.

data would reflect not only these influences but also those stemming from aspects of the system that have implicitly been impounded among the constants—population changes, industrial changes, macro-economic developments, and so on. The measuring procedure might reasonably be as follows: Begin by calculating "normal" land prices for the metropolitan area as a function of critical variables, such as community income and population (with or without breakdowns for demographic characteristics). For example,

Let: $\bar{P}_{s+\bar{s}}$ = "normal price" of metropolitan land.
$Y$ = community income.
$N$ = size of population.

Then:

(8.3) $$\bar{P}_{s+\bar{s}} = P(Y,N).$$

Consider now the period just after completion of the redevelopment project,[5] Period 1.

Let:

$P_{s+\bar{s},1}$ = actual total land price for the metropolitan area in Period 1.
$\bar{P}_{s+\bar{s},1}$ = normal total land price for the metropolitan area in Period 1.
$e_1$ = error in Period 1, containing a stochastic component.

Then:
(8.4) $$P_{s+\bar{s},1} = \bar{P}_{s+\bar{s},1} + e_1 \quad \text{or} \quad e_1 = P_{s+\bar{s},1} - \bar{P}_{s+\bar{s},1}.$$

It is assumed that (8.3) is linear in the arguments and that the same regression holds for $s$ and $\bar{s}$. Therefore:

Let:

$\bar{P}_{s1}$ = normal land price on the site in Period 1.
$Y_{s1}$ = income for inhabitants of the site in Period 1.
$N_{s1}$ = number of inhabitants of the site in Period 1.

Then:
(8.5) $$\bar{P}_{s1} = P(Y_{s1},N_{s1}).[6]$$

[5] This period is chosen because a locational impact does not occur until after the new dwellings and facilities are completed. The term "just after" is to allow lag time for this impact to take place.
[6] As an alternative form, $Y/N$ may be used as the income argument. Comparison of their respective merits is beyond the scope of this study. In addition,

Similarly:

(8.6)                              $\bar{P}_{\bar{s}1} = P(Y_{\bar{s}1}, N_{\bar{s}1})$.

Next, the amount of deviation from these "normal" site and off-site prices due to locational changes will be computed. To do this, total $e_1$ must be distributed to the actual site and off-site prices in Period 1, $P_{s1}$ and $P_{\bar{s}1}$, so as in effect to reflect their "non-stochastic" component. The divergence between these error terms so distributed and $\bar{P}_{s1}$ and $\bar{P}_{\bar{s}1}$ may be treated as a systematic variation due to the locational factor. By applying as a constraint the assumption that the sum of locational effects is zero, $e_1$ is distributed between $e_{s1}$ and $e_{\bar{s}1}$. That is, these conditions are applied:

(8.7)                              $e_1 = e_{s1} + e_{\bar{s}1}$;

(8.8)              $(P_{\bar{s}1} - e_{s1}) - \bar{P}_{s1} = -(P_{\bar{s}1} - e_{\bar{s}1}) - \bar{P}_{\bar{s}1}$.

The difficulty here is one of data and statistical practice. First, a simple linear regression like (8.3) is likely to give a poor fit, considering the important idiosyncratic factors operating in the land market in different cities. This means that $e_1$ can be expected to be large. The larger $e_1$ is, the more dangerous is the arbitrary partitioning into $e_{s1}$ and $e_{\bar{s}1}$. Whatever systematic component there is, is likely to be swamped by error; closeness of fit of (8.3) should not be dismissed a priori. It can be put to the test.[7]

Second, it is questionable whether accurate data necessary for these computations can be obtained. Income figures for cities over a reasonable time interval are not easily available, let alone for met-

---

discussions of the problem of statistical identification is omitted in both regressions (8.3) and (8.5). A brief remark on this is called for, however. Both of these regressions are interpreted as reduced from equations, the demand response being obvious, the supply response being in the form of the amount of land in the metropolitan area—both functions of $Y$ and $N$.

[7] Actually, in the regression that was fitted as part of a numerical illustration of the procedure, a very close fit was obtained. The correlation coefficient was 0.975. The closeness of fit was very likely due to the fact that the period chosen was dominated by a secular linear trend, which strongly affected all of the variables. Indeed, regressing the dependent variable on time alone gave almost as good a fit. Success under these circumstances does not constitute persuasive evidence.

ropolitan areas, and especially not for redevelopment sites. Population figures for redevelopment sites are probably unobtainable over such a time interval.

Third, much hinges on the assumption that locational effects cancel out in the aggregate. The estimates here may well be very sensitive to any deviation from this in the real world. If the amount of locational impact is small, the estimates may be almost entirely an artifact of the data and procedure used here.

In view of these difficulties, the following strategy may be advisable. For small projects, where the locational impact is probably minor, omit any locational adjustment from site price. Assuming that redevelopment typically enhances the location of the site, this would have the effect of overstating redevelopment benefits relating to externalities. For larger projects, or for projects whose specific characteristics make it likely that substantial locational advantages have been shifted, the procedure here can be attempted. An indication of how successful such a procedure will be is the closeness of fit attainable with linear regression (8.3). Of course, the basic regression need not be the one given by (8.3); it may include different and/or more arguments and have different form. In the latter case, some change will be necessary in the rest of the procedure.

## Benefit-Cost and Governmental Profits: The Assumption of Full Employment

The method proposed for measuring site benefits arising out of the internalization of externalities involves largely a comparison between what the local public agency (LPA) pays for inputs and what it receives for outputs. As such, it has some similarity to a method of measurements proposed by Davis and Whinston.[8] They measure costs and benefits as the outlays and receipts of the local government that arise out of the project. Benefits from the project represent the enhancement of the value of the site as a result of the coordination of land-use decisions brought about by governmental assembly through eminent domain, demolition, and preparation. Value is measured in terms of the private market's view of opportu-

[8] Otto A. Davis and Andrew B. Whinston, "The Economics of Urban Renewal," *Law and Contemporary Problems,* Vol. 26 (Winter 1961), pp. 105-17.

nities. The enhanced value of the site is reflected in local government receipts because the LPA can sell site land at a price that will compensate for its new productivity. Diminution of the purchase because of tax capitalization is subsequently captured by the local government in increased property tax revenues. As in the procedure used here, the amount of tax capitalization can be measured by computing a present discounted value of increased tax liability. Davis and Whinston view this measurement as exhausting benefits and costs from redevelopment projects. Therefore, they are willing to adopt as an overall criterion a government budget effect—or government "profit" effect. If the local government's revenues due to the project exceed its outlays, then the project is warranted. Otherwise it is not.

The difficulty with this measurement procedure and criterion—and a major source of the difference between it and the one proposed here—lies in what is considered to be "due to" the project. As costs, Davis and Whinston include LPA payments, not only for the land, but for improvements—structures standing on the land—as well. Similarly, they include as benefits not only the higher value of site land but also the present discounted value of the increase in tax liability on improvements. This latter factor can easily swamp all other components. The structures erected as part of the redevelopment invariably have a far higher market value than those they replace, and probably even disproportionately higher assessed values.[9]

The value of the demolished property is, of course, a cost of the project and will be included as part of the net project cost. But inclusion of the value of the new structures and other improvements as offsetting benefits is improper. It implies that the particular investment in reproducible capital represents a net social gain. This would be true only if its opportunity cost were zero, that is, if it represented the output of resources that would not otherwise have been used. Thus, to include the investment, one would have to argue that the resources used up would not otherwise have been used to produce housing elsewhere, or, indeed, anything else of value.

Some writers in the field do indeed take this view. They argue

---

[9] It has been suggested above that slum structures are apt to be underassessed relative to standard structures.

that one of the purposes of the urban renewal program is as a countercyclical instrument—in other words, that the program puts resources to work that would otherwise be unemployed. But urban renewal is surely a very poorly conceived type of program for this purpose. It takes so long to initiate and so long to complete projects that its timing is of little or no countercyclical help; it may, indeed, aggravate cyclical swings.

For this reason it will be assumed that the program has no net employment effect, either direct or indirect. This does not mean that a building constructed on the redevelopment site precludes another building just like it elsewhere in the metropolitan area, although this may sometimes occur. It means rather an assumption of full employment. Investment on the site displaces other useful employment for the resources used.

The full-employment assumption is not by itself enough to determine the exact magnitude of benefits from site investment. It is possible, after all, for resources to be shifted from less productive to more productive use, while remaining fully employed in both situations. Allowance is made here for widespread competition in the capital market via the full-employment assumption; in addition, highly competitive construction markets are assumed. Together this permits treating site investment as representing marginal (hence homogeneous) resource shifts. The productivity of displaced uses is therefore assumed to equal that of use on the redevelopment site. This assumption, wherever incorrect, biases measured redevelopment benefits downward.

It is not impossible in principle to formulate a more discriminating measure. In principle, a better measure would be one in which differential profitability signifies net benefits as a result of resource shifts to the site. The amount of increased (or decreased) profitability because of shifting is a measure of the generation of net benefits (or costs).[10] In practice, however, this may not be calculable. Unless it is certain that the redeveloper paid the full market price for the site land and has received neither subsidy nor constraint from the government, private profit accounts are not a good measure of differential productivity. Earlier there was reason

---

[10] But profits would have to be calculated gross of any marginal taxes or subsidies involved in financing the project to avoid distorted comparisons. I am indebted to Richard Muth for emphasizing this point in personal correspondence.

to doubt the competitiveness of site disposition transactions. In addition, the "affected-with-the-general-interest" nature of redevelopment often involves various hidden public subsidies to the redeveloper. Finally, as was noted above, public constraints on the pattern of redevelopment *are* frequently imposed in the process of site disposition by the LPA.

## Spillover Effects on Neighboring Real Estate

This leads to the second component of benefits from internalization of externalities. While the full-employment assumption rules out inclusion of redevelopment site improvements (structures) as benefits, it does not rule out certain effects of redevelopment on the value of improvements as well as of land off the site. It was argued earlier that the real value of housing services rendered by any given unit is a function of facilities in the neighborhood as well as of the characteristics of the dwelling unit itself. For any unit near enough to the redevelopment site, redevelopment improves the complexion of the neighborhood and therefore in effect improves the quality of the housing provided by the unit. This externality represents a true technical enhancement of housing quality brought about by the project and, as was indicated above, should be counted as an aggregate benefit. Both the land and the structures, as complementary inputs, share in this enhancement.

Unfortunately there are two complexities that must be unraveled before this can be done. The positive externality generated is a neighborhood effect, and its impact is restricted to the neighborhood. The first concerns the difficult problem of determining how far the "neighborhood" extends. The second is even more serious. It concerns how one should measure the benefits once one has succeeded in demarcating the impact neighborhood. At first glance, it would seem appropriate simply to treat as benefits all changes in the value of existing real property in the impact neighborhood.

The type of technical enhancement involved is not the only effect that redevelopment has on the value of off-site real property. There are, in addition, as has been described above, a general relative price repercussion throughout the housing market and a relative location effect. Unlike the neighborhood externality, neither of these represents an aggregate real income effect. They are redistributive. The trouble is that they are likely to be strongest on just those properties that are most likely to be affected by the neighborhood effect. Locational gains for the redevelopment site fan out, affecting nearby properties most. Price repercussion effects are due to changes in the relative supply of different types of housing. Since most redevelopment sites border other slum and near-slum areas, such areas would be expected to experience greater increases in property values than would most others, due to the relative decrease in the number of low-quality units. Moreover, it is established that most people who are dislocated by a project concentrate on the nearby areas in relocating. The two factors together suggest that bordering areas are among the most strongly—if not *the* most strongly—hit by *upward* price repercussions that do not reflect aggregate real income changes.

The relative housing stock effects are especially likely to be misleading. Consider an extreme case where neighborhood and locational effects are minimal. Suppose the "renewal" project involves simply destroying a large number of substandard[11] units, without rebuilding of any kind or conversion into parkland. That is, no production whatever occurs—only destruction. It is highly conceivable that property values in the adjoining areas will rise. It is even conceivable, given the right demand elasticities and if enough adjoining property is considered, that the increase in the value of existing property through revaluation will exceed the value of property destroyed. Then, if the reevaluations are included as benefits, one would be led to say that a cheap, radical destruction of property (whether slum or not) can produce net social benefits!

If real externalities produced by redevelopment are to be included, they must be demarcated from the effects of housing stock and locational changes. This seems most difficult to do because of the common clustering of all three on the same property. The following rough approximation may be attempted, although it is quite possible that computational costs will outweigh the progress made toward proper demarcation. Thus the approach will simply be sketched out here, and details will be omitted. The main objective is to obtain a measure of price response to the supply shifts in the city at large and to adjust this for the adjacent area in question in

[11] It will be seen below that the argument applies with equal force to destruction of standard units as well.

terms of the substitutability of its housing for that of the redevelopment area. First, an estimate of the demand function for low-quality housing is obtained in order to arrive at a price coefficient or a price elasticity of demand.[12] The total decrease in the low-quality housing supply is applied to this measure of price responsiveness along the demand function. This gives an estimate of price response to the supply shift on the part of the low-quality portion of the stock. Call this $_D\Delta P$ (that is, the demolition-induced price change in low-quality housing).

Now the extent to which the adjoining area feels this effect must be calculated. This depends on the degree of substitutability of the adjoining property for that of the demolished units. In the case of close substitutability this will equal $_D\Delta P$, but will decline toward zero as substitutability diminishes.

Let:

$k$ = the coefficient of substitutability.

$_D\Delta P_A$ = the supply-induced price change on adjoining property.

Then:

(8.9) $$_D\Delta P_A = k_D\Delta P.$$

The degree of substitutability is measured crudely in terms of the closeness of average rental levels (for "comparable" quantities of housing) between the two areas, that is:

Let:

$r_s$ = the average rental level in the redevelopment site.

$r_A$ = the average rental level in the adjoining area.

$0 \leq k \leq 1$ and defined as the step function $\{0, \frac{1}{4}, \frac{1}{2}, \frac{3}{4}, 1\}$ for increasing values of $r_s/r_A (0 \leq r_s/r_A \leq 1)$.

Then:

(8.10) $$k = k(r_s/r_A).$$

[12] It is suggested that the function be limited to that for low-quality housing on the suspicion that the relevant elasticity will differ as between higher-quality and low-quality housing and since this application will concern only the low-quality portion. Availability and costliness of data for such a refinement should of course dictate whether it is worth attempting.

The rationale for this treatment is that the more nearly similar the spillover area is to the units demolished, the more likely dislocated persons are to settle there, thereby forcing the relative supply-demand adjustment on this area; moreover, the less likely is the neighborhood improvement in the redevelopment site to enhance the value of the adjacent property since there will be little interplay between populations and economic activities in the two areas; and finally, the less likely are the new structures on the redevelopment site to compete with property in the adjacent area and so exert a *downward* pressure on property values. So most or all of any price increase experienced in the adjoining area reflects the distributional effect of relative stock changes and not genuine spillover or locational effects. Here $k$ is defined as a step function arbitrarily because of the unfeasibility of any direct way (for example, through estimates of actual cross-elasticities of demand) to link the ratio $r_s/r_A$ to the absolute magnitude of effect.

The total change in prices is now expressed as the sum of neighborhood spillover, location, and demolition-induced relative stock effects, as follows:

$$(8.11) \qquad \Delta P_A = {}_N\Delta P_A + {}_L\Delta P_A + {}_D\Delta P_A.$$

${}_D\Delta P_A$ is measured by (8.9). Then the desired term ${}_N\Delta P_A$ is obtained by assuming, where it is at all reasonable, that locational effects are negligible (that ${}_L\Delta P_A = 0$).

This method is obviously crude, but it helps somewhat to break down $\Delta P_A$. If its crudity does not seem to warrant the work involved and the gross inadequacies of the necessary data, an even cruder approach may be taken. It may be determined qualitatively whether the project is (1) locationally neutral; and (2) small enough to have only trivial relocation and relative housing stock effects.[13] If both (1) and (2) are met, then the entire change in adjoining property values may be assumed to represent a real income effect through neighborhood externalities. If *both* are not met, then revaluation changes can be assumed to contain no real income effects.

---

[13] It must be noted that the more nearly competitive the surrounding property is with the new housing, the smaller must the project be to have no such repercussions. On the other hand, except when the new housing is the untypical low-quality type (that is, public housing), the higher the competitiveness in property, the less relocation concentration is to be expected in adjoining areas.

Erroneous application of the first overstates benefits. Application of the second always understates benefits, but it understates them most seriously when it represents the worse side of the dichotomous choice.

The procedure could be modified for particular benefit-cost strategies. For example, if the investigator wanted consistently to overestimate benefits at each choice point to give the project every chance to justify itself in the face of his prior belief that the renewal program could probably not be justified, then he would want always to assume the first. An opposite strategy (usually based on the investigator's prior belief that the program could easily be justified) would lead to omitting these spillover effects entirely.

A second basic decision must be made so long as the spillover effects are not to be dismissed entirely. This is the question, mentioned earlier, of what property should be included. Any stopping place is arbitrary. Different portions of the market are always responding to a variety of forces. Thus, it is impossible to be sure about the source of a particular price change. There are factors to aid one's judgment, however. Sometimes the physical features of an area, like lakes or parks, or special functional configurations (observable in the pattern of transaction flows), produce clearly delineated neighborhood demarcations. Where such obvious signs are lacking, sometimes one can use as a substitute a demarcation based on the area over which price changes are homogeneously increased. This is more hazardous since property in any area is rarely homogeneous. Property that is more competitive with new units than the average in the area will show a smaller upward revaluation than the average or even a net downward revaluation, despite receiving as much neighborhood advantage from the new units. Thus, the effect of non-externality repercussions can damage the effectiveness of this demarcation technique.

To summarize, it is proposed to measure net benefits due to internalizing externalities as an enhancement in the value of the land forming the redevelopment site. This can be calculated by adjusting for tax capitalization and for changes in locational attraction. The latter adjustment is likely to be crude, and, where one suspects only small changes, it is advisable to drop the adjustment altogether. Unlike in the Davis-Whinston criterion, changes in the value of improvements are excluded, but the value of demolished structures *is* counted as a cost. In general, by adopting an assumption of full employment and wide competition in the capital markets, reproducible investments are viewed as displacing alternative resource uses with equal productivity. Relaxation of this last assumption permits calculation in principle of the advantage of non-marginal resource shifts; but in practice such calculation is likely to be essentially barred. In addition to these benefits reflected in site values, the new land uses that are made attractive produce genuine income spillover effects—enhancing the productivity of property outside the site but within the same neighborhood. These benefits are extremely hard to calculate, because of a concentration of project-generated redistributive effects on much the same outside property. Two crude techniques have been suggested to determine what allowance should be made for these benefits.

One final point must be made. So far only the effects of the redevelopment policy have been discussed and not those of the modified status quo policy. As has already been noted, this is because there is no unique modification policy, perhaps not even a best modification policy. To examine a wide variety of such possible alternatives would be beyond the scope of this book. But the effects of some alternatives will be described briefly in Chapter XIII. In a full-scale empirical application of the present analytic approach a deeper treatment would, of course, be essential. A choice of composite reform measures would have to be decided on. Only after this is done could an alternative set of benefits and costs be estimated to compare with those of redevelopment.

# APPENDIX TO CHAPTER VIII

## Adjustment of Land-Use Externality Benefits for Local Property Tax

This appendix adjusts land price changes for the existence of property taxes in order to calculate the true impact of redevelopment on the productivity of site land.

Let:

$V_0$ and $V_1 =$ the productivity values of the site land just before assembly and preparation, and after, respectively.

$T_0$ and $T_1 =$ the capitalized value of expected taxes before and after.

$t =$ the tax capitalization function relating each $V$ with a corresponding $T$.

$V_L =$ productivity value attributed to locational factors.

$V_E =$ productivity value attributed to nonlocational factors (factors that are subject to the externalities that the LPA project internalizes).

Then:

(8.1a) $$P = P_E + P_L \text{ and}$$
(8.1b) $$V = V_E + V_L.$$

Then, by the theory of tax incidence:

(8.1c) $$P = V - T = V - t(P) \text{ or}$$
(8.1d) $$P_E + P_L = [V_E - t(P_e)] + [V_L - t(P_L)].$$

Since locational values can be distinguished operationally from nonlocational values, it may be assumed

(8.1e) $$\text{a) } P = V - t(P_E)$$
$$\text{b) } P_L = V_L - t(P_L).$$

To calculate $V_{E1} - V_{E0} \equiv \Delta V_E$, substitute (7.1),

$$\Delta P_{sE} = \Delta P_s + \Delta P_{\bar{s}} \text{ (where } \Delta P_s \equiv \Delta P_E)$$

into (8.1e[a]), which gives:

(8.1f) $$\Delta V_E = (\Delta P_s + \Delta P_{\bar{s}}) + t(\Delta P_s + \Delta P_{\bar{s}}).$$

144

CHAPTER IX

# Effects of Changes in the Housing Stock

THE BENEFITS TO BE discussed in this chapter concern not so much the production of real income as its redistribution. Consider Case 2 in Chapter VII, where the replacement structures are basically different from those they supersede. Essentially, one population moves out, another moves in. To facilitate the analysis of redistribution, the effect on four different categories of individuals must be distinguished:[1] (1) those with specific types of assets or goods and services previously being consumed but now removed as objects of choice; (2) those with the same range of commodities open to choice but facing increased prices for some of them; (3) those with specific types of assets or goods and services, hitherto not available, but now made available, and chosen; and (4) those with the same range of commodities open to choice, but facing lowered prices for some of them.

[1] These refer to individuals as consumers of real property, whether they own property or not. The case of real estate owners as owners is discussed below.

## Consumer Groupings

Group 1 are largely residential, commercial, and industrial inhabitants of property that is to be demolished as part of the project. Group 2 are largely inhabitants of structures that are close substitutes for those that are to be demolished. Group 3 are individuals who are potential customers for the new residential dwellings or commercial or public service facilities produced as part of the project. Those in Group 4 are similar to Group 3, except that they need not actually move to the project site to be affected; and, if they do make such a move, it is to structures and services that are similar to those already available. Only the total *quantity* of such structures is affected by the project. But those in Group 3 are involved only where the project has made available novel types of residential, commercial, or public service facilities and include only individuals who have actually moved into them. Since location is sometimes an important aspect of such facilities, those of a kind already available elsewhere but in a distinctly different type of location might be considered novel types.

A specific individual may be a member of more than one group. For example, he may live near a demolished slum and in somewhat similar housing and may shop in stores subsequently demolished as part of the project. He is thus in Group 1 as far as commercial demolitions are concerned and in Group 2 as far as housing is concerned. Similarly, a suburbanite who moves into a new high-rise apartment community created by the project may be in Group 3 with regard to housing and Group 4 with regard to central city cultural services, since transportation costs to such services will have decreased for him. Generally, most multiple group membership is likely to involve Groups 1 and 2 on the one hand, and Groups 3 and 4 on the other.

An important asymmetry must be noted among the groups. Whereas in Groups 2, 3, and 4, any change in behavior is a voluntary response to changes in market signals—lower or higher prices for goods hitherto available, or availability of new goods—only in Group 1 is the change coerced. Inhabitants of demolished structures are forced to move out. They alone are *precluded* from unchanged consumption in housing; others are simply induced to change by the desire to make a better adjustment, but need not if they do not want to.

The welfare impact on these groups is as follows: If it is assumed first that all individuals had been in equilibrium with full information about alternatives prior to the project, then Groups 1 and 2 suffer welfare losses, while Groups 3 and 4 experience welfare gains.

## Effects on Group 1

Each member of Group 1 loses all consumer surplus associated with his ability to consume his first housing choice rather than his second. He loses in addition because the absolute cost of housing has gone up for him, without any price going down. And finally, he unwillingly loses the social capital developed by living in, and becoming adjusted to and part of a neighborhood. Housing location is a crucial part of one's whole pattern of living. It determines the direction in which substantial energies are expended—to learn about the various nonhousing consumption opportunities that are available, and to develop a configuration of social interaction, extending from particular specialized relationships through deep friendships. These investments in knowledge and decision making about consumption and social interaction are largely lost when a family moves out of a neighborhood. Of course, such losses are not per se equivalent to welfare loss for the family. Some prefer the need for such retooling. They like the experience of novelty. But they are likely to seek it by moving voluntarily. Group 1 may include some in this category who would soon have moved on their own in any case. But in a mass eviction such as is being discussed here one must assume that the majority feel that they are losing something on balance. The implication of this factor is that the preference of a family for the chosen—and lived in—housing over its second choice is greater after the family has lived there for some time than at the moment of its choice.[2] Thus, the welfare loss due to forced moving depends on both the heterogeneity of the housing stock (the first factor) and on the accumulated capital of neighborhood adjust-

[2] For a general discussion of neighborhood social interaction capital, see Jane Jacobs, *The Death and Life of Great American Cities* (Random House, 1961), Chaps. 2-4, 6; and Alvin L. Schorr, *Slums and Social Insecurity* (U.S. Department of Health, Education, and Welfare, 1963), Chaps. 1-2.

ment. Either can exist independently of the other. They constitute "moving costs" over and above the sheer cost of transporting property and person. While the first component can be offset *directly* by the relative attractiveness of the new location, the second can be offset to only a lesser extent. But it can be indirectly substituted for.

The second factor, the rise in the cost of housing, has the effect of displacing the dislocated inhabitants away from what would have been their second choice when their first choice was available.[3] With higher housing costs they are likely to consume less housing (or less probably, lower-quality housing;[4] "less probably" because their first choice was presumably near the bottom of the quality ladder).[5]

[3] There are really two stages of impact to be distinguished: first, a transitional impact, then a final impact. The transitional impact is the eviction from existing structures, followed by a period during which these structures are demolished, the site is prepared, and new structures are built. This period of gestation involves considerable lead time, during which only the gross negative effect on the housing stock is felt. Since a project may take as much as eight years from beginning to end, and more than five years during this transitional gestation period, the population as a whole—not only Group 1—experiences tighter housing conditions for a substantial period. It is not until the new structures are completed that Groups 3 and 4 come into being. While new construction always involves the social cost of a considerable period of production, the additional responsibility that is due to a redevelopment project stems from its larger lumpiness relative to individual private construction jobs. First, the gestation period of only gross negative impact may be greater because of the larger assembly task, because of more elaborate and complicated site preparation, and because of the larger and often more intricate character of the new construction. Construction crews are probably less than proportionately larger to conform to the greater task. Second, the relocation load is considerably greater and is thus less likely to flow unobtrusively into the housing market. Placed on the market at the same time, it may well have a nonmarginal impact on housing costs. These characteristics of the project's large size are of course the other side of the coin to the benefits accruing to that size: the opportunity to force the direction of neighborhood effects *from* the project *to* adjoining areas instead of the reverse (as is typical of the small private project).

[4] Except, as noted above, where a vigorous government relocation program exercises strong pressure on families to buy more and/or better housing by allocating a larger share of their budgets to housing. Except for benefits stemming from a decrease in the real costs (often external effects) of slum living, which are considered separately, even this entails the adverse distributional effect, since the price of the better housing reflects the demand and supply shifts resulting from relocation.

[5] This treatment differs from that of Nathaniel Lichfield in *Cost-Benefit Analysis in Urban Redevelopment,* Real Estate Research Program (Institute of Business and Economic Research, University of California, Berkeley, 1962), pp. 24ff. He

It is assumed here that the purely physical costs of moving are reimbursed as an integral part of the redevelopment project. This is a fair approximation to actual practice. Moving expenses are generally reimbursed in connection with the relocation portion of the project.[6] In fact, however, reimbursement is restricted to maximum total amounts that probably fall short of actual expenses for a number of families, though the extent of under-reimbursement would be difficult to discover. However, it is by no means a necessary part of redevelopment, and basic policy should not be influenced by any discrepancy here. Thus, complete reimbursement is assumed.

Legislation adopted in 1964 provides for payment of temporary rent supplements to households in Group 1. In principle these payments could offset or even more than offset the various losses examined here. What matters, of course, is the size and duration of these supplements relative to the size of the losses.[7] On the other hand, just because some of these losses are compensated does not mean that they are not generated by the program. They are so generated, and additional resources—the supplemental allowances— are needed to offset them in part or in full.

Group 1 includes commercial entrepreneurs as well as residential inhabitants. Owners of commercial establishments in the redevelopment area are forced to terminate or relocate their businesses. These businesses generally have "good will value" as going concerns, some portion of which is due to the specific location of the enterprise.[8] Assuming previous equilibrium with full information about alternatives, the firm will relocate if the good will lost along with its chosen location does not reduce earnings below normal profits; it will terminate if loss of location does reduce earnings

---

assumes that the dislocated sustain no loss, that they are fully reimbursed for their moving expenses, and that they are able to find comparable dwelling units at an unchanged price.

[6] Martin Millspaugh, "Problems and Opportunities of Relocation," *Law and Contemporary Problems* (Winter 1961), pp. 8-11.

[7] The substitutability of annual dollar supplements for the kinds of housing options that were foreclosed is not perfect. There are, subtle differences in their impact on marginal decisions. But this is of a lower order of magnitude relative to the magnitude we are considering.

[8] This locational value refers not to special locational values of the land—in which case it would be commandeered in land rent—but to the formation of specific customer attachments. Thus, it has some similarity with the accumulated capital of neighborhood adjustment of residential inhabitants.

below normal profits. In either case, assuming as before that actual moving expenses are reimbursed, eminent domain compensation is designed to meet only the "disembodied" value of the property, not its value embodied in a going concern. Since components of good will that are not directly concerned with a specific location are transferable to a new location, an amount equal to the locational advantages of the preceding site is lost when relocation occurs. A somewhat higher loss may be sustained—namely, the whole value of good will—where termination occurs, because profits would fall below the normal level. As with households, the additional cash grants provided in the 1964 legislation can offset this type of loss partially or fully. But any amelioration comes from incurring additional project costs. It must be pointed out that the loss involved in this category is not a social loss like a net loss of producer's surplus in the economy as a whole. It represents only an undesirable redistribution of wealth.

To summarize for Group 1 so far, three types of loss are envisaged: (1) elimination of the chosen alternative and others in the same neighborhood from the opportunity set of residential inhabitants—the necessity of choosing a less preferred alternative; (2) a rise in the absolute price of the type of housing typically purchased by these inhabitants; (3) a loss of accumulated capital in specific neighborhood adjustment by both residents and commercial enterprises. This analysis has proceeded under the assumption that all agents were in equilibrium, with full information, before demolition occurred. It was argued previously in this study, however, that the conditions for such an equilibrium, especially the requirement of broad information, were very unlikely to be met in a slum area. The difference this makes to the delineation of welfare losses must now be examined.

If inhabitants were not in full equilibrium prior to eviction, then it no longer follows that after eviction they would necessarily choose an inferior alternative within their opportunity set. Their search among alternatives, many of which they may never have scanned before, or a search conducted on their behalf by a relocation agency, might lead them to improved housing. While some families may benefit—for example, perhaps some of those who are admitted to new public housing constructed for the purpose—the fact that a sizable number of families are simultaneously thrown onto the market makes it more likely that many will be forced to accept choices inferior to their first (inferior in the sense of a quality-quantity-price package comparison, where quality includes location). Thus, the effect of previous disequilibrium is to decrease the extent of loss when the first choice must be superseded by second choice alternatives.[9] The other two sources of loss are not affected greatly, however. The price rise can be expected to occur and worsen their situation. Because their forced move out of the demolished neighborhood eliminates most of their accumulated neighborhood adjustment capital, a capital adjustment cost is imposed on them.

Measurement of these losses is quite difficult. If the heterogeneity of the housing stock is not so great as to produce significant first-choice–second-choice welfare discrepancies,[10] then the effect of the second loss factor, the price rise, can be roughly approximated for Group 1 residential inhabitants by a conventional method. An attempt can be made to estimate their demand function for housing and compute from the function the area of lost consumer's surplus due to the price rise (the so-called "welfare triangle").[11] Heterogeneity would prevent this by making dubious any identification of movements along this function with actual before-dislocation and after-dislocation choices. On the basis of the argument of the last paragraph, welfare losses due to heterogeneity, depending as they do on the extent of any preceding disequilibrium (at least, on the paucity of information), may be only moderate. It will be assumed that they are negligible, and that therefore the housing transfers may be treated as taking place between homogeneous packages.[12] The valid-

[9] If the alleged existence of significant external diseconomies in slum living is characterized as a social disequilibrium—in that the inhabitants do not know the true costs, even for themselves, of the choice they make—then the offset to loss *may* be much greater than is indicated here. But such further offset does not come about if the dislocated simply shift from one slum to another, or help to create a new slum by their large-scale transfer. In any case, the question of the diminution of the social external costs of slums will be considered in Chap. X.

[10] The problem is not heterogeneity per se, but only idiosyncratic heterogeneity —that is, housing differences not reflected in price differences.

[11] Producer's surplus is not relevant here, since Group 1 refers only to housing consumers. See the discussion below concerning property owners.

[12] Losses to small business entrepreneurs due to liquidation cannot be so easily dismissed. It has been argued that true *transferable* profits are simply redistributed. But there is good reason to believe that the retention of some of these enterprises is not so much a question of obtaining real profits as of buying a way of life

ity of this assumption can be tested by sampling some of the dislocated to discover to what extent they were worse off for the transfer,
*abstracting from price changes and moving costs.* Both the size of
the price effect and the existence of an adjustment cost welfare loss
are easy to conceptualize. Actual measurement is considerably
more difficult. The first entails estimating a demand function for
housing for those who formerly lived on the project site. An aggregate function (for a given community) is not too hard to obtain, but
the paucity of data on the project site dwellers is a real barrier. One
may have to proceed by attempting to disaggregate the aggregate
relation.

The adjustment cost is a different story. This represents a capital
item—a stock, unlike the two preceding items, which are flows and
must therefore be converted to present value terms to be comparable.
It is probably not highly related to the quantity or even the quality
of housing consumed; and it is probably largely conserved by household moves within the given neighborhood. To simplify the problem,
suppose that the size of the resource commitment involved does not
depend greatly on social class or type of neighborhood, but that the
money value of the adjustment varies only for the marginal utility of
income. In this way, relevant data may be obtained on the whole
housing market, instead of only on the dislocatees. Estimates will be
made of the money value of the minimum housing improvement necessary to induce families to move from one neighborhood to another.
The sample must exclude, if possible, families that like novelty.
Whether this means that moves to comparable neighborhoods are
more appropriate for the purpose here than moves to "better" neighborhoods is not clear. Both types may be permissible in the sample.
But in this connection, see the discussion below.

Thus in the discussion of the welfare effects in Group 1 a price
effect and a capital adjustment cost are computed. In addition, it is
indicated that these understate total losses by the (unmeasured) size
of the first-choice–second-choice discontinuity. The analysis of the
other groups will proceed on similar lines, but will have some

---

befitting their condition—say, old age. It relates in detail to their utility functions.
Such enterprises can be treated as consumer goods. Being forced to terminate
them counts as a distinct *aggregate* (not redistributive) loss of utility due to—
in this sense—significant commodity heterogeneity. They are forced to give up a
first choice commodity (the family business) for distinctly inferior alternatives.

differences stemming from the basic asymmetry between Group 1 and the others.

## Effects on Group 2

For Group 2, those who suffer only the price rise effect, this loss is measured by the same means used for Group 1.[13] The difficulty here, as with Group 1, is to estimate a demand function applicable to just this group. To facilitate computation, a symmetry assumption may be made—namely, that household demand functions depend on family composition and income level.[14] Thus families comparable in these respects have similar demand functions, regardless of the particular neighborhood in which they live. Group demand functions have to be aggregated from this kind of information. No adjustment cost is included because some of the affected families do not move; those who move, do so voluntarily. Therefore, it may be assumed that the advantages of moving at least offset the adjustment cost.

## Effects on Group 3

Those in Group 3 experience a quality change effect—a new housing opportunity is available. In addition, they experience a price effect, but indirectly. Since by definition they move into project housing, they do not take advantage of changing prices for dwellings that they relinquish. But they take advantage of the *effect* of these prices on the prices ultimately charged by the new project housing. The prices of the two kinds of accommodation will tend to adjust to a relationship where the difference is accounted for by differences in quality. Thus, the price of the package represented by project housing reflects the fall in the real cost of housing to this group. Since, by definition, the members of Group 3 move, they are subject in addition to first-choice–second-choice discontinuity and neighborhood adjustment costs. In this case the latter two

[13] Strictly speaking, idiosyncratic heterogeneity complicates matters here too. But it is less serious here because the alternatives that are foreclosed from availability are not the first choices of the respective families. They may well appear in an irrelevant part of the opportunity set—*that is,* they may not directly influence choice at all.

[14] For elaborate estimation on this basis, see Margaret G. Reid, *Housing and Income* (University of Chicago Press, 1962).

operate in opposite directions. Group 3 gains a new first-choice alternative added to its opportunity set—a welfare improvement; while the adjustment component of the move imposes a cost. However, since the move is voluntary, the new first-choice advantages must exceed the moving costs (where, as always, flows are implicitly converted to present capital values to prevent comparison with changes in capital values).

The distributional welfare gains due to enlarging the opportunity set of families in this group cannot be ignored. It will be assumed that a competitive market process distributed the new units among the interested families, so that the price set on these new units is just high enough to equal the marginal purchaser's valuation. There almost always results an increase in satisfaction for those who moved. (Only perfect price discrimination could prevent this.) In principle, this increment can be approximated by aggregating consumer's surplus from the adjusted set of demand functions. In practice, such a procedure is hopeless. Actual computation here requires drastic simplifications.

The following assumptions will be made:

1. The demand for standard housing is log-linear—that is, with constant elasticity. $P_1 = b_1 Q^a$, or $\log P_1 = \log b_1 + a \log Q$ (where $a$ is the price elasticity).

2. The demand for the new type of housing package is also log-linear and has the same elasticity, but is more desirable than the average package. $P_2 = b_2 Q^a$, or $\log P_2 = \log b_2 + a \log Q$ and $b_2 > b_1$.

3. The introduction of novel housing has an impact on the demand for traditional housing only.

From (1) and (2), $P_2/P_1 = b_2/b_1 > 1$. Figures 3a and 3b show the analysis. $D_{11}$ is the original demand curve, $S_1$ is the original supply curve. $D_{22}$ is the demand curve for the novel housing package, $S_2$ the supply curve for novel housing.

Equilibrium before the project is given by point 1 in Figure 3a. After completion of the project, $S_2$ has been added; so $S_2$ and $D_{22}$ exist. Equilibrium here is shown as the pair of points 2 in Figures 3a and 3b. In Figure 3a, $D_{12}$ has declined due to introduction of the novel commodity.

To measure the change in consumer's surplus as a result of

**FIGURE 3a. Traditional Housing Package**

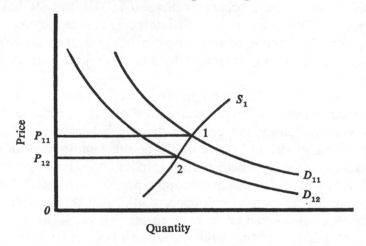

introducing $S_2$ requires that $D_{11}$, $D_{12}$, and $D_{22}$ be estimated[15]; and that the change in surplus areas under the demand curves in moving from point 1 to point 2 be calculated. Toward this end, point 1 and point 2 are observable, elasticity $a$ has been obtained by statistical estimation of $D_{11}$, and similarly $b_1$. Thus, substitution of these magnitudes in the equations of assumptions (1) and (2)

**FIGURE 3b. Novel Housing Package**

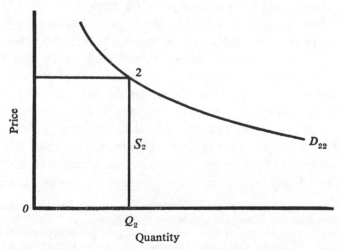

[15] Producer's surplus is not relevant here, since Group 3 does not include project property owners.

leaves only $b_2$ as unknown; and $b_2$ is found by solving: $P_2/P_1 = b_2/b_1$. A last problem occurs whenever $D_{11}$, $D_{12}$, and $D_{22}$ have no intercept on the price axis. Such intercepts can be approximated by arbitrarily selecting corresponding points with high price on all three and generating intercepts by linear projection from these points.[16]

Group 3 is subject to neighborhood adjustment costs as well. But their extent is different from that of Group 1. Since Group 3 moves are voluntary, not only are they on balance advantageous, they are likely also to involve a selection of families that may not mind moving to a new neighborhood; indeed, they may even like it. Such moves may often involve moving upward—to a "better" neighborhood. The challenges and opportunities that this provides may themselves often entail an increase in satisfaction. Thus, there are real grounds for treating adjustment costs here as negligible, as a good first approximation.

The price effect experienced by Group 3 will be the same as that for Group 4, since the conglomerate effect of choosing the new product housing is partitioned into a price and a quality component. The price effect will be discussed under Group 4.

*Effects on Group 4*

Group 4 is partly symmetrical with Group 2. Members of this group are affected by whatever price changes result from Group 3 moves. But Group 3 is likely to come into existence only in rare projects. In most projects the new construction is not novel enough to warrant the elaborate analysis of new commodity introduction. Rather, while heterogeneity of course exists, it is probably easily subsumable as a quality variation within the basic housing category. Quality differences are reflected more or less appropriately in price differences; so that one can tolerably treat different qualities as simply different *quantities* of housing. For situations where this holds, the chief effect of the project is on relative prices. And a Group 4 comes into being here as well (even though there is no Group 3).

[16] This overall procedure would be available for measuring Group 1 loss of first-choice opportunities, except for the anticipated existence of "suboptimality"—inadequate information, etc., as discussed above—in the pre-project situation. There is less reason to suspect similar prior suboptimality in the segment of the housing population in Group 3.

Thus, a Group 4 is generated whenever a Group 3 is generated, and even more frequently when no Group 3 exists. Under the first, the introduction of a new kind of housing competes strongly with some portions of the traditional stock. It thereby affects this stock typically by lowering its prices. Members of Group 4 may either move, in order to take advantage of these price changes, or be able to benefit maximally without actually moving. Under the second situation too, the change in the size of relative stocks lowers the relative prices of houses competitive with those of the project, and members of Group 4 are families who purchase in those parts of the market where prices fall, whether on the project site or in areas vacated by families moving to the project site. They may benefit either by moving or by not moving. Where they actually move in response to price changes, they are likely to move either within the same neighborhood or to a "better" one. Thus the argument about the size of the neighborhood adjustment costs for Group 3 probably holds here too. These costs can be treated as negligible.

The price effects for Groups 3 and 4 can be calculated by the method suggested for Group 2. It should be noted that, despite this basic similarity, there is an asymmetry. Members of Group 2 cannot move either from or to the project site; members of Groups 3 and 4 can. Such moves are not treated as incurring sizable neighborhood adjustment costs, however.[17]

## Other Effects

For Groups 2, 3, and 4 only effects on residential consumers have been mentioned. Effects on business enterprises are much the same. The only adjustments necessary are to translate impacts into effects on profits and to treat any moves as involving some locational losses. The capital value of these losses, appropriately budgeted over time, is an offset to, or aggravator of, advantageous or disadvantageous rental changes.

[17] Included in Groups 2 and 4 are, in the first situation, families that move out of the neighborhoods impacted by slum dislocatees due to their rising prices, and, in the second, families moving into neighborhoods experiencing lower prices due to the attractive competition from the project site construction. Moreover, the families doing such moving are likely to be disproportionately those that like to move. For these reasons neighborhood adjustment costs for such movers are treated as negligible also.

This discussion of welfare effects on Groups 2, 3, and 4 has been based on the assumption of optimal adjustment prior to the project. Dropping this assumption made a difference in the case of Group 1. To drop it with respect to the other three groups, however, has far less importance. What was crucial in the case of Group 1 was not a matter of computational nicety but of fundamental qualitative inferences. If a family had not made an optimal adjustment previously, it *might* end up better off (abstracting from price effects) by moving to a different neighborhood—although moving against its will—in contradistinction to the unambiguous inference to be drawn under prior optimality. Groups 2, 3, and 4 differ critically in that all moves embraced within them are voluntary and therefore represent at least anticipated improvements. It makes little difference that families in these groups could have been better off prior to this move by having made a different move under the old circumstances. After the circumstances change, the fact that families do move signals improvement over a failure to move under the changed circumstances. And it is only the extent of this improvement that needs to be measured, not the improvement that would have occurred *if* families had been otherwise situated under the prior circumstances. So no ambiguity is introduced into the inferences by dropping the assumption of prior optimality.

Two last brief points should be made. First, the four groups do not include property owners. These may be included and classified into three categories: (1) owners of real and improvement project site property; (2) owners of improvement property patronized by Groups 1 and 2; (3) owners of non-site improvement property patronized by Group 4. The first gain a producer's surplus whenever their transaction with the local public agency (LPA) does not involve a perfectly discriminating all-or-nothing arrangement. The second group gain quasi-rent by reason of the increased demand for the improvements. The third lose symmetrically by reason of decreased demand (that is, due to the competition of the additional supply). Methods for calculating these effects are essentially the same as those discussed above for consumers.

Owner-occupiers are composites of property owners and consumers. Their gains as one are offset by their losses as the other. On balance, their owner role predominates since their opportunities as owners are more nearly immobilized there (through capitalization) than are their opportunities as consumers.

Finally, the treatment above omits distributional effects arising from the effects of the project on interest rates for different kinds of securities. Given the crudity of our estimating techniques, these are considered to be negligible.

# CHAPTER X

# Reduction in the Social Costs of Slum Living

IN THE AREA COVERED by this chapter, costs and benefits are extraordinarily difficult to measure, and their very existence is subject to intense controversy. Because of the great difficulty of quantitative exercise here, a really useful statement of the problem and its possible solution would require a scale and degree of detail that is beyond the scope of this study. The treatment will therefore be brief.

## The Status of the Social Costs of Slums

In Chapter III a number of types of external social costs that slums are alleged to generate were listed. Slums are said to (1) increase fire hazards, (2) increase the menace to health, (3) breed crime, and (4) generate individual personality difficulties. These are all areas where quantitative measurement is difficult, but some are more tractable than others. In most cases the problem is either that

160

it is not clear exactly what should be measured, or that even if that is known, measurement is inaccessible.

Except with regard to fire hazards, the mechanism by which the existence of slums is supposed to "cause" these effects is neither well understood nor widely agreed upon. Moreover, in terms of what is understood, the causative process is broad, diffuse, and long-acting. It is not a case of a one-shot exposure to the "cause" at a specific time and place giving rise to a specific instance of the "consequence." The process at any one time is nearly invisible. It operates as a continuous setting of complicated interrelationships, an environment which slightly enhances the probability of some kinds of behavior and slightly reduces the probability of others. Thus, it is a stochastic, long-continuing process. Moreover, many of the alleged effects are also said to be influenced by a variety of other factors, which also generally operate in much the same diffuse, long-continuing way. The picture is often complicated further because these factors are often interrelated among themselves and related to the existence of slums. For example, health is influenced by income level, occupation, ethnic background, age, and physical surroundings. Moreover, these influences are themselves interrelated. The slums contain a far higher proportion of individuals who are poor *and* old *and* ill *and* poorly employed *and* members of minority groups than the national average. So causal relationships are, at best, difficult to unravel.

A last difficulty on the purely qualitative level is that even where a certain effect does occur, it is often difficult to detect. Personality and family difficulties are extremely hard to discover. Even aggravations of crime and illness, apparently so observable, are not easy to become informed about, since information about them, whether quantitative or even qualitative, is notoriously imprecise. Finally, the processes are so intrinsically stochastic that it is not at all obvious when a significant and not simply chance variation has occurred. These are important limitations.

Thus, it is not hard to see why the very existence, let alone the magnitude, of these social costs is controversial. Studies have been undertaken in search of the answers to these perplexing questions.[1]

[1] For a list of some of these studies, see the bibliography at the end of Chap. III. The 1951 article, "The Social Costs of Slums," by Jay Rumney, who was

Many of them are deficient. One type of study simply compares the incidence of disease, fire loss, crime, delinquency, etc., in slum areas with that in non-slum areas, or in the city or nation as a whole. This is clearly misleading. Since the slum population is a highly selective one, as suggested above, the method completely fails to abstract out the effects on these observed behaviors of the very pertinent charac-

---

himself an active empirical investigator in this field, summarizes many of the statistical studies produced in the period 1933-45. They cover thirteen cities, mostly northern. In city after city, the slums are shown to be the areas with the most disease, fire, crime, and social disorganization compared with the rest of the city. Slums and blighted areas are correlated with indices of social pathology, such as rate of juvenile delinquency, illiteracy, relief cases, disease, etc. These do not establish causal relationship, of course. Most of the studies simply adduce gross associations with no attempt to correct for the influence of special population and other qualifying factors. A few, however, do try to correct for some factors—roughly poverty—by comparing slum dwellers with public housing dwellers; but other selective characteristics of public housing inhabitants are not adjusted for in these more carefully controlled studies (1933-45), which show that public housing dwellers had a better record than slum dwellers. In the presence of a 1947 study, which compared the same families first in a slum and then subsequently in "decent" housing and found that transplantation resulted in substantial improvement in behavior, these better-controlled findings add persuasiveness to the hypothesis that slums themselves—not for example, poverty alone—cause social costs. (F. Stuart Chapin, *Experimental Designs in Sociological Research* [Harper, 1947].)

One consequence of the differentials in performance or incidence of costs between slum and non-slum areas is that the city government spends more on public services for slum areas than it receives from them in the form of revenue. Rumney presents data on these expenditures and revenues for the thirteen cities. The average ratio of expenditures to revenues is 5.8, with only one city falling below 3.3. The government "losses" implied by these ratios are sometimes considered the social costs of slums. From the treatment in this study it is clear that these "losses" have no implications whatever for the existence of true social costs. *Most* government programs have redistributive effects, especially in a progressive direction. These do not at all indicate that social costs have been incurred. Indeed, not only is a government "loss" with respect to any particular population group not indicative of social cost, a governmental "loss" with respect to the entire population does not indicate social loss either. Net borrowing by government has no diagnostic significance whatever for this purpose. Government simply is not in business to make "profits." The discussion in Chap. V on potential benefits from governmental profits is not relevant for countering this point. The differential needs of different segments of the population, or the decision to finance projects by borrowing, are not per se related to the constraints against efficient decision making that were mentioned in the earlier discussion.

Besides, the figures cannot be taken even as an indication of the size of net governmental "profits" that might be realized through the elimination of slums, since they do not separate expenditures required because of a particular housing pattern from those required because of the character of the population living in the slum but subsequently simply relocated elsewhere in the city.

teristics of slum dwellers—such as poverty, minority race, old age, primitive rural background.

Another kind of study tries to meet this objection by looking at the same population in both a slum and a non-slum situation, generally by following a group from a slum to public housing.[2] This is misleading too, but at least in one direction. It systematically understates the effects of slum living in the categories studied. Whatever its strength in fact, the influence of slum living, compounded typically with the overall subculture of poverty, must be a deep-seated diffuse one within the individual's psyche. A move into a better environment after long immersion in the slum, *other elements of poverty being unchanged,* is unlikely to have important, immediate effects on his deep cast of personality or even his physical health. He will probably bring his behavior patterns and his ailments with him into the new surroundings. This is especially likely if groups of families move together from one site to the other. Each family will reinforce the other in retaining behavior traits generated in their former circumstances. New influences are likely to have an impact only very gradually over time. The strongest effect of a radical change in environmental benevolence is to be seen in the development of the new generation. This effect may be of great importance; yet it is likely to be missed in many studies, since they typically take a much shorter time perspective.

To summarize so far: the measurement of social costs generated by slums is hampered because the causal process is complicated and interrelated with other causal factors; because outcomes are difficult to read; because in any serious attempt to isolate the effects of slums one must be prepared to separate out the influence of the other, strongly correlated factors; because changes in the arguments of the functional relationship are likely to have only minor, short-run effects, the important effects being truly long-run ones; and finally, because even where effects are isolated, they are likely to be discerned only qualitatively. Quantitative measurement, especially in terms of dollar values, is extremely difficult.

Despite these formidable obstacles, it is worth examining briefly

[2] For example, Naomi Barer, "A Note on Tuberculosis Among Residents of a Housing Project," *Public Housing* (August 1945); *Ibid.,* "Delinquency Before, After Admission to New Haven Housing Development," *Journal of Housing* (December 1945-January 1946); and F. Stuart Chapin, "An Experiment in the Social Effects of Good Housing," *American Sociological Review,* Vol. 5 (December 1940).

the prospects for more detailed cost estimates. Of course, one should make every possible use of empirical studies, employing them as suggestive at least, where their results cannot be formally used. The objective here is to find the money value of resources that the affected individuals would be willing to pay to avoid the costs imposed on them. Where this is not possible, an attempt is made to find the magnitude of the cost consequences in terms of the original dimensions—such as number of days of serious illness, or deaths, or robberies. Each of the five categories of cost is considered briefly from this viewpoint.

### Fire Hazards

The amount the community pays for fire protection in the form of fire department services is not equal to either the value of protection from fire hazard or the cost of fire damage. The fire department does not prevent all fires; it limits their destructiveness. For a measure of the cost of fire hazard, therefore, the value of destroyed and damaged property and loss of life through fire is sought, and also the value of the services which prevent that damage from being greater than it is. It may be assumed that fire protection services (the fire department, the hydrants and water facilities used, etc.) are just worth the value of the property and life that they protect. This is not a stringent assumption, since differences in levels rather than absolute levels are of interest here.

The general measuring procedure is to compare the total value of fire damage and protective services in slum areas with that in non-slum areas, adjusting for relevant differences in their respective populations. There are a number of specific decisions that must be made in order to formulate a specific procedure. First, the value of property damage should be obtainable from fire insurance company material records.[3] The value of human life lost and damaged is more difficult to obtain. Medical expenses are not a good estimate of the cost of human disability. As with fire protection services, medical services do not prevent or even totally cure fire-connected disability, and they thus fall far short of measuring the cost in human suffering. If anything, medical expenses should be added to

---

[3] This is not easy in practice since property is not separated out by slum and non-slum areas. Moreover, even differential premium rates are not easily obtainable to enable differential damage to be approximated. See Chap. XI.

personal valuation of suffering to get a meaningful total. Loss of human life, while seemingly more difficult, may actually be more tractable to measurement. The personal valuation aspect of costs is largely bypassed (except in the suffering imposed on relatives and friends of the deceased) because the personal evaluator is eliminated. In its stead is the valuation the community places on human life, reflecting both lost productivity and some inherent worth of person. This valuation can be read off explicitly in court damage decisions, and implicitly in certain substitution relations embedded in provisions of social services. For example, it can sometimes be calculated how many lives have to be lost in a dangerous stretch of roadway before structural changes will be made to eliminate the hazard. Social provision of medical services can also sometimes be analyzed to reveal implicit social valuation of human life. Admittedly, the several sources can be expected to reveal quite different valuations. If an investigator is lucky, the variability of these estimates will not be intolerably large, so that the mean value will be reasonable as a rough estimate.

A second question concerns the use of public service levels in the comparison. An attempt is made to measure fire damage *potential*. Actual damage is a stochastic process. The provision of public fire protection services is generally a monotonic function of the size of this potential. An index of the change in the potential—as well as simply a component—is therefore the change in the provision of these public services. This may entail a bias. Examination of the actual provision of public services to slum and non-slum areas may tend to understate the difference. To use public services as an index assumes that they are provided at the needed level. But it is frequently argued that the level of public services of all types provided to slum areas—including fire protection—is significantly inadequate when compared with the services provided to non-slum areas. Thus, where slum areas require a higher level, the deficiency will not be reflected in differences in actual services provided.[4]

If the change in fire protection needs due to redevelopment is measured by a before-after service level comparison, the change would be understated since the "before" (and presumably higher) figure would have been below actual needs. The same is true of

---

[4] Max R. Bloom, "Fiscal Productivity and the Pure Theory of Urban Renewal," *Land Economics* (May 1962), p. 140.

slum–non-slum cross-section comparisons. But this bias is offset to some extent by the fact that inadequate protection leads to higher damages. One might even argue crassly that the political determination of service levels marginally equates the extra cost of service with the "social value" of additional expected fire damage, so that the bias is exactly offset. Less crassly, the absence of the necessary data to disentangle these opposing forces[5] makes the assumption of total offset attractive for simplicity's sake.

A third decision to be made—that of the units in which services should be measured—also concerns the use of public service levels as an index of the level of potential. Should the comparison be carried out in terms of public services provided per square mile, or per capita, or per $1,000 of assessed valuation of property? Each has something to be said for it. Since population density in slums is higher than the average, the first would show high slum needs, the second low, the third something in between. If it is assumed that fire protection is chiefly concerned with the protection of property, the third basis seems most appropriate. It indicates the per unit cost of carrying out its function. It has the additional advantage of bringing comparability to protection levels for commercial and industrial establishments, as well as residential areas.[6]

The most important problem is raised by the need to separate the fire hazard effect of the slum from that of its particular population. Separation is necessary because, while redevelopment eliminates structures, it simply relocates the population. Granted that slum buildings are fire traps, to the extent that fire hazard is influenced also by the *kind of use* made of these structures, and this in turn influenced by population characteristics, relocation of this population may well mean a repetition of the same kind of use elsewhere, thus offsetting the diminution of overall community hazard. A gross association between fire and slum will thus overstate the net relationship.

[5] If one were to try to disentangle the two, one should not, of course, simply project "adequate" slum needs on the basis of non-slum service levels, since this would assume away the whole problem of possible real differences in per unit needs between the two kinds of areas.

[6] This approach differs from a preference for per capita measurement in Guy I. Kelnhofer, Jr., "Slum Clearance—Its Costs and Benefits," *The Tennessee Planner* (April 1955), pp. 153-58. The per capita method is also cited approvingly in Bloom, *op. cit.*, pp. 140-41.

Isolating the net effect of the slum proper on fire hazard should be helped by a multiple regression analysis, in which needed public fire protection per $1,000 assessed valuation ($Y$) is made a function of family income level ($X_1$), population density per square mile ($X_2$), and percentage of substandard dwellings in the area ($X_3$). The last variable bears the weight of slum influence.

Isolation of the slum impact makes it possible to treat another question, the question whether social cost changes should be measured by means of cross-section comparisons between slum areas and non-slum areas, or of time series comparisons between the same area before and after redevelopment. The cross-section approach generates far more data than the time series approach for running a multiple regression and is therefore to be preferred. A difficult problem is how to measure "needed" services for each type of area. As before, no very satisfactory solution suggests itself. Given the contrary forces noted above, the assumption that "needed" services equal "actual" services may be the best one can do.

To summarize, the procedure preferred here is to take the total cost of fire damage and fire protection services (as well as whatever estimates are available for the cost of human suffering), expressed per $1,000 of assessed valuation, and estimate regression coefficients for this as a function of family income level, population density per square mile, and percentage of substandard dwellings in the neighborhood. The coefficient of the last figure gives the marginal impact of slums on fire hazard—assuming that relocation creates no new slums and does not worsen others already in existence. The effect of this assumption can be included in the procedure by the following modification. After the regression has been estimated from cross-section data (the first approach), it becomes the estimating equation for the actual temporal process of redevelopment. The before-project value of fire hazards associated with the slum is calculated by substituting the value of $X_3$ that characterizes the slum. The after-project value is calculated first by substituting $X_3$ for the renewed area, and then adding to this the value of $\Delta Y$ for a change in $X_3$ in any neighborhood affected by relocation.

The result of these calculations is likely to contain a sizable error, as a reflection of the varied pitfalls that have been noted along the way. But it may give at least some indication of the fire hazard savings involved in non-slum over slum areas. The estimate is probably low due to the fairly consistent direction of bias that has been noted in the various steps in making the estimate. On the other hand, the bias in the estimate of how these savings are affected when allowance is made for the possibility that relocation will spread slums elsewhere is not determinable a priori.

## Health Hazards

As was noted above, medical services do not prevent illnesses perfectly, or even cure them perfectly. They limit the ravages more or less. Thus, as with fire hazards, the measurement here contains two components: (1) differential protective, therapeutic services, (2) differential morbidity and fatality.

Measuring these components is considerably more difficult than measuring the corresponding ones for fire. The first should be measured by the value of medical goods and services, but these are not easy to obtain for the specific geographic population. There is considerable migration across neighborhood lines in the use of medical facilities—especially hospitals. Moreover, sliding scales of charges for medical services are especially applicable to slum dwellers, and these complicate the question of the value of services rendered. In addition, expenditures on drugs and medicines would have to be included—especially nonprescription items—since there is some evidence that the poor are likely to use these medicines in many instances as *substitutes* for professional medical services rather than as complements to them, as do those in higher income groups.

On the other hand, it is not easy to point out a bias in the adequacy of *public* health and medical services for slum and non-slum inhabitants. A disproportionate amount of these go to slum dwellers. A number of free medical care programs are available only to the indigent and medically indigent. This is certainly not to suggest that slum inhabitants get more than they "need" while others get less (or some combination of this), but simply that a strong case for bias in either direction is not easy to make.

Morbidity and fatality figures are even more difficult to obtain for the slum dwellers, since they are likely to seek medical care in a smaller percentage of illnesses than do non-slum households. Specific sampling studies might be required. The problem of giving human illness and death a monetary social valuation is the same here as with fire hazards. In this category, of course, it represents the total substance from which benefits are generated; in the earlier category it represents only a small part of that total, the rest being directly expressible in money terms. Thus, this category is likely to be far less precise than the other.

As with the fire category also, the effect of slums proper must be isolated from that of the selective characteristics of the slum population since the latter essentially remain—though geographically redistributed—after redevelopment. The population influence is probably greater here than for fire, but it is difficult to separate out. Two approaches may be mentioned: (1) to establish gross statistical association between housing characteristics and illness, supplemented by knowledge of a generally accepted mechanism of transmission; (2) to establish net statistical association by abstracting out coordinate influences statistically.

There are a number of studies that use an approach similar to the first.[7] Among the most notable are those of Daniel M. Wilner and his associates.[8] The method used most is to study the effect of housing on specific illnesses. The understanding of causative connections between housing and specific illnesses supports a net causal interpretation of its gross association with total morbidity and mortality. A summary of some of Wilner's (*et al.*) findings, as cited in Schorr, is quoted below.[9]

1. Acute respiratory infections (cold, bronchitis, grippe), related to multiple use of toilet and water facilities, inadequate and crowded sleeping arrangements.

2. Certain infectious diseases of childhood (measles, chicken pox, and whooping cough), related to similar causal factors.

3. Minor digestive diseases and enteritis (typhoid, dysentery, diarrhea), related to poor facilities for the cold storage of food and to inadequate washing and toilet facilities.

[7] Some are listed in the bibliography at the end of Chap. III.

[8] For example, *The Housing Environment and Family Life* (Johns Hopkins Press, 1962); "Housing Environment and Mental Health," in Benjamin Pasamanick (ed.), *Epidemiology of Mental Disorder,* Pub. No. 60 (American Association for the Advancement of Science, 1949); "The Effects of Housing on Health, Social Adjustment and School Performance," *Proceedings* of 39th Annual Meeting of American Orthopsychiatric Association, 1962; "Housing as an Environmental Factor in Mental Health: The Johns Hopkins Longitudinal Study," *American Journal of Public Health,* Vol. 50 (January 1960).

[9] Alvin L. Schorr, *Slums and Social Insecurity* (U.S. Department of Health, Education, and Welfare, 1963), p. 14. Other ailments, such as rat bite and certain filth-borne diseases, also are closely associated with slums.

4. Injuries resulting from home accidents, related to crowded or inadequate kitchens, poor electrical connections, and poorly lighted and unstable stairs.

5. Infectious and noninfectious diseases of the skin, related to crowding and facilities for washing.

Other diseases that, one may be confident, may be caused by poor housing include lead poisoning in children from eating scaling paint, and pneumonia and tuberculosis.

This approach could separate out much of the influence of specific population. But a sizable interplay may remain. While certain housing characteristics may raise the probabilities of specific disorders in perfectly straightforward ways, the extent of the impact may well depend on population characteristics that were not allowed for (systematically controlled) in the investigations. The second approach can help to disentangle this interplay, because it can examine non-slum populations with many of the same characteristics that slum dwellers have. Thus, the two approaches are not so much competitive as complementary.

The second approach involves multiple regression. Morbidity and mortality per capita[10] would be dependent variables, and family income level and the percentage of substandard dwellings (which includes overcrowding) would be independent variables, the last reflecting slums. In order to gain insight, the slum variable might be broken down into an overcrowding variable (number of persons per room) and a structural dilapidation variable (number of major repairs needed).

## Crime

Unlike the preceding two categories, public protective services here do have a substantial deterrent effect. The level of police protection authorized by the political process bears a closer relation to the amount the public is willing to pay to *avoid* losses due to crime than do services under the preceding categories. The relation is far from perfect, since it is probably criminal apprehension as much as deterrence that is increased by enlarging the level of police services, and not even apprehension is dependably related to budget size.

[10] Per capita rather than per dollar of assessed valuation (as with fire) because public service programs in this field are oriented toward people, not property.

But if it is assumed that the police budget, say, is a fair first approximation measure, then some very difficult problems can be by-passed that concern the human cost of crime—assault, robbery, rape, murder, etc.—where such cost probably far exceeds the value of any property that might be involved.

The method used here, which is subject to a considerable margin of error, compares slum with non-slum police costs per capita. The measuring procedure is much like that for the earlier categories, with per capita units preferable to area or value of property units.

Once again the question must be faced: How much of the gross association between slums and crime represents a *net* effect of housing proper? Many statistical studies show large gross associations between slums and crime.[11] But they fail to control for important variables.[12] The need for such control is illustrated by a study referred to above, that of Bernard Lander on juvenile delinquency.[13] Lander found significant simple correlations between juvenile delinquency and both overcrowding and substandard housing. However, after extracting the effects of percentage of non-whites and median educational level, the net relationship with the slum variables became zero. The only variables that maintained significant *net* associations with delinquency were racial heterogeneity and the percentage of homes rented rather than owned, which Lander rationalized as factors contributing to anomie (social rootlessness).

Characteristics of the slum population, and of their social interaction stemming from other than housing conditions, must play an important role in crime. The complex of poverty, poor education, low morale, and discrimination—and its ramifications—must be an important explanatory and predictive factor. It should be remembered too that this complex influences the housing market to produce slums. So causation is highly complicated and involuted.

An elementary statistical analysis would introduce variables like family income and median education along with slum variables like

[11] They are included in the literature discussed in note 1 to this chapter.

[12] For a critique of many of these studies, see John P. Dean, "The Myths of Housing Reform," *American Sociological Review*, Vol. 14 (April 1949).

[13] *Towards an Understanding of Juvenile Delinquency* (Columbia University Press, 1954).

overcrowding and dilapidation (or simply percentage of substandard dwellings) as independent variables regressed against crime incidence (in per capita terms). It is not expected that such a regression will completely untangle the strands of causation. But it is not essential that they be untangled for policy purposes. The factors do not have an independent impact on crime, but one rather that results from influencing and being influenced by the whole cluster of forces. The policy problem is to manipulate *salient* factors; and salience is not equivalent to net statistical significance. Housing could be a salient factor in the complex. At any rate it *can* be manipulated on a substantial scale. This may make it more strategically accessible than is poverty, or discrimination, or morale.

### Personality Difficulties

In the previous categories, private or public expenditures that suppressed undesirable outcomes could be identified. This is not so easy here. The difficulties themselves are rarely deterred and—for this socioeconomic level of the population—rarely treated or cured. Only when they reach the level of severe psychosis is even a third level of action resorted to: custodial or mildly adjustive care. For what may well be a wide ocean of unhappiness, despair, misery, frustration, anger, and fright, there are no operational measuring rods. Broad qualitative judgments about both psychic states and the processes that might bring them into being are all that are available. But there is an imposing literature on the subject, producing a body of evidence that is perhaps nowhere definitive, but together forms a persuasive whole.[14] To indicate the flavor of the findings, a summary of Schorr's survey of the literature may be quoted:

Though the evidence is scattered, taken as a whole it is substantial. The type of housing occupied influences health, behavior and attitude, particularly if the housing is desperately inadequate [*i.e.,* "dilapidated" or lacking a major facility]. . . . Housing, even when it is minimally ade-

---

[14] A number of these works are listed in the appendix to Chap. III. In addition, for example, see James S. Plant, "Some Psychiatric Aspects of Crowded Living Conditions," *American Journal of Psychiatry,* Vol. 9 (March 1930). Also see the survey of the literature in Schorr, *op. cit.,* pp. 14-31, as well as a useful bibliography.

quate, appears to influence family and social relationships. . . . Those influences on behavior and attitudes that have been established bear a relationship to whether people can move out of or stay out of poverty. The following effects may spring from poor housing: a perception of one's self that leads to pessimism and passivity, stress to which the individual cannot adapt, poor health, and a state of dissatisfaction; pleasure in company but not in solitude, cynicism about people and organizations, a high degree of sexual stimulation without legitimate outlet, and difficulty in household management and child-rearing; and relationships that tend to spread out in the neighborhood rather than deeply into the family. Most of these effects, in turn, place obstacles in the path of improving one's financial circumstances.[15]

They decrease both the range of opportunities and the mobility of families in response to differential opportunities.

The problem of measurement here is especially difficult. By analogy with previous categories, one might look to social welfare services that are designed to ameliorate or prevent these personality difficulties: family social work, settlement house activities, neighborhood club house activities, etc. There is probably some prevention and some amelioration. On the basis of slight information, it would appear that the combined impact is less than for the other categories that have been treated here. Thus, by far the greater part of the personality problems associated with slums will be untouched by including social work budgets as a measure of these costs. The submerged part of the iceberg will be omitted.

Moreover, it does not help much that the objective here is to measure only changes in levels of costs, not absolute levels themselves. Measures of cost changes can be misleading. For example, with radical upward changes in the socioeconomic level of the population inhabiting the renewed site, the whole organizational apparatus for certain social work activities hitherto operating there will move out. The needy population will typically move into neighborhoods like their own, where social work organizations are already in being. Suppose this displaced population needs social work activities as much as ever. It is quite likely that the increased case loads falling on existing organizations will require the use of more resources—but not as much as was dismantled from the renewal

[15] Schorr, *op. cit.*, pp. 31-32.

site, since these latter included overhead resources which are no longer needed. An examination of budgets will suggest a diminution of total need, whereas all that occurred was an organizational economizing of resources due to greater geographic concentration of the needy population.

Thus, for a variety of reasons the use of social work budgets is not at all satisfactory for estimating changes in social costs in the present category. It is not clear what kind of measurement would be tolerable. Selective population characteristics will very likely have an important impact that cannot be isolated, perhaps even more so than for crime. Yet Schorr's summary calls upon studies that purport to find a distinguishable slum influence as well. It must probably be concluded that changes in social costs in this category are, at least at present, unmeasurable.

The existence of slum-generated costs cannot be definitively established here, nor can changes brought about by redevelopment be measured even tolerably well. But if they were excluded from consideration, given this body of evidence, a possibly important aspect of social costs generated by slums would be neglected. In the particular context of redevelopment, when account is taken of the consequences of relocation, it is more difficult to make judgments about the size—or conceivably even the direction—of bias. If it is reasonable to assume that the extent of slum living typically decreases somewhat on balance under redevelopment, then exclusion of this category imparts a downward bias to estimates of redevelopment benefits. Ultimate policy makers should take notice of this category when making project decisions.

## Summary

The external social costs allegedly generated by the existence of slums probably exist, but it is extremely difficult to find out even roughly how important they are. And the need for measurement is even more urgent in determining how these social costs are affected by the redevelopment project as a whole, taking into account the effects of relocation on other neighborhoods. Any empirical solution obtained to this problem must be presented with real reservation. As has been noted, some components are easier to measure than others. It is worth trying to press the inquiry in whatever directions and to whatever extent possible. But one should not take any magnitudes obtained too seriously when comparing them with magnitudes obtained from the two other main categories of effect here.

The reservation about even the direction of change stems from the possibility that the tendency of massive relocation to spread slums could significantly offset the effects of redevelopment in eliminating them. If in particular projects or even in general, empirical findings should indicate that the former effect is slight, then the procedures suggested here would be more useful—since then most remaining biases would run in the same direction of understating the benefits from redevelopment, and there would then be a lower bound estimate. The formulation of a conceptual framework cannot carry the inquiry that far. Really useful conclusions must wait upon the empirical application.

A final point should be made. Some observers believe that this category of social costs of slum living is the most important of all. Urban renewal programs will stand or fall ultimately on how significant these benefits are. It is difficult indeed to obtain relevant dollar figures here to use as offsets to project costs. To base important policy decisions on only the dollar amounts that *can* be computed, simply because they are the only dollar amounts, would be most dangerous. Underestimating the most truly distinctive benefits of the program might be crucial. Wherever possible, therefore, the money costs should be supplemented by those that are not measurable in money terms: for example, serious illness days, murders, incidence of psychosis. While the investigator may not be able to discover unique consensual trade-offs in the community among these different kinds of consequences, society has the option of discovering them by a form of simulation: the governmental decision making process.

# CHAPTER XI

# A Numerical Example[1]

THE EXAMPLE THAT FOLLOWS is not intended as a serious empirical application of the method suggested in this work. It is only an illustrative exercise, designed to indicate in a preliminary fashion the directions that statistical procedures might follow, the difficulties that might be encountered, the scale of operations that might be necessary to obtain different types of information. Because the scale of the inquiry was very small, there are areas covered by crude, over-simplified techniques that in a more adequate study would be handled more appropriately. Because the study is so rough, with substantial areas left uncovered entirely, due to limitations of scale, the estimates made should not be considered very significant, nor should they be used to get an approximate—even preliminary— sense of the ultimate benefit-cost comparisons to be made. The data here were not produced in a context of trying to give a best guess as to the magnitude of the relevant benefits and costs in actual redevelopment projects. Rather, they represent an effort to approximate statistical techniques. If anything, this is a preliminary examination of observational and procedural availability.

The subject of the study is five projects in Chicago: Michael Reese (also known as Prairie Shores), Hyde Park "A" and "B," Blue Island, and Lake Meadows. Hyde Park "A" and "B" are two

[1] Robert Puth collected the data and made the calculations for this example.

176

portions of a larger Hyde Park-Kenwood project. Hyde Park "B" is a small redevelopment strip, the first portion of the overall project completed. Hyde Park "A" represents the core and major part of the overall project. Other, more disparate portions were nearing completion in 1965.

These five projects were chosen because they were the only completed ones. Three of them, Michael Reese, Hyde Park "A," and Lake Meadows are really substantial projects; the other two are small. The starting date is 1956 for Michael Reese and Hyde Park "A" and "B" and 1959 for Lake Meadows and Blue Island. Thus, for the first three the pre-project situation is assumed to be that in 1955, and for the last two, that in 1958; the post-project situation is assumed to be that in 1962 and 1963.

For each project three types of benefits are of interest: (1) internalization of externalities in neighborhood land use and their resulting neighborhood spillovers; (2) income redistribution effects through changes in the structure of the housing stock; and (3) changes in the social costs generated by slums.

## Internalization Benefits

### Site Benefits

Consider the very simple model of equation (7.1).

Let:

$\Delta P_s$ = the total land price change in the redevelopment site.

$\Delta P_{sE}$ = the land price change in the redevelopment site due to internalization of externalities.

$\Delta P_{\bar{s}}$ = the total land price change elsewhere in the metropolitan area (assumed due only to changes in locational advantages).

Then:

(7.1) $$\Delta P_{sE} = \Delta P_s + \Delta P_{\bar{s}}.$$

This model neglects explicit treatment of tax capitalization in the manner indicated by equation (8.2).

Let:

$\Delta V_E$ = the change in land value in the development site due to internalization (value differs from price because of backward shifting of capital values of expected taxes).

$t(\Delta P_s + \Delta P_{\bar{s}})$ = the capitalized value of the anticipated increase in property tax liability due to the increased real value of the land.

Then:

(8.2)                    $\Delta V_E = (\Delta P_s + \Delta P_{\bar{s}}) + t(\Delta P_s + \Delta P_{\bar{s}}).$

The tax adjustment will be neglected for convenience. Consequently, since this term is positive so long as land value is enhanced, a downward bias is imparted to the measures. This can be rectified rather easily by estimating a tax capitalization factor.

It may be remembered that the term $-\Delta P_{\bar{s}}$ is a measure of value changes in the redevelopment site due to a changing locational significance. The calculation of this is complex but crude, with statistical "noise" masking all but very significant locational changes. Three of the projects chosen—Michael Reese, Hyde Park "A," and Lake Meadows—are large enough and located strategically enough so that shifts in relative locational advantage might have occurred.[2]

They were probably not so large as to be unambiguously isolable by means of the technique suggested in Chapter VIII. But this guess is, of course, no substitute for empirical examination. Unfortunately, the scope of the present illustration does not allow for such an examination, but it should be done in a formal evaluation. In the present case a correction for locational change is omitted, assuming that no significant valuation change due to location occurred.

(11.1)                              $\Delta P_{sE} = \Delta P_s$

The problem here is to measure the change in the land site value after the redevelopment project. Because of long gestation periods this means for the Hyde Park "B" and Reese projects a comparison between 1955 and 1962; for Blue Island, 1958 and 1962; for Hyde Park "A," 1955 and 1963; and for Lake Meadows, 1958 and 1963. These are time intervals long enough for the general forces that determine land values in the city to have brought

[2] Michael Reese-Prairie Shores and Lake Meadows reinforce one another since they are contiguous.

about noticeable changes in these values, abstracting from redevelopment. Only those changes in land values over and above the changes that can be explained by these more general forces may be ascribed to redevelopment. Calculation of these influences is very difficult. Given the small scale of this study, it has had to be done in a very rough, and probably unsatisfactory, way.

It is assumed that an important part of land price variations can be explained by per capita income and population changes. The following equation is used:

Let:

$_{YN}P$ = "$Y-N$ explained" land prices, which will be referred to as "$Y-N$ explained values."

$Y$ = per capita income.

$N$ = population.

Then:

(11.2) $$_{YN}P = a + b_1Y + b_2N.$$

The problem is to obtain the appropriate data for the redevelopment sites. The availability of data here becomes the limiting factor. In order to estimate coefficients $a$, $b_1$, and $b_2$, time series observations of $P_s$, $Y_s$, and $N_s$ for the project area going back many years are needed. No such direct observations of $Y_s$ are available. A series of this sort could be approximated laboriously for $N_s$ (through census tracts) and for $P_s$. Nonetheless, indirect approximations could be assembled for all three. The more statistical resources devoted to this, the better the approximation. The scale here allows only the roughest approximation. A more complete study should certainly improve on this.

Since it is very difficult to get data for the redevelopment area, estimates are made from only one form of direct observation of the area. The rest is pieced together from observations of a much broader geographic area. The object is to measure that portion of the change in land prices in the redevelopment area that is not accounted for by variations in $Y$ and $N$.

Let:

$_R\Delta P_s$ = redevelopment-induced value change in the site.

$_{Y,N}\Delta P_s$ = income-and-population-induced value change in the site.

Then:

(11.3) $$_R\Delta P_s = \Delta P_s - _{Y,N}\Delta P_s.$$

$_{Y,N}\Delta P_s$ is obtained indirectly from Cook County data by assuming:

(11.4) $$\frac{_{Y,N}\Delta P_s}{_{Y,N}\Delta P_c} = \frac{\text{mean } (P_s)_{0,1}}{\text{mean } (P_c)_{0,1}}$$

(where subscript $c$ refers to Cook County data; and subscripts 0, 1 are the pre-project and post-project dates).

Coefficients $a$, $b_1$, and $b_2$ are then estimated for computing $_{Y,N}P_c$ in (11.2). This, together with the mean of pre-project and post-project $P_c$, gives the Cook County percentage change in explained value (using $P_c$ as base). The actual percentage gain in site prices is obtained directly, that is,

$$\frac{\Delta P_s}{\text{mean } (P_s)_{0,1}},$$

and, since (11.4) can be rewritten as:

(11.5) $$\frac{_{Y\ N}\Delta P_s}{\text{mean } (P_s)_{0,1}} = \frac{_{Y\ N}\Delta P_c}{\text{mean } (P_c)_{0,1}},$$

and (11.3) can be rewritten as:

(11.6) $$\frac{_R\Delta P_s}{\text{mean } (P_s)_{0,1}} = \frac{\Delta P_s}{\text{mean } (P_s)_{0,1}} - \frac{_{Y,N}\Delta P_s}{\text{mean } (P_s)_{0,1}},$$

then:

$$\frac{_R\Delta P_s}{\text{mean } (P_s)_{0,1}}$$

and, therefore, $_R\Delta P_s$ can be computed.

Assumption (11.4) looks outrageous at first glance. One would surely expect slum land values to respond differently from those of the city as a whole to city-wide per capita income and population variations. For example, because of selective immigrations, one would expect a city-wide per capita income change to be less than proportionately reflected in slum incomes, with no assurance whatever that the relationship is linear.[3] Population changes are more difficult to gauge; but there have been variations in slum density over the period and an uneven rate of spread of erstwhile site dwellers to other areas, thus suggesting that slum and city-wide experiences in population and income changes are not even co-linear, let alone proportional. To use city-wide income and population movements as proxy arguments determining $_{Y,N}\Delta P_s$ would therefore seem foolish. However, assumption (11.4) postulates similarity only for the period of gestation during redevelopment. From the start of redevelopment on, the site partakes less and less of the character of a slum and more and more of that of a "typical" central city area. Indeed, the land itself is not occupied during gestation. So either it has no character—if it is large enough to be a self-contained neighborhood, as perhaps the Michael Reese-Lake Meadows complex is—or, if this is not the case, it partakes potentially of the character of the surrounding non-slum neighborhood (as in Hyde Park "B"). In either case, assumption (11.4) may be a reasonably good approximation.

CALCULATION OF $_{Y,N}P_c$. The calculations are as follows: To estimate coefficients in equation (11.2) for $_{Y,N}P_c$, the years 1947-61 were used. The income variable used was net after-tax income for Cook County, as compiled by *Sales Management*. The population figures are for numbers of inhabitants of Cook County, also compiled by *Sales Management*. The population figures are not especially reliable for non-census years, being obtained largely, through interpolation. For this reason, aggregate rather than per capita income data were used. The latter are derived by dividing aggregate income by population data. While the use of aggregate income along with population muddies the interpretation of the relative size of $b_1$ and $b_2$, it avoids compounding errors of measurement in *both Y and N*; therefore it improves the overall fit of the equation.

The series for land values in Cook County is the real stumbling block. This should refer to true market values. An approximation to such values is available on a lot-by-lot basis in *Olcott's Land Values Blue Book of Chicago*. Unfortunately no aggregate figures are given. The project scale here is obviously too small to permit totaling the individual items. On a larger scale it might be worth the

---

[3] For example, the income of Negroes has risen less rapidly than that of whites.

**TABLE XI-1. Land Prices, Aggregate Income, and Population, Cook County, Illinois, 1947–61**[a]

*(In thousands)*

| Year | Land Prices | Aggregate Income | Population |
|------|-------------|------------------|-----------|
| 1947 | $18,399,558 | $ 7,416,982 | 4,225.7 |
| 1948 | 19,666,323 | 8,176,791 | 4,305.8 |
| 1949 | 19,574,018 | 8,425,620 | 4,522.7 |
| 1950 | 19,984,798 | 8,137,803 | 4,490.7 |
| 1951 | 22,045,478 | 8,967,124 | 4,548.8 |
| 1952 | 22,052,150 | 9,173,481 | 4,601.8 |
| 1953 | 22,448,690 | 9,583,494[b] | 4,607.1 |
| 1954 | 22,839,805 | 9,993,506 | 4,667.5[b] |
| 1955 | 22,947,800 | 10,769,380 | 4,727.9 |
| 1956 | 25,716,518 | 11,476,197 | 4,866.1 |
| 1957 | 27,345,985 | 11,684,475 | 4,881.8 |
| 1958 | 28,316,530 | 11,757,304 | 4,944.8 |
| 1959 | 31,196,125 | 12,814,366 | 5,049.1 |
| 1960 | 31,543,940 | 13,428,844 | 5,119.8 |
| 1961 | 32,199,125 | 13,352,979 | 5,165.7 |

Source: Column 1 from Cook County, Illinois, Tax Assessor's Office; Columns 2 and 3 from *Sales Management.*
[a] $Y_{,N}P_c = a + b_1Y_c + b_cN_c.$
[b] Value interpolated.

trouble. The alternative may be seriously deficient. Assessed values of land from the Cook County Tax Assessor's office have had to be used, and these have been inflated to a market value basis on the assumption that they are 40 percent of true market values. Assessed values are well known to be poor approximations to market values, with respect to both level and change in level. There are idiosyncratic elements in the assessment at any one time and important lags, during which market values change without a corresponding adjustment in assessed values.

The relevant time series are reproduced in Table XI-1. The estimating equation was found to be:

$$(11.7) \quad _{Y,N}P_c = -\ 10,857,084 + 1.79\ Y_c + 3554.76\ N_c.[4]$$

[4] This estimating equation proved to have very close fit—an $R^2$ of 0.951 (an $R$ of 0.975). The closeness is to be accounted for largely by a substantial upward linear trend in all the variables considered. Indeed, while this "complicated" explanation showed better fit than a simple linear trend, the improvement was very small—the correlation coefficient of fitted trend was 0.969. Thus, this example should not be thought of as providing strong evidence that the intricate isolation of locational effects suggested in Chap. VII can be performed.

**TABLE XI-2. Changes in Standard Lot Land Values During Redevelopment, Five Chicago Projects**

| Item | Hyde Park "B" | Michael Reese | Blue Island | Hyde Park "A" | Lake Meadows |
|---|---|---|---|---|---|
| 1. Pre-project[a] land value | $12,500 | $ 5,750 | $5,000 | $10,000 | $ 6,125 |
| 2. Post-project[b] land value | $20,000 | $10,500 | $7,250 | $20,000 | $11,900 |
| 3. Average pre-project and post-project land value (based on lines 1 and 2) | $16,250 | $ 8,125 | $6,125 | $15,000 | $ 9,012 |
| 4. Absolute increase | | | | | |
|   a. Amount (line 2–line 1) | $ 7,500 | $ 4,750 | $2,250 | $10,000 | $ 5,775 |
|   b. As a percentage of average land value (line 4a÷line 3) | 46 | 58 | 37 | 67 | 64 |

Source: Olcott's *Land Values Blue* Book *of Chicago,* Vols. for 1955, 1958, 1962, 1963.
[a] For Hyde Park "A" and "B" and Michael Reese, this is 1955. For Blue Island and Lake Meadows, it is 1958.
[b] 1962 for Hyde Park "B," Michael Reese, and Blue Island; 1963 for Hyde Park "A" and Lake Meadows.

CALCULATION OF $\Delta P_s$/MEAN $(P_s)_{0,1}$. The data obtained for all projects is the market value of a standard lot ($100' \times 125'$) in the pre-project and post-project years. All data were obtained from *Olcott's Land Values Blue Book of Chicago*. Figures for the five projects are given in Table XI-2.

CALCULATION OF $_R\Delta P_s$. The relevant computations are presented in Table XI-3. In lines 5 and 6 a figure for either the beginning *or* the end of the period was obtained directly. The other was calculated by applying the growth percentage due to redevelopment, taking care to adjust for the fact that the growth percentage was derived from a base that was the *mean* of beginning and end figures.[5]

Table XI-3 shows very marked differences in absolute benefits among projects, with Hyde Park "A" and Lake Meadows by far the most productive projects in this regard. There is variation in growth percentages as well, but not as much. Here too Lake Meadows exceeds the others.

### Spillover Effects

The second aspect of internalization benefits is that the dramatic change in land use made possible can induce a reversal in the di-

[5] Since the growth percentage was calculated as $g = (e - b)/(e + b)$, where $g =$ growth percentage, $e =$ end of period value and $b =$ beginning of period value, either the beginning or end figure can easily be found: $e = (b + bg)/(1 - g)$ and $b = (e - eg)/(1 + g)$.

**TABLE XI-3. Changes in Redevelopment Site Land Values Due to Redevelopment ($_R\Delta P_s$), Five Chicago Projects[a]**

| Item | Hyde Park "B" | Michael Reese | Blue Island | Hyde Park "A" | Lake Meadows |
|---|---|---|---|---|---|
| 1. Actual percentage increase, $\Delta P_s$/mean ($P_s$) | 46 (actual site mean = $16,250) | 58 (actual site mean = $8,125) | 37 (actual site mean = $6,125) | 67 (actual site mean = $15,000) | 64 (actual site mean = $9,012) |
| 2. Percentage change explained by Y and N, $_{Y,N}\Delta P_s$/mean ($P_s$) | 23 (explained Cook mean = $28,434,954) | 23 | 13 (explained Cook mean = $29,704,660) | 39 (explained Cook mean = $29,788,101) | 22 (explained Cook mean = $31,061,302) |
| 3. Percentage change due to redevelopment, $_R\Delta P_s$/mean ($P_s$) (#1 −#2) | 23 | 35 | 24 | 28 | 42 |
| 4. Absolute change due to redevelopment, per standard lot, ($_R\Delta P_s$) | $ 3,738 | $ 2,844 | $ 1,470 | $ 4,180 | $ 3,788 |
| 5. Initial total market value of acquired land ($L_0$) (adjusted for Y and N) | $49,506 | $1,596,433 | $45,559 | $ 6,449,063 | $ 8,776,585 |
| 6. Terminal total market value of acquired land ($L_1$) (adjusted for Y and N) | $79,080 | $3,315,618 | $74,333 | $11,465,000 | $21,487,500 |
| 7. Total increase due to redevelopment ($\Delta L$) (#6 −#5) | $29,574 | $1,719,185 | $28,774 | $ 5,015,937 | $12,710,915 |

Source: Line 1 (including means) from Table XI-2 above. Line 2 from Table XI-1 and equation (11.7) above. Line 4 from Olcott's Land Values Blue Book of Chicago, 1955, 1958, 1962. Lines 5–7 from Olcott's, 1955, 1958, 1961, 1962, 1963; Col. 2 from Chicago Land Clearance Commission, Michael Reese-Prairie Shores Redevelopment Project: Final Project Report, 1962. For Cols. 1, 3, 4, 5, $L_0$ is the figure adjusted for Y,N; Col. 2, $L_1$ is the adjusted figure.
[a] See Table XI-2, notes a and b, for period covered for each project.

rection of neighborhood effects. Instead of the character of the surrounding area affecting values in the site, the changed character of the site affects values in the surrounding area. These reverse externalities, or spillovers, affect both land and structure values. In Chapter VIII the difficulty of identifying these spillover effects in the face of other—but not aggregate income—influences impinging on the same real estate was discussed. In the light of that discussion the procedure used here stems from assumptions about the magnitude of locational and relative housing stock changes. It has already been assumed—for better or worse—that locational changes are not important for the projects under consideration. In the next section it will be argued—on somewhat deeper grounds—that relative housing stock effects are also negligible in the present context. Therefore, changes in surrounding real estate values may be ascribed solely to spillover effects (adjusting, of course, for general influences on property values, like per capita income and population during the gestation period—as with site value changes).

To begin with, Hyde Park "B" and Blue Island are excluded because they are too small to have any noticeable adverse neighborhood effect. Hyde Park "B" has the further defect of being surrounded by a large renewal area in which other projects are under way, so that nearby property is being impinged upon by other renewal activities as well. Hyde Park "A" is to be excluded also, because even this much larger redevelopment project is embedded in a larger renewal area in which a variety of activities are occurring. It would be very difficult to allocate the overall effect on neighboring real estate among the several influences. Finally, Michael Reese and Lake Meadows have a common boundary on one side. It is therefore useful to treat them as a single unit in generating neighborhood effects. Indeed, they very likely enhance one another's effects on the surrounding area.

An effort was made to obtain estimates of spillovers that would be comparable with the estimates of effects on the redevelopment site. Since assessed valuation figures are generally thought to be very misleading for this purpose, figures from *Olcott's Land Values Blue Book of Chicago* were used. For this reason Olcott's figures were used for neighboring land as well. This source has two disadvantages. First, no aggregate data are available, only figures for individual plots. Thus, sampling is necessary. As in the derivation of the redevelopment site figures, representative plots were sampled to obtain before and after values. Second, market values of improvements (structures, etc.) are not available. It is possible, but rather hazardous, to proceed by obtaining an "average" ratio of improvement value to land values and then projecting the land value increment onto improvement value, tacitly implying that the two components are affected proportionally. One would wish first to examine relative movements of the two under a variety of circumstances. The scope of this study does not permit any such investigation. Consequently land price changes alone will be presented, and they will be paired with the comparable changes in values on the redevelopment site.

A final difficulty in calculating spillovers is that there is no clear boundary demarcating the affected from the unaffected area. As was suggested above, moreover, this demarcation cannot generally be made by examining the geographic pattern of price changes— inferring causes from consequences—because a given pattern is the result of a myriad of special and general forces. A larger study might examine the pattern, however; by chance, regularities attributable to the forces under discussion *may* be clearly discernible.

**TABLE XI-4. Spillover Effects: Changes in Market Value of Standard Lot on Land Neighboring Michael Reese-Lake Meadows Redevelopment Sites, 1955–63**

| | Location of land with respect to project site | | |
|---|---|---|---|
| Item | Adjacent | One block distant | Five blocks distant |
| 1. Pre-project land value | $5,000 | $4,000 | $4,000 |
| 2. Post-project land value | $9,580 | $8,000 | $8,000 |
| 3. Average pre-project and post-project land values (based on lines 1 and 2) | $7,290 | $6,000 | $6,000 |
| 4. Absolute increase | | | |
|     a. Amount (line 2—line 1) | $4,580 | $4,000 | $4,000 |
|     b. As a percentage of average land values (line 4a ÷ line 3) | 63 | 67 | 67 |

Source: *Olcott's Land Values Blue Book of Chicago*, Vols. for 1955 (pre-project year) and 1963 (post-project year).

The more modest procedure here does not even raise the question of how much property is involved. Rather a price impact on samples of property taken at three different distances from the redevelopment site—across the street, one block away, five blocks away is indicated. Thus, the treatment of spillovers is clearly preliminary and meant only to be suggestive. The data are presented in Table XI-4.

These figures are not adjusted for per capita income and population change. An interesting characteristic of Table XI-4 is that the spillover impact appears to be as strong for land five blocks away as for land much nearer the project.[6] This is either of some importance to the size of total benefits or a hint that in fact not spillovers but

[6] Column 1 is less significant for this judgment than column 2, since the former has a larger proportion of commercial property than either the site or the more distant land.

some other effects have been isolated. These figures may be compared with those referring to the redevelopment site itself. From Table XI-3, Michael Reese shows a 35 percent value change adjusted for income and population, Lake Meadows a 42 percent adjusted change. If it is assumed that the relevant period for the Michael Reese-Lake Meadows complex was 1955-63 and 39 percent is taken as the correction factor for this period (from col. 4, line 2, since this was also the period of the Hyde Park "A" project), then spillovers accounted for a 28 percent increase. Spillovers therefore are nearly as substantial as site effects, given this limited sample. The total increment in property values (including improvements) may be quite substantial, perhaps exceeding total site benefits, when account is taken of the entire area over which the spillover effect occurs. But of course nothing very persuasive even of a qualitative nature can be presumed from the rough and fragmentary evidence presented here. One can say that a neglect of spillovers in making policy decisions carries a real risk. And much more of a quantitative nature could be discovered from a more painstaking study.

## Income Redistribution

This type of effect concerns transfers of real income through the price changes attendant on changes in the structure of the housing stock. In particular it has been suggested that dislocatees are likely to lose on balance and that the group that subsequently moves into the redeveloped area is likely on balance to gain. Since the former, but typically not the latter, largely include the poor, many of them members of racial minority groups, any noticeable worsening of their condition through redevelopment has strong political implications. It is on this group, therefore, that the present section focuses chiefly.

The prediction of an absolute worsening for the former group is not unqualified. Significant prior suboptimality of choice (due to ignorance and/or lack of mobility), along with an active relocation program by the local public agency, could well bring about improvement for most dislocatees. Moreover, real worsening is likely to occur only if the number of dislocatees simultaneously thrown onto the housing market is significant relative to the size of the market (its "thinness"). A small redevelopment project will have no appreciable effect on prices (rentals) elsewhere in the market. The dislocatees will be marginal to other housing transactions and will leave real prices unchanged.

Over and above these qualifications of principle is the question of the circumstances under which a predicted worsening can be detected. If the housing supply is very tight or is tightening, any such effect is probably noticeable. On the other hand, a loose or loosening market may well be characterized by lags in price adjustments. Instead of prices falling, some considerable time may pass during which the ease is reflected only in a high or growing vacancy rate.[7] In such a situation, a nonmarginal increment of low-quality demand, coupled with a decrease in the supply of such housing, may result only in a decreased vacancy rate, rather than in a noticeable change in prices (rentals). At best, a market that is significantly loosening due to other forces, if fully price-responsive, will adjust to a nonmarginal dislocatee demand through prices that fall less than they would have in the absence of redevelopment. Such a differential effect is likely to be too subtle to be detected by most statistical procedures.

In the real world situation all three qualifying features are to be found. Prior disequilibrium is suspected; there has been an active relocation program; the number of dislocatees is not especially great;[8] most important of all, a significant loosening was occurring in the entire housing market in Chicago beginning in about 1955. The 1960 Census shows an 11 percent increase in Chicago housing units during a period when population was declining due to suburbanization. The vacancy rate in slums has risen over this period and is quite high—much higher than the average for the city as a whole. If the earlier suppositions are correct, it is doubtful whether the much smaller tightening forces due to redevelopment could show up at all in the data.

Measurement is made even more difficult by the types of procedure imposed by the small scale. Two procedures suggest them-

---

[7] William G. Grigsby, *Housing Markets and Public Policy* (University of Pennsylvania Press, 1963).

[8] It should be pointed out that in the Michael Reese project the number of new dwelling units constructed is more than double the number demolished—a rather unusual situation (Evelyn M. Kitagawa and Karl E. Taeuber, eds., *Local Community Fact Book, Chicago Metropolitan Area, 1960* [Chicago Community Inventory, University of Chicago, 1963]).

selves: (1) to use the records of relocation authorities to discover what rental differences were encountered by actual relocatees; and (2) to compare rentals paid on the redevelopment site before dislocation occurred and those paid subsequent to dislocation in areas where the flow of dislocatees is largely concentrated. The period of dislocation-relocation is considerably shorter than the redevelopment process as a whole. Therefore (unlike with land values in measuring internalization benefits), there is no need to be too concerned with the influence of large general forces during its operation.[9] But some adjustment can be made for whatever such larger movements occurred by comparing this change in rental levels with changes in areas similar to the ones studied, but receiving few relocatees. To facilitate this adjustment, relocation-impacted rental changes can be measured entirely in terms of the changes that took place in the relocation-impacted area, without reference to rents paid in the redevelopment sites. This latter kind of measure would incidentally indicate costs imposed on Group 2[10] as well as on Group 1.

Application of the first procedure has had to deal only with aggregates. Figures are not available on the projects explicitly being studied, but the Relocation Office of the Renewal Assistance Administration in Chicago does have aggregate figures for more recent projects. The median rent paid by all relocatees in their relocated housing exceeded the median rent paid in their original housing by six dollars a month. Interpretation of this figure is extremely difficult, because for most relocatees the quality of housing is improved through relocation. For example, in Hyde Park "B," 98.3 percent of the housing was substandard, yet 82 percent of the relocatees from this section subsequently obtained residence in standard dwellings.[11] Much the same is true of the other Chicago projects. And, as was noted earlier, this is true for the nation as a whole. Through June 1963, of the 87 percent of 157,000 relocated families about whom the information is available, over 92 percent moved into "decent, safe and sanitary housing," yet most of them

[9] It must be remembered that the short-run effect is more severe than the long-run, since, in the short run, dwellings are demolished and *no* new dwellings of any type have yet taken their place.

[10] Inhabitants of dwellings like those demolished, and living in relocation-impacted areas. See pp. 145-46.

[11] Relocation Office, Renewal Assistance Administration, Chicago, Ill.

had come from substandard housing.[12] Thus, without further information, no inference can be drawn about the real rental paid by the dislocated.

Again, a study of larger scope could extract more useful information from this type of procedure. The relocation experience of specific families could be followed up. Rental changes for families moving to comparable units could be computed directly. Where quality changes occurred, rental differentials could be compared to what seem to be the price differences established in the market as a whole for particular quality gradations.

The second procedure is even less promising, especially since the scope here is small. But even in a larger-scale study the substantial loosening in the market and the locational and population differences among areas superficially similar in terms of housing would probably overwhelm systematic impact effects with statistical "noise." Figures could not be obtained that would permit an adjustment to be made for these complications.

There are no persuasive, let alone decisive, data available. But for all their paucity and ambiguity, they may be consistent with the tenor of the remarks made above that the combination of small size relative to the market, prior suboptimality, and a substantially loosening market suggest that dislocatees were not hurt much, if at all, by relocation (except for their attachment to their original dwellings). It will be assumed, therefore, that in this particular situation the redevelopment projects had no important adverse redistributional effects to offset advantages to those who *eventually* moved into the new units (in the "long run"). It must be emphasized that this assumption is prompted not by lack of data but by the import of the qualifying circumstances mentioned above. Lack of data may well appear in studying other projects, but circumstances there may make a similar assumption entirely unwarranted, even dangerously misleading. Lack of data does not warrant the assumption of zero effects. Attendant circumstances could well favor strong impacts. This distinction between the unavailability of data and the assumption of zero effect will be considered further below. It is a distinction of great importance for policy recommendations in this area.

[12] William L. Slayton, "Report on Urban Renewal," *Urban Renewal,* Hearings before the Subcommittee on Housing, House Committee on Banking and Currency, 88 Cong. 1 sess. (November 1963), Pt. 2, p. 410.

## Social Costs of Slums

This is the area that may give rise to the most distinctive types of benefits of urban renewal. The benefits—if they exist—affect the level of national income and not simply its distribution. Furthermore, they may be of considerable magnitude. It is an area where facts are extremely important, yet are most difficult to come by.

There are four types of benefits, each connected with the amelioration of a slum-generated social cost (typically reflected in a market externality): (1) decreased fire hazards, (2) decreased illness, (3) decreased crime, and (4) decreased damage to personality development.

Some of the voluminous literature has been cited in the bibliographical appendix to Chapter III, and methods of quantification on the twin problems have been discussed in Chapter X: (1) slum generation of social (external) costs, and (2) the extent to which redevelopment and public housing programs decrease these costs. Many treatments have been suggested for portions of these problems. But there are no definitive studies, using appropriate controls, that would permit reliable quantification of the magnitudes involved—not simply magnitudes in terms of money, but even those in terms of the natural dimensions involved, as, for example, patient days, or homicides, or number of psychotics. It is clearly beyond the scope of this study to try to make such a definitive study from primary sources. Indeed, it is probably even beyond the scope of an expanded empirical study. Primary reliance for data must probably remain on the manipulation of secondary source materials. One must hope for more penetrating and relevant major studies coming out of sociology, psychology and psychiatry, medicine, and criminology.

An effort was made to obtain some Chicago data on these categories of social cost, but with little success. The fire hazard category, seemingly the most straightforward, did not yield anything of value to a study of the limited scope of this one. Fire department records give differential experience for areas which can be laboriously broken down into slum and non-slum areas. But the unit of experience is the service run. So amount of damage, or number of dwellings, or even number of fires cannot accurately be determined.

Fire department budgetary allocations might be more helpful, but they were not available for use here.

The property damage records of insurance companies should be a rich source, but they are not broken down by slum and non-slum areas. Thus, substantial work would be required to put them into usable form. Even differential premium rates, which one might consider using as a short cut, involve difficulties. By law, companies are not allowed to discriminate in their rates between slum and non-slum units, or, indeed, between high-risk and low-risk clients in general. A lumping together of risks is the general rule. Companies that set deviating rates do so by specializing in a selected group of insurers and setting a single rate for this group. But this represents a differential for selective *low-risk* insurers. Non-restricted entry companies have too broad a clientele to be considered the comparable high-risk group. Differential rates may be charged, however, in terms of physical characteristics of the property being insured. Slum property may differ in such characteristics on the average from non-slum property. But differential risk from type of use would not be reflected. It is possible that insurance companies obtain a premium differential in fact to offset this by misclassifying slum property into higher-risk categories than their physical characteristics would warrant. Or the real premium difference might be reflected in a differential ability of slum property owners to buy insurance. Companies may simply refuse to insure very adverse risks.

Some quantitative information should certainly be available on fire hazards. But a good deal of work will probably be necessary to obtain it.

Some sketchy data on differential crime rates in Chicago was obtained and is shown in Table XI-5.

The data are crude, however, and they probably understate the slum–non-slum differential because offenses are recorded by locale of the crime rather than by residence of the criminal. They are subject to the substantial biases suspected of police reporting, and they tell the familiar story of gross association that was discussed in Chapter X. They do nothing to separate the effect of slums from other—partly intertwining—variables.

Since no idea about the size of these effects in the Chicago situation can be given, it might be useful at least to cull some of the general literature as well as the sense of the analysis in earlier chap-

**TABLE XI-5. Crime Rates per 1,000 Population in Selected Police Districts in Chicago, 1955**

| Police district | Future redevelopment project relevant | Population | Crime rate (offenses per 1,000) |
|---|---|---|---|
| A. Districts with slum areas | | | |
| District 6 | Hyde Park "A" and "B" | 101,678 | 31.8 |
| District 2 | Lake-Meadows— | | |
| | Prairie Shores | 100,801 | 25.7 |
| District 22 | Blue Island | 72,570 | 21.7 |
| B. Non-slum district | | | |
| Rogers Park | | | 9.3 |
| C. Chicago average | | | 14.8 |

Source: City of Chicago Police Department.

ters of this book, to indicate something about direction and order of magnitude of these types of effect. Very probably slum concentrations increase fire hazards appreciably. The physical configuration and use characteristic of slums would indicate this very strongly. Buildings are not maintained, wiring is often overloaded, cooking stoves are used to supplement inadequate central heating, and the buildings are old and not fireproof. Moreover, since the sheer area of such physical concentration is an important variable, redevelopment probably removes considerably more hazard than it adds by relocation.

Overcrowding and filth demonstrably increase the incidence of illness. Insofar as relocation moves dislocatees into standard housing, these two physical variables are clearly affected by redevelopment. Health hazards due to poverty and group practices will be largely untouched. In Chapter X data were presented suggesting that redevelopment decreased substandard housing use. Thus, one expects to find some influences tending to reduce the incidence of disease but none tending to increase it. On balance, therefore, one can expect redevelopment to reduce social costs in this area.

Crime is much more specifically related to population and its behavior than to physical surroundings. Thus, poverty and group characteristics must surely explain an important part of the higher incidence of crime in slum areas than elsewhere. But the physical environment may well have an effect on economic productivity through illness, deterioration of aspirations, etc. Or the slum itself, through homogeneous population concentration, can encourage crime by providing opportunities for subculture values (including criminal cultural values) to become important. Here, too, redevelopment might curb crime due to the latter factors but not that due to the former. The criminals—actual and potential—and the "causes" of crime would simply have changed location. Indeed, if the dislocatees ended up in a slum much like the one they left, then, even if their presence did not worsen the slum (that is, even if they had only marginal impact on the slum—so that, for example, they were no worse off in terms of real rentals), redevelopment could not even count on diminishing crime due to situational factors. In the present case, the scanty data on relocation cited above is used to infer that some improvement in neighborhood was achieved.

Even where this last is so, however, the dislocation process, by uprooting individuals from their accustomed locale, could have a traumatic effect and increase criminal propensities. How much, of course, is a question; but it would involve only a transitional effect and would disappear as new roots were fixed.

Thus, on balance, so long as dislocation has only a marginal impact on the immigrant neighborhoods, redevelopment might be expected to have a slight ameliorating effect on crime—an effect likely to become apparent only after some time, when the long-run impact of the slum on behavior is gradually moderated with the development of new generations.

Much the same can be said about the remaining category. The presumed higher incidence of individual and family difficulties in slums can be explained in significant measure by the limited opportunities associated with poverty (both as cause *and* as effect) and the idiosyncratic factors that result in poverty. Group subculture characteristics may also be explanatory factors. But here, too, the physical-functional complex that is a slum has some generative force. Environment does influence individual and group interactions. Depressed, unhealthy, overcrowded surroundings can warp both individual and family processes. It may be that unhappiness and mental illness belong to dimensions that do not possess a threshold discontinuity like that of criminal-noncriminal behavior. As a result, degrees of unhappiness and mental illness may more easily be evoked by unfavorable influences than is crime.

To summarize, the admittedly poorly documented conclusion is drawn that relocation did not noticeably spread or aggravate slums elsewhere because of small numbers and a loosening market, and that indeed improvement in housing quality was attained. On the basis of this, it is inferred that improvements are likely to have been impelled in all of the four categories of slum-generated social cost, offset to some extent temporarily by the loss of neighborhood capital. These improvements are most probable in fire and health, least probable in crime. In all categories, however, quantification is beyond the scope of this study, even in terms of the dimension natural to each kind of social cost, let alone in terms of money.

These benefits may be very important. The approximate magnitude of the gains from internalizing the externalities in land use have been seen. This is brought together below with estimates of the cost of redevelopment. The costs are generally *much greater* than the land gains. Thus, despite the downward bias of the gains figures, redevelopment is not generally justified in terms of land productivity alone. If it is justified, it is chiefly because the eradication of slum-generated social costs is sizable. Thus, in a real sense, the basic political decision depends on just how important this category of benefits is. The intractability of data cannot be used as an excuse for neglecting the category. This would summarily dismiss urban redevelopment as a justifiable object of resource expenditure. While redevelopment may turn out to represent an unwise use of resources even when this category is considered, it would be dangerously misleading to think one is giving redevelopment an impartial hearing if the category is omitted. This warning holds especially for the comparison of redevelopment with the status quo; but it also holds, though in lesser degree, for comparison with the modified public policy package as well, because the configuration of effects on slums differs under the two alternatives.

## Benefit-Cost Summary of Numerical Illustration

While the findings have been sketchy, a summary of the numerical example should give some idea about the relationship of the various elements to the overall policy evaluation. (See Table XI-6.)

The structure of the table derives from the following basic relationship:

**TABLE XI-6. Benefit-Cost Summary of Numerical Illustration**

*(In thousands of dollars)*

| Benefit and cost categories | Blue Island | Hyde Park "B" | Hyde Park "A" | Michael Reese | Lake Meadows |
|---|---|---|---|---|---|
| 1. Resource cost of project | | | | | |
|   a. Gross project costs (GPC) | 396 | 638 | 10,534 | 6,235 | 16,761 |
|   b. Less initial value of land | | | | | |
|     ($L_0$), equals | 46 | 49 | 6,449 | 1,596 | 8,777 |
|   c. Total resource costs (TC) | 350 | 589 | 4,085 | 4,639 | 7,984 |
| 2. Benefits produced by project | | | | | |
|   a. Increased productivity of | | | | | |
|     site land ($L_1 - L_0$) | 29 | 30 | 5,016 | 1,719 | 12,711 |
|   b. Increased productivity of neighboring real estate (spillover) | + | + | + | + | + |
|   c. Decreased social costs associated with slums ($\Delta SC$) | + | + | + | + | + |
| 3. Total costs not offset by site land benefit ($1c - 2a$) | 321 | 559 | −931 (gain) | 2,920 | −4,727 (gain) |

Source: Line 1a from U. S. Housing and Home Finance Agency, Urban Renewal Administration, *Urban Renewal Project Characteristics*, 1962 and 1963 vols. Other data from Table XI-3.

Let:

    $GPC$ = gross project cost.
    $AC$ = cost of acquired real estate in site (Acquisition Cost).
    $L_0$ = market value of land acquired in site.
    $I_0$ = market value of improvements acquired in site.
    $R$ = resource expenditures in project other than acquisition cost.
    $TC$ = total resource costs of project.

Then:

(11.5a)  $$GPC = AC + R$$
(11.5b)  $$AC = L_0 + I_0$$
(11.5c)  $$TC = I_0 + R$$

(since $I_0$, but not $L_0$, is lost to society through the project).

So:

(11.5d)  $$TC = (AC - L_0) + R = GPC - L_0.$$

And total benefits (*TB*) is given by:

(11.5e)      $TB = (L_1 - L_0) +$ (spillover effects)
$+$ (change in social costs of slums).[13]

To simulate a decision-making context, site land benefits are subtracted from total resource costs on the bottom line, so as to indicate how much spillover and social cost benefits would have to be worth to decision makers for the total to exceed total costs from the projects listed, *relative to the status quo only*. Benefits associated with subsidization to achieve "public goals" (like population heterogeneity, university expansion, architectural beauty) would appropriately be added at this point to determine the grand balance.

Although no claim of accuracy can be made for the particular figures in Table XI-6, it may tentatively be concluded that there are economies of scale in these redevelopment projects. The deficiency of measured benefits relative to resource costs steadily declines as the scale of gross project costs increases, until the benefits actually exceed resource costs. This tendency is less certain with respect to total resource cost, which is a better index of project size, but it is not absent. This is an interesting tendency in light of the fact that percentage impacts on land prices are not dependably greater for the two larger projects than for the others. The greater profitability seems to consist in a proportional economizing of inputs necessary to produce internalization benefits. This suggests the existence of certain relatively fixed inputs in the redevelopment process. But again, our evidence is meager, and even this lesson must not be taken too seriously.

[13] Any net distributional gains by families moving into redeveloped units, not offset by distributional losses by the dislocated and those buying competitive units, are being neglected.

PART THREE

*Issues of Public Policy*

CHAPTER XII

# Major Criticisms of the Redevelopment Program

THE BENEFITS FROM urban renewal that have been treated in the preceding chapters were suggested by examining the ostensible goals of the program. Their appropriateness and inclusiveness can be checked by examining an apparently opposite source—the criticisms leveled at the program in recent literature on public policy, with attention primarily to criticisms of redevelopment. The aim would be to see whether discussion and resolution of these criticisms require benefit categories in addition to, or instead of, those developed here. This can be done only roughly, since it is in principle inconsistent to attempt a comprehensive discussion of policy issues before any concrete benefit-cost study is made while at the same time preaching the crucial relevance of a benefit-cost analysis for policy making.

The following criticisms will be considered: (1) Private enterprise can do the job; (2) the government subsidy involved in redevelopment is too large; (3) redevelopment projects are too slow; (4) the targets have been improperly distorted, the priorities are inadequate; and (5) the poor, especially slum dwellers, have been hurt, not helped, by redevelopment programs.

In Chapter XIII the claim that there are better ways of accomplishing the aims of redevelopment will be examined.

## The Adequacy of Private Enterprise

The major conclusion of a recent, widely publicized, detailed work in the field—and one that probably represents a considerable body of opinion—is that the whole renewal program, redevelopment and rehabilitation, should be discontinued. The problems of substandard housing, of housing shortages, of raising housing standards throughout the country have already been considerably ameliorated by free market activity in the years since 1950 and will be substantially solved by a continuation of this trend. Redevelopment programs, it is claimed, made little, if any, contribution to this.[1]

This argument is critical of the analysis in this book, since it suggests that the achievements of private industry in this regard, with which renewal should be compared, will in fact soon represent a nearly optimal resource use. Any external tampering, its proponents feel, would generate not gains, but actual gross losses—over and above the costs of the tampering.

### Postwar Building Activities

The argument is based on the record of substantial private construction and rehabilitation activity of the postwar period, especially from 1950 to 1960. Data in the *U.S. Census of Housing* (1960) show that the proportion of the housing stock meeting minimum standards increased from 63 percent in 1950 to 81 percent in 1960. This was due partly to an increase in the overall number of standard units (a 63 percent increase from 29.1 million to 47.4 million) and also to an absolute decrease in the number of substandard units (a 36 percent decrease from 17 million to about 11 million). Moreover, the really poor housing, classified as dilapidated, decreased from 9.8 percent of the housing stock in 1950 (3.9 million) to 5.2 percent in 1960 (2.4 million).[2]

This is an extremely impressive, but also an unusual, accom-

[1] Martin Anderson, *The Federal Bulldozer; a Critical Analysis of Urban Renewal, 1949-1962* (M.I.T. Press, 1964).

[2] Figures cited in Martin Anderson, "Fiasco of Urban Renewal," *Harvard Business Review* (January-February 1965).

plishment. Even the book in question recognizes its uniqueness, terming it the greatest improvement in housing quality in American history.[3] The major source of improvement was the boom in new construction, associated largely with suburbanization. The latter meant a considerable shifting of populations, with higher-income households moving out of cities and releasing their dwelling units to lower-income groups, both those already living in poorer units and those migrating into the cities from rural areas. Thus there was considerable filtering, and quality improvement became attainable for many households. Overcrowding in substandard units decreased, and vacancy rates rose, thus making voluntary renovation and repair an attractive investment for property owners.

## The Extent of Poor Housing

The relevant question for this study is not the reality of the improvement, but the effect it has had on the problems considered here, and what its effect is likely to be in the future. Moreover, the magnitude of the problem for policy purposes may be misleading when looked at solely through percentage figures. While substandard units decreased from 37 percent to 19 percent of the housing stock, and dilapidated units from 9.8 percent to 5.2 percent, about 9 million American households are still living in poor housing, and of these, 2.4 million are living in extremely poor conditions. If the tremendous outlays under federal agricultural programs affect directly no more than 5 million farm families, certainly the sheer numbers of people affected by poor housing call for an evaluation of the redevelopment program on its merits.

Indeed, the affected group is even more politically significant than its numbers would indicate. It consists disproportionately of minority racial groups, such as Negroes and Puerto Ricans. While nonwhite groups showed an improvement in the quality of their housing during the 1950's that compared favorably with that of whites,[4] much of this can be accounted for by the fact that many of them were migrating from extremely dismal housing conditions in

[3] Anderson, *The Federal Bulldozer*, pp. 219-20.

[4] The proportion of nonwhite-occupied units that were standard rose from only 28 percent in 1950 to 56 percent in 1960; while the comparable figures for whites were 68 percent and 87 percent. (U.S. Housing and Home Finance Agency, *Our Non-White Population and Its Housing: The Changes Between 1950 and 1960* [1963], p. 14, cited in Anderson, *The Federal Bulldozer*, p. 210.)

the South to northern and western cities, where conditions were not as bad. Moreover, almost one-half of their housing units were still substandard in 1960.[5] These groups find the private housing market much stickier than do whites. Their ability to range over the market to take advantage of filtering is seriously hampered by racial discrimination, quite aside from income difficulties. Thus, it takes especially powerful market forces to include them in any housing gains. Yet their continued concentration in slums threatens social stability.

### Quality Improvement and the Elimination of Slums

The problem to which the quality improvement figures are relevant is, of course, the elimination of slums. This is related to, but is not exactly the same thing as, the elimination of substandard dwelling units. The difference is important. It was argued earlier in this study that slums represent a suboptimal use of resources, not so much because they contain inferior quality housing, but because their *concentration* of extreme inferiority is generated out of neighborhood effects, and that same concentration in turn generates certain social costs. On the other hand, individually inferior units might well be part of an appropriate resource response to poverty and housing technology. What do the figures say about slums?

First, it is important to note that the heavy building and repairing activity between 1950 and 1960 was not the result of purely private incentives. It was significantly subsidized by the federal government. Government mortgages and mortgage insurance, income tax advantages, and vast highway construction connecting suburbs with other suburbs and the central city were important influences helping to shape market responses.

Second, the actual decline of substandard units during the period must be studied to see how market forces remove slums. During the period 1950-56, the number of substandard units in the United States decreased from 14.8 million to 10.2 million, a 31 percent decline. The three most important sources of the decline were *net* quality appreciation of "same" units,[6] involving 19 percent of the substandard stock; demolition, involving 10 percent of the stock;

_____

[5] In 1950, fully 87 percent of all nonwhite-occupied units in the South were substandard, as opposed to only 56 percent in the north central states and 41 percent in both the Northeast and the West (Anderson, *The Federal Bulldozer,* p. 120).

[6] That is, units occupied both at the beginning and at the end of the period.

and *net* vacancies, involving 7 percent of the stock.[7] These figures show that only small portions of the substandard stock were touched. Data covering the period 1950-59, but involving only units in the seventeen largest metropolitan areas, are even less persuasive. Here the overall increase in standard units was 38 percent, the decrease in substandard units 15 percent. The relative magnitudes of these changes are comparable to the 1950-60 United States figures given earlier. But here, with a finer breakdown of substandard into "dilapidated" and "deteriorating," the more seriously inferior "dilapidated" category, presumably characteristic of slums, showed no decrease at all from quality changes and conversions. In fact, there was a net increase of 84,000 out of a 1950 total of 675,000 units. Only demolition, combined apparently with vacancies, succeeded in decreasing the total, by a net amount of 137,000.[8] Yet a considerable portion of this must be due to urban renewal demolitions and induced vacancies, since these are the areas on which the program concentrated in the 1950's.

The two sets of figures are consistent with the conjecture that quality improvement may not have been focused on really poor housing units in central cities, but may often have involved easier jobs of repair and renovation on less decayed units, for example, correcting minor structural deficiencies. Moreover, where really poor units were involved through demolition, a considerable part may have been due to the urban renewal program. Finally, where a decrease in substandard use resulted from vacancies in units, due largely to filtering, these vacancies may not have led to abandonment and private demolition. The structures, less fully used, may well have remained standing. So clustering of slum structures may have persisted nearly intact.

## The Future of Private Slum Elimination

This conjecture bears on the prediction of what the market can be expected to do about slums in the future. It stems from the analysis of slum formation and persistence made earlier in this study, which argued that important neighborhood externalities help gener-

---

[7] Figures derived from *National Housing Inventory* of 1956; cited in William G. Grigsby, *Housing Markets and Public Policy* (University of Pennsylvania Press, 1963), pp. 176, 254.

[8] Figures from *U.S. Census of Housing* (1960), cited in Anderson, *The Federal Bulldozer*, p. 201.

ate slums and help prevent their removal by purely private means. Thus, slum *occupancy* (not the existence of slum structures) is likely to be subject to filtering, but not much to direct physical transformation under private auspices. This argument is especially relevant for rental property, though less so for owner-occupied property. But rental property constitutes the more serious problem in slums.

This may be tested by examining data on the 1950-60 owner-occupied and rental categories. In 1950, rental units comprised 46 percent of the total for the United States.[9] Forty-one percent of rental units were substandard as against only 31 percent of owner-occupied units. Besides, while the former showed a 36 percent decrease in substandard units over the period, the latter showed a 46 percent decrease. It is especially interesting that most of this difference occurred in the latter part of the period. Substandard owner-occupied units were subject to an average annual decrease of 345,000 in the period 1950-57, and 323,000 in the years 1957-60, an almost constant rate. But while substandard rental units had a comparable rate of decline during the period 1950-60 (by 329,000 annually), the rate dropped sharply thereafter (to 215,000 annually).[10] Thus, the market impetus to eliminate occupied substandard rental units—the backbone of slums—tapered off significantly even in the midst of a massive housing boom. It is important to note that this is not influenced solely by construction and renovation of *rental* units, but, through filtering, by the whole complex of forces in the housing market. This apparent inability of the market to act in a strong, sustained way on the substandard rental sector during a period of market ease is consistent with the earlier analysis in this study.[10]

From the foregoing, the analysis here of the inherent suboptimalities in the private resource decisions that generate slums seems

[9] But by 1960 had fallen to only 38 percent due to a 39 percent expansion in owner-occupied units, as opposed to only a 0.05 percent expansion in rental units during the period. This shows to what extent market forces favored expansion of owner-occupied units at the expense of rental units. All figures are from the *U.S. Census of Housing* (1950), the *National Housing Inventory* (1956), and Preliminary Reports from the *U.S. Census of Housing* (1960). They are cited in Grigsby, *op. cit.*, p. 254.

[10] Rehabilitation experiences of private groups in slums bear this out. The Citizen's Housing and Planning Council (New York City) quit its attempts after heavy losses over two years. The deficits were laid to vandalism, high maintenance and material costs, and inability to charge adequate rentals. Large government subsidies to landlords and tenants were urged to make such efforts viable. (*New York Times,* March 9, 1967).

persuasive. There *are* barriers against purely private actions correcting these suboptimalities. While there is some improvement when the housing market is eased through extensive construction, important inefficiencies remain. Thus, even if there were a continuation of the expansive trend of 1950-60—an assumption certainly not supported by the present substantial (albeit policy-influenced) decline—there would still be a task to be performed by a government urban renewal program.

## Land Assembly Without Slum Clearance

Foremost among the forces hampering private efforts to rectify inefficiencies associated with slums is the difficulty of large land assembly at the core of the central city. It not only influences the existence of slums, but also probably lends an important impetus to vast urban sprawl, due to the far easier availability of large land parcels in fringe areas than in dense, central areas. Thus, some government intervention seems necessary, particularly through the use of eminent domain, to decrease the real cost of large-scale land assembly.

In view of this, and since it has been argued that most of the real difficulties with the redevelopment program lie not in the land assembly portion of the program, but in the government-operated slum clearance and disposition portions, it might be useful to reconstitute the program as one of land assembly only. The local public agency (LPA) would use the power of eminent domain to assemble sizable parcels of land and then, without interposing in any way on their existing or prospective use, would dispose of them to private interests in lot sizes determined by the criterion of maximizing proceeds.[11]

### Advantages of Land Assembly Only

One alleged advantage of this proposal is that it would eliminate a superfluous subsidy. Private interests, it is said, do not need the writedown subsidy—the excess of acquisition, demolition, and site preparation costs over disposition proceeds. All they need is an economically feasible opportunity to manage land plots large enough to internalize the market externalities. Internalization per-

[11] The suggestion that the program be limited to assembly comes from Mr. Leo Grebler in a private communication, 1965.

mits more profitable use after than before assembly. Therefore, private buyers could pay more for the batch than the LPA had to pay to assemble it, since fair market price for individual small components does not comprehend the additional productivity of the assembled batch. As a result, not only would the LPA not have to sustain net project cost, it would earn a profit on the transaction. No federal support would be needed, and the program could be entirely local. This does not mean that every conceivable assembly of a substantial land area would automatically be profitable. There are many batches—possibly a majority of them—where assembly would not be productive, and where the resource costs that would have to be incurred to bring about assembly would result in a net loss. Each area proposed for assembly would have to be carefully selected with an eye to profitablity. And profitablility refers to privately appropriable values.

The alleged advantages of this proposal are, then, that it would strike at the core of the private market externality, making possible more efficient resource use (including a re-evaluation of the relative advantages of suburban and city development), while necessitating no vast, complicated, government subsidization machinery, and indeed restricting the required government intervention to the local level only.

### Disadvantages of Land Assembly Only

The defects of the proposal are very close to its alleged advantages. The LPA would in effect be scouting the land market, as a middleman with monopsonistic powers, for opportunities to make strictly middleman's profits by buying and selling. Use of a profitability criterion by government has been criticized in Chapter V, and the reasons for the criticisms are especially clear in this case. Profitability here reflects only private valuations of land productivity, which would ignore the social costs of slum living. Since the government would not directly influence land use under this proposal, the decision about subsequent land use, and consequently the value of the batch to a prospective owner, would not take these costs into consideration. Thus, as was argued in Chapter VII, slum elimination (whether by demolition or rehabilitation) would by no means be guaranteed under this land-assembly-only proposal. The demolition and site preparation portions of the present program serve to guarantee that the slum structures will in fact be removed. It is uniquely appropriate to the role of government that it consider valuations for benefits and losses that are not appropriable through private market transactions.

## Relevance of Cost-Benefit Analysis

But while the social costs of slum living may justify slum elimination in particular cases, this will not always be true. The transformation from slums to non-slum use—however it is brought about—will cost resources. And the benefits, even though they are substantial, may not be worth the costs. Or the benefits may be worth the costs of one type of transformation but not of another. The present redevelopment program assumes that in each case chosen, the costs of the favored method of transformation—redevelopment—are less than the benefits to be obtained. Indeed, the benefit-cost analysis of this book was developed to determine whether this is likely to be so for each prospective project.

The benefit-cost analysis here has a related use as well. It examines the question whether some other means of bringing about transformed land use would be even more advantageous than redevelopment. One can strongly suspect that while the general types of benefits of slum removal are associated with a variety of projects, both the benefit mixes attainable and the relative costs of producing any one mix differ significantly for different classes of projects. It is probably not so much a question of finding the one best way of removing slums in every kind of circumstance, but rather of finding the best method for each particular kind of circumstance.

## Land Assembly as a Supplement

It has been argued above that the pure assembly function should not be adopted as a *substitute* for the present program. But the same argument can be used to suggest that it should be considered as a possible *supplement* to the present program. It was argued above that redevelopment should not be used unless the benefits of slum removal would be great enough to warrant incurring the costs of that method of attaining it. But there will be instances where they will not warrant the cost, yet the benefits of land assembly alone will warrant its much smaller costs. The present program does not permit this kind of flexibility, though it might very well be desirable.

However, there is a political difficulty connected with a supplement of this kind. While by its very nature it does not entail net costs that must be met by either the national or the local taxpayers, it does effect a redistribution of income, except in the unlikely case that the LPA is able to dispose of the land on the same terms as would be obtained by a perfectly discriminating monopolist and squeeze all of the buyer's prospective profits out of the sale. The government would be taking land by coercion from one group and giving it to another, on terms that would not help the former but would help the latter. Indeed, the former might even contend that the transaction hurts them, on the grounds that, without government interference, they might eventually have disposed of their property privately on more favorable terms. This is especially likely if the government, instead of paying the owners the capitalized value of slum earnings, paid only some lower "fair market price" that disallowed such earnings. Yet such a forced redistribution is apparently not connected with performance by the government of any public service. The internalization-of-externalities argument may well be too subtle for political persuasiveness. Thus, it is easy for the public to feel that the government is merely acting as a private land broker on behalf of a privileged private interest group. A pure assembly supplement would scarcely be acceptable under those circumstances and indeed might destroy the political acceptability of the renewal program as a whole.

## The Extravagance of Public Subsidy

This criticism takes two forms. The first asserts that one of the main alleged justifications for the urban renewal program is that it is an effective pump-priming device. That is, a small amount of government investment is supposed to induce a large amount of private investment. Critics argue that in fact the program has been a poor pump primer. The second form of the criticism is really intertwined with a number of other criticisms of the program, notably the regressive effects on dislocatees and other poor families. It asserts that the size of the land writedown subsidy to redevelopers is too great, not because the redevelopers do not pay the local public agency enough, but because the LPA pays too much for the land it assembles.

## Urban Renewal as a Pump Primer

The first argument is essentially that the relative and absolute magnitude of the federal support for the urban renewal program is much greater than has been generally supposed. In addition to the two-thirds share of net project costs and the full amount of relocation costs, which are met by the federal government, the Federal Housing Administration insures a sizable amount of redevelopment mortgages, and the Federal National Mortgage Association has purchased a significant number of these FHA-insured mortgages. Adding these makes a big difference in the size of the public dollar–private construction dollar multiplier. Instead of the 1:3.65 ratio estimated by federal renewal officials (1:5.11 as the federal dollar multiplier), this adjustment has been estimated to bring about a 1:1 ratio.[12]

There are two critical steps in this calculation. First, the figures on FNMA involvement are based on its portfolio holdings as of December 1962. This was the very high figure of 53.5 percent of the FHA-insured mortgages on urban renewal private construction, and it is simply projected into the future, with the assumption that these holdings will be concentrated in poorer quality mortgages rejected by private lenders.[13] The key to this projection is that 27 percent of the mortgages on multi-family dwellings held by FNMA were delinquent, a proportion that it was assumed would continue in the future. Assuming that FHA would continue to insure 79 percent of urban renewal residential mortgages, the federal government would be involved in long-term loans on 35 percent of the total privately owned construction on urban renewal sites. Second, estimated federal lending as a percentage of total—public and private—project cost (27 percent) is obtained by accepting the size of private construction as derived from the RAA ratio, 1:3.65. This federal lending is then added to the direct public payment of 21 percent to ob-

---

[12] Anderson, *The Federal Bulldozer*, pp. 138-40.
[13] *Ibid.*, p. 133.

tain a total public involvement equal to almost one-half of the overall costs of redevelopment.[14]

It has been noted above (Chapter I, note 8) that the underlying
conception of the role of FNMA on which these calculations rest is
misinformed. Events subsequent to 1962 would appear to bear this
out. By September 1964 only 4 percent of the relevant FNMA-
held mortgages were delinquent (instead of 27 percent), and its
holdings of such mortgages (especially as a percentage of the
total) were radically decreased.[15] Thus the above estimates seriously
overestimate the extent of federal long-term lending.

The second step is open to even greater misunderstanding. The
argument is couched in terms of "public money" and "private
sources." Since it is private builders who use the loan portion of this
"public money," it suggests that they are being subsidized by government to the amount of the "public money." But the amount of
actual subsidy, even where the federal government does in effect
make long-term loans to redevelopers through FNMA holdings, is
far less than the amount of such holdings. It is reflected only in the
difference between the private mortgage rate that would have had
to be paid and the actual rate that was paid due to the government
mortgage purchase. The resulting subsidy is of a different order of
magnitude entirely; only the much smaller capital value of the
mortgage rate differential should be added to direct government outlays for net project costs to give the extent of federal resources com-
mited for urban renewal.

This discussion of the efficiency of redevelopment as a pump-
priming device to encourage private construction, and of the absolute
extent of government subsidization of what may alternatively be
completely a private function, is somewhat of a digression from the
main purpose of this study. The absolute size of the government
commitment is irrelevant to the question of whether benefits exceed
costs. The encouragement of private construction is not obviously a
benefit at all in a full employment situation. Supporters and critics
of urban renewal have treated it as such because they see the program as an instrumentality of macro-economic fiscal policy. In this
study, it was decided instead to adopt the full employment assumption, because, whether or not the economy is actually at full em-

[14] *Ibid.*, pp. 133-39.
[15] "Rebirth for Cities?," *The Economist* (London, Feb. 6, 1965), p. 542.

ployment, the program is considered too cumbersome to be used for fiscal policy purposes. Its inflexible and extended timing could easily aggravate the problem of high-income stability for the economy. Thus any impact on investment can be disregarded, assuming in effect that comparable income consequences could have been (and would have been) produced by more appropriate fiscal tools.

Criticism concerning the relative extent of federal and local participation is also essentially a digression. This really refers to alleged administrative violation of the spirit of the program. It will be remembered that the city may contribute part or all of its share of net project costs in the form of public facilities dedicated to the benefit of the redevelopment site. It is alleged that the city often donates facilities that were in no sense triggered by the project and are not used exclusively, or sometimes even mainly, by site dwellers. The actual relevant city participation in the program is thus less than it should be.

This is a criticism of the administration of the program. There have been many others of this sort, concerning bureaucratic red tape, local political maneuvering, poor planning, errors, etc. They are very hard to evaluate and often depend on controversial theories of public administration. The economist's welfare tools are not adapted to scrutinizing many of these claims, although the claims *are* relevant to proper administration, and even to the question of the program's very existence. Some programs that in principle would yield net benefits cannot be administered without dissipating their substantive advantages. Therefore, though administrative efficiency is certainly important, it will not be dealt with here.

## The High Price of Land Acquisition

The second main form of the argument about the extravagance of the government subsidy contends that the government writedown subsidy is too great because the local public agency pays too much for the land acquired. It assembles land that is still in great demand for shelter by poor families. Use density is too great; the vacancy rate is too low. Thus, property owners make good returns on their property, and the fair market price is high. Furthermore, successive sites to be redeveloped are often near one another, and since the redeveloped structures generally raise the quality level of each narrower neighborhood substantially, property values in adjacent areas scheduled for later redevelopment are likely to become inflated. This increases the cost of the subsequent government assembly.[16]

The superfluous assembly costs partly represent waste in the form of a surplus to property owners that has no social function, and partly they represent deeper characteristics of resource allocation under the program. They reflect, for example, a policy of willingness first to displace substantial numbers of slum dwellers during demolition and subsequently to discourage the displaced from returning by constructing units far above their economic reach. Both of these facets concern the regressive distributional effects of redevelopment. This aspect will be considered further below.

The proposal is to attack the first problem by having the LPA select only sites where density of use has already fallen substantially. That is, redevelopment would be restricted to only those areas that have been "rejected by the market"—areas characterized by high vacancy rates, private abandonments, and declining property values. Moreover, in such areas property values can be depressed even further, as a matter of public policy, by strict enforcement of zoning regulations and health and building codes. This changes resource use, but not unwarrantedly, since it represents the imposition of social cost accounting on property that has hitherto been used solely in terms of private cost accounting.[17]

The second problem would be attacked partly by introducing strict code enforcement into the adjoining areas as well and partly by changing the mix of new construction so that more new units represent only moderate quality inflation and are therefore competitive with units standing in the adjoining area. Both forces should prevent speculative inflation in the neighboring areas and indeed should even force prices down. Here too such price influences do not mean unwarranted distortions of resource allocation.[18]

---

[16] See Grigsby, op. cit., pp. 315ff.

[17] Ibid.

[18] Ibid. Grigsby actually couples the modification with his major prescription: encourage a substantial increase of new residential construction. Through filtering this will ease the slum market and produce not only areas that move progressively toward private abandonment but also higher-quality units into which the dislocatees can move. This constructive proposal will be treated in a later section, but it can be eliminated from this discussion because even with heavy new construction there will be both dense slum areas and areas that are being extensively abandoned. Redevelopment policy must still decide which of these should have priority for demolition.

At the outset, it is clear that code enforcement and construction mix are not at issue. Code enforcement could supplement present policy as well as a change in the construction mix. Indeed, it is already supposed to be part of the present program. Similarly, the specific construction mix is not a real issue, unless one understands by it a radical effort to subsidize new low-income housing. Recent changes in the present program aim at increasing the proportion of medium-income and low-income units in the mix by extending federal lending to lower-quality levels than have so far been affected. Control of the mix has always been a proper function of the LPA. At no time has the agency been required legislatively to dispose of land on the basis of the highest private bid. Disposition can be channeled to meet any social purpose reflected in the mix of new construction. Of course, the marketability of site land depends on the new uses, and higher-income units (as well as commercial construction) have usually proven more attractive to redevelopers than has a broader mix. To require a wider mix would probably reduce the proceeds that the LPA could command and thus increase the writedown subsidy. Any differential in proceeds would be the cost of realizing the social purpose.

The principal problem is to make a better selection of redevelopment sites in order to minimize acquisition costs and the extent of relocation. One difficulty is that while the present method of site selection certainly does not follow the criterion suggested above, it is not clear what alternative criterion it does follow. One of the real weaknesses in the administration of the program has been the lack of any federal guidelines for priorities in project selection. Decentralization has been so complete and local practices so varied that this is not easy to generalize even *ex post*. The residential-nonresidential issue in selection will be considered below. The discussion here is confined to the residential sector. In view of the difficulty in characterizing present practices, the issue posed in this criticism can be formulated as whether or not it is wise to hold open the option of selecting dense, high property value slums for demolition.

Following the proposal would mean lower government resource costs and a lower burden of relocation. On the other hand, relative to clearing denser slum areas, it would mean a smaller decrease in slum occupancy per acre cleared—subject to the qualification that the *net* reduction in slum living for dense slum clearance is still

greater, even when any possible spread of slums due to a larger relocation burden has been considered as an offset. If slum living entails heavy social costs and the local housing market does not make
acceptable relocation very difficult, the comparison may well favor
clearance of dense slums.

More intuitively, application of the proposal implies waiting for
the private market to do most of the work of solving the problem of
slum living. Government could, of course, hasten the process of
market rejection by encouraging new construction, but this would
help the situation under both policies. For any given total housing
stock, the extent of slum living is a negative function of the efficiency of filtering—the degree of perfection of the market and absence
of external influences (systematic tax incentives, capital market imperfections, discrimination). The more efficient the housing market,
the more reason there is to step in after market forces have decreased slum occupancy in every respect other than physical clearance. The less efficient the market, the more reason there is not to
trust market forces to lead the way. As a postscript, if the housing
market worked very efficiently and did in fact substantially "reject"
erstwhile slum areas, then this rejection would in itself weaken the
forces that prevent private land assembly and clearance. In such
cases government intervention to clear "rejected areas" would be
nearly superfluous.

To conclude, site selection in accordance with the suggested criterion does not clearly recommend itself as a general principle. But
its advantage in specific situations can be tested by applying the
kind of benefit-cost analysis presented here. An extreme interpretation of market rejection is not recommended, however, since it is
likely to lead to superfluous intervention.

## The Speed of Redevelopment

The average gestation period for a redevelopment project initiated before 1961 was slightly less than 12 years, 2½-3 years for
planning and about 8½ years for execution, the latter including the
public functions as well as the new construction by the redeveloper.[19]
These are estimates, since most projects were not completed when the

[19] Anderson, *The Federal Bulldozer*, Chap. 5.

data were collected. The length of time required decreased substantially as experience was gained, and appears to be a positive function of the size of projects. The duration of projects, it is said, is extremely long and is a major defect of the program. This problem must therefore be examined.

## The Planning Period

A long planning period does not itself have untoward effects. Indeed, it may be the best guarantee of a worthwhile project. Redevelopment is a complicated process, with many layers of action that must be interrelated, not the least of these being the selection and conception of the project. Deep, unhurried planning is probably necessary if the project is to economize resources and secure the most substantial benefits attainable.

## The Land Assembly Stage

A long assembly stage does not itself represent waste either. It may simply indicate a delicate and intricate transactional process. Government performance at this stage probably does not compare badly with a "comparable" effort by private interests. Indeed, for reasons given above, it may be far more expeditious. If the duration of this stage is very long (perhaps compared with average private projects), it is because government redevelopment projects are considerably more complex and larger in scope than are private projects.

## The Relocation Stage

A lengthy stage of relocation has two types of consequences. On the one hand, it tends to decrease the redistributional effects of relocation. Fewer households are thrust onto the market at any one time, and more time is available to seek alternative housing in standard units without appreciably higher rentals. This alone tends to improve the benefit-cost balance of projects. But a second type of consequence probably operates in the opposite direction. As relocation proceeds, a growing proportion of living space in accumulated structures becomes and remains vacant, and the structures themselves are allowed to deteriorate. Resources are wasted, and living conditions in these units become—although on a transitory basis—even worse than before LPA assembly. Which of the two effects predominates depends partly on the state of the housing market (which measures the relocation gain from gradual displacement) and the importance attached to the welfare of the dislocatees relative to land productivity. In evaluating the net effects, it is important to discover whether the actual duration is the result of an explicit LPA decision about relocation burdens versus property waste or simply the result of administrative considerations having little to do with this question. Administrative inefficiency could well give rise to net losses on this score.

### Demolition and Site Preparation

A long period of demolition and site preparation gives rise only to economic losses. The land is unused and hence wasted. Moreover, market conditions may be changing, so that some potential private redevelopers—who also must plan in advance—find it too risky to try to plan construction for redevelopment land in the light of particular expected market conditions. The land's availability is too far in the future. Concrete interest in renewal land is likely therefore to be restricted to redevelopers who can postpone specific planning to a period close to or even after the emergence of the land. As a result, the next stage—construction—is likely to be lengthened as well. Thus, duration at this government action stage is the most critical of all, since time represents resource waste, and delay both weakens the market attractiveness of the land and tends to make the reconstruction stage longer by inhibiting advance planning.

On the other hand, there are not strong reasons in the nature of the project itself to expect this stage to be unduly long. If it appears to take longer than in private projects, this may be due largely to the typically larger scale of the public project. There is perhaps one danger spot. Site preparation, unlike the preceding demolition, involves coordinated action by several public authorities—as, for example, where streets, lighting, sewer systems, and schools must be installed. Problems of interagency coordination may sometimes significantly extend total action time in a way not connected with the purely technical aspects of the operation. But this is not inherent in the program and would have to be evaluated in particular circumstances. Conventional judgments about management efficiency are enough to gauge net losses associated with operational delays.

## Disposition

Disposition may be another danger area. Here, too, delay represents economic waste. Insofar as the preceding stages are variable as well as long, disposition is not likely to be arranged much in advance of the land's actual availability. Moreover, a number of factors connected with disposition itself may protract negotiations. (1) The LPA often prefers to dispose of the site as a single package. The resulting capital requirements for purchase leave few developers interested and make it harder for the LPA to initiate serious negotiations. (2) The LPA typically lays down conditions on the character of proposed land use that lengthen negotiations. (3) Partly because of the first two factors, and partly because of the complexity and large scale of proposed development, negotiations often bring in additional government authorities at a variety of levels.[20] This is reported to involve serious delays. However, one must be careful to distinguish the extra time necessary because of the complexity and size of the project from delays due to administrative inefficiency. Public redevelopment is designedly more complicated and larger than most private projects. The additional cost one pays in time is not a waste but a necessary input to produce something not attainable in the smaller, simpler projects. Whether this "something" is worth the cost can be measured by the benefit-cost approach.

## Private Redevelopment

The final stage is that of private redevelopment. Operational time here is not a waste except when it results from delays extraneous to the physical characteristics of the project. There may be interagency political complications, as suggested above. But they must be abstracted from the amount of public coordination that is essential to secure the public purposes of the project. And again, the time resulting from the unusual project scope is not a waste but a necessary input to the overall "commodity" being produced.

To summarize, the absolute length of a gestation period tells very little about the gains and losses involved. Extra time at one stage and for one reason may reflect net gains, at another stage and

[20] These widenings of negotiations sometimes take place at the following stage of private development instead of the disposition stage.

for another reason, net losses. This is not to argue that the length of gestation of urban renewal projects is or is not too great. But, for one thing, some apparently wasteful delays in operations may result from the unique character of urban renewal projects, by which they differ from private projects and from which specific benefits are generated. This character sometimes requires the additional productive input of time. For another thing, there are as yet no data on how much time is spent at each stage, and for what reason, though such information is obtainable.

## Residential-Nonresidential Mix and the Problem of Priorities

There have been many complaints that the wrong kinds of projects are being carried out. One group lays greatest emphasis on slum clearance and so deplores the recent relative increase in downtown commercial projects. Another group is concerned primarily about the low standard of living of slum dwellers and so attacks both the commercial projects and the residential projects that replace slum dwellings with high-income housing units. Another sees the paramount problem as one of easing the desperate financial plight of central city governments and so deplores the disproportionate resources still going into predominantly residential projects. Another is concerned chiefly about the lack of adequate overall city planning and wants renewal projects to pay more attention to larger constellations of harmonious interaction in the city or metropolitan area as a whole. Still another is convinced that more resources must be devoted to housing, both in absolute terms and relative to other industries, and so wants urban renewal to focus more on increasing the total of new residential construction.

### Project Choices

Clearly, not all of these criticisms can be met, since a truly effective formulation of the program in any one of these suggested directions would make the program less well adapted to fulfilling the other goals. If it were possible to give values to the fulfillment in varying degrees of these different goals, then in principle it would be possible by a benefit-cost analysis to decide which direction should in fact be paramount or, more appropriately, what mix of fulfillment would give the best compromise. But most of the goals represent "public purposes" on which analysis does not help to place values. Therefore benefit-cost analysis cannot be used to adjudicate among these criticisms, nor can the criticisms be used to supplement the analysis.

This does, however, raise a question that has been touched on here from various points of view—the question of criteria for the choice of projects. The urban renewal program is a national program, yet its substance is determined very largely on the local level. The requirement for local formulation of a Workable Program, the insistence on explicit provision for relocation, and the statutory maximum for federal contributions to nonresidential projects (from 10 percent, to 20 percent, to 30 percent of the total federal aid to renewal) are the most notable elements of central influence. The really critical features of renewal administration are in local hands.

## Local Determination of Criteria

Local authorities decide the residential-nonresidential mix, criteria on the seriousness of blight, whether blight removal is directed to help slum dwellers or property values, the sequence of intervention into different areas, the extent to which downtown commercial attractiveness should be subsidized, the identity of the population whose interests are to be considered, and most of the other fundamental questions that shape actual redevelopment. It has already been suggested above that local responsibility for deciding which is the relevant population imparts a bias to decision making that belies the national scope of the program. It leads to a maximization of jurisdictional advantage instead of a broader social advantage. It might be argued that a lack of uniform criteria for other dimensions of the program violates the spirit of the program as well. The criteria for the relative urgency of different projects, for example, ought to be properly stipulated centrally, especially for projects within the same category. This would not interfere with evaluation by the localities of their own problems but would help prevent decisions from being influenced by issues foreign to the spirit of urban renewal—as for example, a selection of slum areas influenced by policy toward location of minority racial groups. But this would not change matters much, for interpretations by local bodies of each legitimate goal, and their differing preferences for various combinations of these goals, would still account for most of the variation in emphasis of redevelopment projects. There is not likely to be any general agreement about the proper goals of the program so long as the federal government fails to set national criteria.

### Possible Federal Imposition of Criteria

There is a circumstance, not very farfetched, that might elicit such federal specification of criteria. The momentum of renewal has by now affected a considerable number of cities, and the total of accumulated federal aid commitments presses close to the authorized ceiling. This might induce the RAA to formulate criteria other than the inefficient one of "first come, first served" to ration its scarce aid capacity. These criteria would implicitly or explicitly reveal national valuations now lacking. Even to stipulate that the criterion is benefit-cost would require formulating such national valuations, since the several local requests would have to place valuations on the various "public purposes" in each project mix, and these valuations would be based on the respective preferences of the different localities. The local valuations would have to be adjusted by a common national scale of valuations in order to make them comparable.

National criteria would lead to a difficulty of some magnitude in the use of the benefit-cost analysis. In the absence of national criteria it has been assumed that each participating jurisdiction has its own set of criteria and selects projects with an eye toward maximizing total fulfillment, as defined by these criteria. Hence, when a given project is evaluated, it can be taken for granted that it represents the best use of resources for a project of its type—that is, it is compared with alternative *types* of resource use, but not explicitly with other projects of the same type. However, where the federal government has enunciated criteria and these differ from those of the particular locality, then the given LPA may select projects that will rate *acceptably* on the federal criteria but lower than other alternatives open to it, because the selected projects rank higher on their own criteria than the rejected ones. One can never be sure that a selected project is the best of its kind in terms of the national criteria. When there is a scarcity of grant funds, a rejected project is a precluded project.[21] .

## The Burden of Redevelopment on the Poor

Probably the most widespread criticism of redevelopment is that it not only has not helped those who were thought to be the intended beneficiaries—the slum dwellers, the poor—but has actually concentrated most of its real costs on them.[22] This argument has been treated extensively above. Any regressive redistribution of income due to redevelopment is listed as a co-equal consequence with level-of-income effects. A few further comments are in order to link this factor with public policy issues.

It will be remembered that there are three main sources of redistributive effect: (1) the adequacy of the relocation program in meeting the real costs of dislocation; (2) the absolute and relative changes in the composition of the housing stock; (3) the disruption and dispersion of whole neighborhoods with their established patterns of orderly social processes.

### Adequacy of Relocation Programs

The relation of redevelopment to this factor is the most straightforward of the three. Redevelopment necessarily incurs real costs of removal—the expense of moving households and businesses and also the costs of being forced to change from existing arrangements to new ones, such as the loss of locational advantages, of accumulated investment in social capital, of special characteristics of existing units. The question of the adequacy of relocation concerns only slightly the possibility of decreasing the overall size of these real costs. For the most part, it concerns the distribution of the costs among the total population. Their size can be influenced

[21] That is, precluded for the period in question. Since the evaluation of an alternative concerns benefits and costs over a specific time, postponement of inception generally means a change in the present value of benefits and costs.

[22] See, for example, Grigsby, *op. cit.,* Chap. VII; Anderson, *The Federal Bulldozer,* Chap. VI; Herbert J. Gans, "The Failure of Urban Renewal: A Critique and Some Proposals," *Commentary* (April 1965); Jane Jacobs, *The Death and Life of Great American Cities* (Random House, 1961); James Q. Wilson, "Urban Renewal Does Not Always Renew," *Harvard Today* (January 1965). Many popular discussions of urban renewal focus on this aspect.

by the relocation program only insofar as the additional information it creates about housing wants and availabilities in the market improves the use of the existing housing stock by more than the cost of supplying the information. And this in turn depends on the degree of imperfection of knowledge prior to redevelopment and the scope and effectiveness of the relocation efforts.

The distribution of the costs is the real issue. In the early days of the program the requirement that a conscientious effort be made to relocate slum dwellers was sometimes not taken seriously. Since the housing market was tight as well, frequently substantial relocation costs were borne almost entirely by those least able to afford them, the slum dislocatees. Relocation standards have subsequently become more demanding, and housing markets have loosened, with the result that the costs are now shared somewhat by the population at large. But dislocatees still bear most of the psychological and social costs of being uprooted.[23]

While the generation of these costs is inherent in redevelopment, no particular distribution of them is. Any distribution can be achieved (assuming that even approximate measurement of the costs can be carried out) without affecting the transformation of land use characteristic of redevelopment. So the program can further decrease the burden of dislocation on the dislocatees to any desired degree, simply by increasing the intensity of search activity and social services and the amount of the monetary compensation. This is being done. How far it should go is more controversial, but it does not bear on the question of whether redevelopment is worthwhile.

## Compositional Changes in the Housing Stock

This is a factor that is more variably, but intimately, related to redevelopment. To repeat the relationship, redevelopment demolishes dwelling units near or at the lowest quality levels in the housing stock and substitutes for them a smaller total number, disproportionately located in the middle-income or upper-income level; or it substitutes nonresidential units. Thus, although the average quality level of the housing stock is made to rise (and its age to

---

[23] The rental increase effect, which stems from changes in the composition of the housing stock, will be discussed below.

fall), the *number* of units in the lower-quality class declines while that in the higher-quality class increases. The price (and rentals) of lower-quality units rises, that of higher-quality units falls. The poor as a whole, using mostly units in the lower level, are faced with higher real costs for housing; the rich are faced with lower real costs.

A pattern like this is inherent in redevelopment because, since new construction is left to depend to an important degree on private incentives and initiative, the pattern of transformed land use reflects market forces. The government can, of course, influence these forces to produce other mixes, but its means of doing so either involve subsidies or negatively affect the value of the opportunities represented by the prepared land, thus leaving the overall effect on benefits and losses in question.

More concretely, the government has recently begun trying to change the reconstruction mix more toward moderate-income and lower-income dwelling units as against commercial and high-income units. This is being done by extending the types of units that are eligible for subsidized loans and mortgage insurance. Assume that this extension of credit aid redirects private incentives enough so that all of the newly prepared land can be disposed of to redevelopment with the allegedly more socially desirable mix and at the same prices as heretofore. Then the new mix produces higher total benefits than before—but at the cost of the increased subsidies. The net effect depends on the particulars of the situation. Alternatively, suppose no new subsidies are given, but instead disposition is channeled in the new direction by having the LPA sell only to redevelopers who agree to construct the new mix. Then the extra benefits from the new mix have to be offset by the extent to which the decreased profitability to redevelopers from using the land in the prescribed way is reflected in lower bids to the LPA. Again the net effect depends on particulars.[24] Thus, the attempt to modify

---

[24] Some critics of the urban renewal program believe that a policy of this sort would not be easy to bring about. One of the reasons for the problem in the first place is that local governments seem to value high disposition proceeds more than the welfare of dislocatees. They sell to the highest bidder (or nearly highest) and do not want to spoil the market by setting conditions for land use radically different from what developers want. Any decision by the federal government to change the mix in the interest of the poor by setting down disposition conditions would run into the alleged lack of sympathy of the LPA. In such an eventuality, it is suggested by Grigsby (*op. cit.*, p. 328) that the granting of

the impact of redevelopment on the composition of the housing stock (at least so long as the reconstruction is left to the private sector) is not neutral, except by accident, toward the whole structure of costs and benefits.

There is a method whereby this impact is not changed but simply bypassed. It has no direct effects on resource use but only indirect effects stemming from income redistribution. This is to allow whatever change occurs in the composition of the housing stock and then to compensate the poor for this negative income effect through rent supplements—either as a flow or as a capital value. Compensation could be paid not only to the dislocatees but to the larger group of poor who consume housing that is competitive with what was demolished. The former would presumably receive the larger sums. By this method, any desired degree of compensation could be given, either on unrestricted terms or explicitly for housing outlays. In the latter case it would presumably enable the affected group to take advantage of any filtering that occurred due to new construction coming onto the market.

Present public policy is moving in this direction. Not only is there an effort to change the reconstruction mix, but also in 1965, Congress authorized a rent supplement program to aid low-income families who could not obtain standard housing with their limited incomes. (Dislocatees had already been included in 1964.) By making up the difference between the market rent for modestly designed dwellings and 25 percent of the occupant's income, the rent supplement program makes possible the construction and management of decent low-income housing by private enterprise. Congress appropriated $12 million to initiate the program in 1966. In addition, sentiment has been growing to try to transform slums in ways that will significantly decrease the magnitude of household dislocation. But this would involve a decrease in the use of redevelopment and will be discussed below. In sum, there is recognition that slum removal in the past has imposed undesirably heavy burdens on slum dwellers, and changes are being made to correct this. They can be pushed further within the framework of redevelopment.

---

federal aid (its two-thirds share of net project costs) should be made conditional on formulation of projects by the LPA that show the more desirable mix. Projects with basically regressive distributional effects should get no federal subsidy.

## Disruption of Neighborhoods

Removal costs are unavoidable under redevelopment, but their distribution can be changed at will without affecting resource use. The income distribution effects of housing stock composition can be avoided, but only by a non-neutral influence on resource use. Neighborhood disruption creates another unavoidable social cost but one that cannot easily be set right with transfer payments. Redevelopment projects on any substantial scale do tend to disrupt whole neighborhoods by removing substantial portions from complicated social networks. They destroy, not simply redistribute, the interconnected, long-time maturing, extremely valuable social investment in a going community. Massive and intensely subtle systems of social transactions are dispersed.

The loss by individual households of their investment in social capital has been referred to above. These are the individual adaptations each has made for itself to existing on-going social processes. One can conceive of situations where a number of households suffer this cost individually by moving away from their neighborhood, while the neighborhood itself remains viable. However, when a group representing a substantial portion of the neighborhood (residential, commercial, social, religious) moves, those remaining find community processes barely if at all viable. The loss to the families that move appears to be the same in the two cases. Yet the two situations are different. Something more is lost in the second case, not because dislocatees have to attach themselves to other ongoing communities or to new agglomerations of people and things attempting to form new communities,[25] but rather because their move imposes external costs on the portion of the neighborhood that remains—a crippled, stricken community. They find it difficult, if not impossible, to continue to support schools, churches, commercial establishments, and other amenities. And important personal relations have been broken.

---

[25] The implication here is that such resocializing, whether for the individual or the group, entails social costs. This is not necessarily true for pioneer groups, who voluntarily seek the adventure of social creativity. Indeed, their opportunity to forge newness should be considered a social benefit. But the relevant group here is involuntarily being made to tear up its roots. Newness to them is more likely to be seen as a burden to be overcome rather than an opportunity to be enjoyed.

To show that this is the nature of the disruptive costs, suppose that redevelopment dislocates not simply a vital portion of a neigh- borhood but the neighborhood as a whole.[26] The dislocatees dis- perse to join existing neighborhood communities elsewhere. Every- one moving bears the loss of invested social capital, and the total loss is encompassed in this category. Any special character pos- sessed by the old neighborhood (for example, an ethnic flavor) which cannot be recaptured in the new communities indeed repre- sents a loss, but a loss exactly subsumable under the category of loss of first preference housing. (The uniqueness of the preferred hous- ing, in the earlier analysis of distributional effect, was always in- tended to include locational, ethnic, and other amenities that form the setting, and therefore influence the character, of the housing services provided.) Thus, in this extreme situation there are no ex- ternal costs involved, and the previous analysis holds. Only where the neighborhood has been decimated but not completely eradicat- ed is a special category of costs produced.

For purposes of public policy it is important to consider the possible long-run effects of large-scale neighborhood disruption, whether on the dislocatees or on those who remain. In brief, while neighborhood disruption can cause inconvenience, loneliness, and unhappiness, these may not be the only ill effects. It has been argued that the severing of neighborhood supportive roots for those who must leave, and the near-destruction of these roots for those who stay, can make it seem too difficult or even unnecessary to some to make the substantial investment in community accommo- dation once again. They remain improperly socialized thereafter, and show their lack of commitment to their subsequent surrounding neighborhoods by careless, irresponsible, and noncreative behavior. Both the remaining communities and those to which the dislocatees dispersed would contain human time bombs—individuals who sim- ply do not care for their community, cannot be made to care, and even sporadically turn to acts of violence. Since the original groups were sizable, the number of those who behave in this rootless man- ner could be considerable. Their presence in any community might

[26] It is assumed that for topographical, cultural, income, or other reasons the boundaries of the neighborhood are clear-cut. The neighborhood stops abruptly rather than trailing unobtrusively and indefinitely in a series of overlapping linked clusters.

therefore be more serious than simply a nuisance. Thus, a sequence of redevelopment disruptions might succeed in filling community after community with unstabilizing forces.

Unlike the first two sources of regressive distribution, the disruptive influence of redevelopment on neighborhoods is both intrinsic to redevelopment and capable of generating socially destructive forces that are neither easy to measure (even in principle) nor easily dealt with. It is hard to imagine government compensating their victims or suppressing their effects. While uncertain, they do bear upon the overall desirability of redevelopment.

Thus, the criticisms that have been examined highlight some of the aspects of the redevelopment program that call for special attention in a benefit-cost analysis. Redevelopment along the lines sketched in this study deserves to be examined closely on its merits; and the present approach to this examination has not been shown to be inadequate by these criticisms. Throughout the book it has frequently been suggested that the appropriate way to test the program is to compare it with alternative ways of accomplishing the same goals. In the next chapter, some of these alternatives will be described, and an attempt will be made to distinguish the potential effect of the alternatives from that of the present redevelopment program.

# CHAPTER XIII

# Some Alternatives to Redevelopment

THE MAJOR CHALLENGE to redevelopment comes not from the criticisms discussed in Chapter XII, but from the alternative programs that could accomplish many of the goals of redevelopment. Six types of alternatives will be considered: (1) measures that operate through an influence on the demand for housing; (2) measures that operate through an influence on the supply of housing; (3) measures that attempt to moderate market imperfections and inadvertent external interferences; (4) alternative forms of renewal; (5) measures designed to ease the financial difficulties of central cities; and (6) proposed new directions in the present program.

## The Demand for Housing

Early in this study reference was made to the argument that the chief problem is poverty, that slums are only a byproduct. Eliminating poverty will solve the problem of slums, and to try to solve it without tackling the problem of poverty is doomed to failure. Redevelopment is based on a significantly different view. The problem is seen as one, not of the income level of slum dwellers, but rather of land use, with little attention to, and even—in the early years of the program—neglect of, the slum dwellers. Some redress of the early imbalance has been sought in the program, by compensating the dislocates for some of the losses they suffer in the process of transformed land use but not for the broader losses they suffer by being poor.

## Types of Income Supplements

The first type of alternative program would place the focus at the other end. It would supply the slum dwellers with additional purchasing power and allow their increased demand for housing to initiate any change in land use. Improved living standards of the poor would be the entering wedge. Any diminution of slum living would be an indirect resultant of forces set in motion by the increased demand.

Two versions of this type of program must be distinguished: (1) The subsidies may be in the form of rental allowances, where the funds are earmarked for the payment of rent alone, and the amount given is based on the difference between what poor families spend on the average for housing and what they would have to spend to obtain a "decent, safe, and sanitary" level. (2) Since this type of program focuses on raising low living standards, however, it is also possible to give subsidies to improve living standards generally. The funds would not be earmarked for any particular purpose, but could be used as each poor household prefers.

It was argued in Chapter IV that there are grounds for preferring general to specific grants, except where there are strong externalities that bias household choice significantly. Slum living may well involve important externalities and on this ground warrant such special treatment. But other categories of expenditures (for example, for education, medical care, and even food) may also involve important externalities for the poor. The opportunity cost of earmarking in one direction may be the loss of leverage against other biases in household choice. A possible solution to multiple biases is a *set* of earmarked grants. But this becomes extremely complicated and suffers from excessive rigidity in prescribing for the great variety of ills in different households. General unearmarked grants seem a preferable solution. No particular form is urged here, but rather it is suggested that if grants are to be given to the poor at large instead of simply to slum dwellers, it may prove politically unattractive to link them solely to housing.[1]

## Earmarked Rent Allowances

Some of the results of an earmarked rent allowance may be sketched briefly. Poor households, with more money to spend on housing, will seek larger and better housing units. But the increased demand is likely to be in such a price range that it will best be met by units already in the housing stock, although a small part of it may compete for, and therefore generate, new construction. The increased demand therefore will bid up the prices of existing standard units. This will mean a rejection of slum units to some extent, and a decline in slum prices will result. The higher prices for low-level and moderate-level standard units will accelerate conversion downward from higher quality levels. The lower prices (or higher vacancy rate) on slum units will encourage some upward conversion toward—but not invariably *to*—a standard level. Finally, inhabitants of units whose prices have risen as a result of the new demand find that the lower price differential between these and higher-level or new units makes an upward move attractive to them. This will tend to spread prices upward along the stock and thereby encourage new construction in the quality ranges where construction is an important and responsive element in the supply.

It is clear that some of these outcomes differ markedly from those under redevelopment. Some new construction takes place, probably less than under redevelopment (for comparable scales of operation), but distributed similarly with regard to quality. However, slightly more of the construction takes place at a lower quality level than has been the case in the past under redevelopment.[2] Hence, there is less upgrading of the average quality level of the housing stock through new construction than under redevelopment. This differential is decreased to some extent by the upgrading through renovation and repair of slum properties in an effort to

[1] To give grants solely to slum dwellers penalizes households of similar income levels who have assumed the extra financial burden of higher-quality housing.

[2] But, it will be remembered, it is presumed that the redevelopment program will from now on lay somewhat greater emphasis on similar construction at lower quality levels.

compete for the subsidized demand. The effort, however, is hampered by the usual asymmetrical barriers against private slum upgrading or replacement.

It must be pointed out that the upgrading of slums will be limited, and in general the quality improvement achieved by subsidized households will be less than might be expected from the size of the subsidy, for a significant reason. The availability to erstwhile slum dwellers of standard but still inexpensive units depends mainly on a many-linked filtering downward of such units from within the existing stock, which in turn depends on the responsiveness of conversions. It is widely argued that the filtering process works fitfully, unevenly, and with some important lags. One of the causes—imperfection of information—will be less operative here, however, since the source of transformation—the rent subsidies—will be widely known. But all in all, filtering is likely to be imperfect, and as a result there will be a considerable raising of prices for the units most sought by recipients of the subsidy, these price rises shading off in both quality directions with the degree of demand and supply substitutability. The increase in prices uses up part of the subsidy and leads some subsidized and other affected families to buy smaller and/or lower-quality units than they want or in fact than they previously occupied.

In short then, subsidy recipients improve their housing standards somewhat either by moving to standard units or by remaining in erstwhile slum units that have been upgraded. There is no forced mass dislocation of households nor significant neighborhood upheaval. Price rises extend upward to upper-quality levels, thereby imposing some costs on upper-income groups, who get no offsetting gain from the process. Their loss is not great, since there is no actual decrease in the housing stock as a whole but probably an increase, concentrated mostly in the units sought by subsidy recipients. The increased competition for standard units does create a virtual shortage, which will be partly offset by new construction. Thus, the income redistribution is progressive, and the quantity and quality of housing are increased without any incentive to exacerbate slums at any point.

On the other hand, for expenditures comparable to those under redevelopment, the overall quality appreciation is only moderate. Many slums are not cleared up. Various market imperfections continue to bias resource allocation. The program cannot be used to solve particular land-use problems facing cities, especially those involving nonresidential activities and relations among metropolitan jurisdictions. But it does help the financial situation of central city governments through increases in assessed valuations.[3] Thus the focus is on subsidizing poor households, rather than on subsidizing land uses and city governments.

The pattern of resource costs differs greatly from that under redevelopment. The major government outlays—the subsidies—are not factor payments but only transfer payments. Nonetheless they do entail some real resource costs, the incentive effects of raising additional revenues through marginal taxation. These taxes fix a liability which is a function of the amounts of certain economic activities (like earning income, buying excise tax commodities, etc.), while the outlay purposes are not related in an offsetting way to these same activities. Categories that account for most of the resource costs of redevelopment—planning, assembly, demolition, site preparation—have much smaller costs attached to them here, because large-scale clearance and elaborate re-uses are largely absent. Where replacement on the site occurs, it is likely to involve only spot clearance. Much of the new construction is likely to take place in suburban areas, where assembly, demolition, and site preparation are much smaller tasks. In any case, these functions are exercised by the private sector, unlike with redevelopment. Thus, the pattern of resource costs differs greatly, but it should not be assumed that this is a "cheaper" program. A different set of commodities is being bought. Only by comparing what is bought with what has had to be paid for it can one tell which program is the better bargain.

*Non-Earmarked Grants*

Much the same kind of analysis applies to general non-earmarked grants to poor households, except that here a much smaller amount of additional purchasing power will be injected into the housing market. In view of the imperfections of filtering and the

---

[3] Despite the fact that the impetus comes from subsidies financed by increased taxation. This is because the taxation is federal, and while a large share of the burden falls on city dwellers, it is not *as* city dwellers that they must pay but as income earners. There is no incentive to change jurisdictions. Thus, these federal subsidies to households act indirectly as intergovernmental grants.

asymmetrical barriers against slum upgrading, a small increment of demand will have a disproportionately smaller impact on quality and quantity. Even the mobilization of attention to higher demands by the poor, which were predicted in the first case, will be largely missing here, so that various imperfections of information would aggravate other reasons for slight market responsiveness. Much of the effect may therefore be dissipated in price increases, concentrated now at a lower quality level than before, since on the average each family will allot a smaller increment to housing.

Subsidizing the poor obviously has a different complex of effects than does redevelopment. One cannot tell a priori which type of program will show a better benefit-cost performance. Much depends on both the specifics of market responsiveness and the relative weights given to progressive income redistribution as opposed to moderating certain housing market imperfections and subsidizing particular land uses and central city activities.

## The Supply of Housing

The preceding alternative operates through demand, not so much as the best way to end slum occupancy but as the best way of subsidizing the housing demand of the poor. The next type of alternative is closer to the goals of redevelopment in that it has specific housing aims, but it also shares some of the relative emphases of the preceding alternative. The argument is that the major effort ought to be to expand the overall supply of housing, first because it is a particularly efficient way to end slum occupancy without hurting the poor, and second because however efficient new construction may be in removing slums, it serves the direct additional goal of increasing total resource commitment to the housing stock. The population as a whole is inadequately housed, and this requires a larger total resource outlay on housing.

### Effectiveness of the Supply Approach

The consequences of this approach depend on the methods used to induce an increased supply.[4] Writers generally make some obei-

[4] For more extended discussions of methods that might be used, see William G. Grigsby, *Housing Markets and Public Policy* (University of Pennsylvania Press, 1963), pp. 185-223, and 288-334; and Herbert J. Gans, "The Failure of Urban Renewal: A Critique and Some Proposals," *Commentary* (April 1965).

sance to public housing, urging that the number of units authorized for federal construction be enlarged. But they believe that the bulk of new construction should come from the private sector, with the government assisting by subsidizing credit.

They want the federal government to make available long-term loans at interest below market rates, with or without an accompanying extension of eligibility for FHA mortgage insurance. Sometimes this loan availability is asked only for special categories of construction, such as rental units for the aged, or low-income units, or cooperative apartment buildings. Sometimes it is asked for more general categories.

Besides federal loan subsidies there are suggestions that relate to neighborhood-effect barriers to new construction, especially construction of low-income housing in slum and near-slum areas. Such construction is presently discouraged by the presence of neighborhood factors that depress the value of even new property.[5] Government can remove some of these nuisances through spot renewal and rehabilitation programs, as well as by providing public improvements like parks, schools, etc. These, along with the provision of low-cost credit, might be enough to change the balance of incentives and elicit additional construction of the desired type. It should be noticed that spot renewal and rehabilitation operate here as complements to, not substitutes for, the program of housing stock expansion.

Assume that low-cost credit, *not* rigidly restricted to special categories,[6] is to be the mainstay of the program. What consequences can be expected? Suppose that the degree of subsidy has been so scaled as to elicit construction in approximately the volume desired. The construction mix is likely to be similar to that usually preferred by the private sector. But it will be remembered that this bears imperfectly on the relative patterns of demand in different parts of the housing stock. In particular, strong medium-income, and especially upper-income, demands are more frequently met by

[5] These neighborhood effects contribute heavily to the scarcity of private credit for such ventures.

[6] Special categories like housing for the aged, or even cooperative housing, are not likely to prove adequate to remove enough slums. Even the addition of low-cost housing is likely to be too scanty, given the private builder's lack of interest in this category.

new construction than are low-income demands. So greater impetus can be expected to construction in the former categories than in the latter. But this will be less marked than usual to the degree that the credit subsidy loosens an erstwhile tight credit market. The availability of credit for low-income units, especially in slum and near-slum areas, on ostensibly the same terms as for upper-income units represents a proportionately greater subsidy for the former than for the latter. Any additional discrimination in rates in favor of low-income and medium-income units will further stimulate their production. But this implies, of course, a higher total government subsidy for any desired number of new units.

The new construction has an impact on slums through filtering that in the lower-quality categories tends to reduce prices in that segment of the stock. Units become more attractive to households dwelling at adjoining quality levels, some above but most of them below. This spreads the price decline largely downward through the stock, with an accompanying shift of occupancy upward. Each upward shift releases units to dwellers at a lower occupancy level. Finally, the process reaches downward into the stock deeply enough so that some slum dwellers find better units available to them at more attractive prices. They shift upward out of slum occupancy. Assuming no new immigration, the slum vacancy rate rises, and slum prices fall. New construction at higher-quality levels produces the same type of process, but many more intermediate filtering linkages must be made for the effect to reach the slums.

If the filtering process worked rapidly and without friction, the location of new construction in the stock would be a matter of indifference. But the process works imperfectly. There are important time lags, and some linkages fail to be made.[7] This accounts for the special emphasis given to the construction of new units at low-quality levels and especially in decaying neighborhoods. Fewer filtering links need to be forged, and the closeness of the units to existing densely situated slum dwellers provides rapid information about their availability and hence a quick response. In addition, since they are in the same neighborhood, slum dwellers are able to

[7] Some observers claim that filtering operates at some quality levels mostly through vacancy rates, not through price changes. This represents a more wasteful adjustment process.

move without having to abandon their heavy social investment in the community.[8]

The imperfection of filtering means that both the distribution of price declines within the stock and the reduction in slum occupancy that results from a given volume of new construction (or even a given total value of construction) depend importantly on the quality and site distributions of this construction. The more heavily it is concentrated at low-quality levels and physically near existing high-density, low-quality areas, the greater will be the decrease in slum occupancy and the greater the real income improvement of the poor generally because of decreasing prices of the units most relevant to them. But such concentration is difficult to elicit, because it goes against the normal market incentives of builders. In order to bring it about, the schedule of subsidies must discriminate in favor of such construction, and the average amount of subsidy per dollar of new construction will have to be greater than if subsidization were neutral with regard to quality distribution.

Comparing this with redevelopment, considerably more new construction is needed here to eliminate a given number of slum units. The quality distribution of these new units, however, is probably not very different, unless discriminatory subsidization has been deliberately and extensively followed. The pattern of price changes is notably different. Price declines will tend to occur generally throughout the housing stock, being most notable for units that are most competitive with the units just built. Thus, the poor will generally experience a real income improvement. Of non-slum benefits only one category—aid to city finances—will approach the magnitude produced by redevelopment, but even here, not if most of the new units are in the suburbs.

## Costs of the Supply Approach

The costs of the program are those of the credit subsidy and those associated with construction.[9] Both exceed the financing and resource needs to replace housing for the former slum occupants. A much larger number of new units must be built than slum units re-

[8] Grigsby suggests that many of these units should be for owner-occupancy rather than for rentals, because owner-occupied units are generally much better maintained than rental units, since they enlist deeper commitments to belong to the community (*Op. cit.*, Chap. VI)

[9] Still assuming full employment.

leased, because the latter number depends on intermediate filtering linkages being filled. For each of these new units there are not only construction costs but also assembly, demolition, and site preparation costs, as under redevelopment, but they are financed privately. As with construction induced by subsidized demand, wherever new construction occurs on low-density land (for example, in suburbs), some of these costs will be less than under redevelopment. This may be offset somewhat by scale economies in the generally larger redevelopment projects.

The loan subsidy involves an expansion even beyond this construction multiplier. In order to encourage additional construction, subsidized financing must be offered to any project within the general category, even if it would have been instituted without the subsidy. Many projects will thus be subsidized unnecessarily, the total number receiving the subsidy being much in excess of the net additions induced by the program (and this latter is much above the number of slum units released). Of course, a loan subsidy does not represent an equivalent resource cost. Its cost concerns its impact on the capital market and is usually expressible as the amount of alternative investment (public or private) that is foregone.

Subsidized supply expansion is not an especially efficient means of decreasing slum occupancy. The disproportionate effect on alternative investment through resource outlays and heavy commitment of the economy's loanable funds argues against the first of the justifications on its behalf. It is therefore only where the second justification—the alleged special desirability of a significant expansion of the housing stock relative to other commodities—can be supported that the substantial extra resources drawn into the housing industry can be considered as generating more benefits than their costs. Yet it is not obvious that this case can be made. The controversial status of the case was discussed earlier.

## Moderating Market Imperfections

In Chapter III some forces acting on the housing market that contributed to the formation and continuation of slums were discussed. They included scarcity of credit for lower-quality residential areas; the pernicious effects of the local property tax and the federal personal income tax; the inadequate enforcement of zoning regulations and building and health codes; and discrimination against minority racial and ethnic groups in substantial parts of the housing stock. Suppose now that the correction of these forces can be considered as a single-package alternative of public policy. Since in the earlier discussion the contribution that each of these factors made to slum occupancy was traced, it may further be supposed without repeating the earlier discussion that their joint correction will simply eliminate these influences. Beyond this, a few remarks are in order.

### The Package as a Supplement

While the various policies already discussed and those to be taken up below can be considered as alternative approaches to the same complex of problems, this package is in a very real sense not a substitute but a complement to them all.[10] Indeed, code enforcement will be treated herein as an integral part of the rehabilitation alternative. It is presented as an alternative to redevelopment chiefly because it enhances the effectiveness of the substitutes to redevelopment—including the "status quo" alternative—more than it does redevelopment. The effectiveness of the substitutes depends much more importantly than does redevelopment on free mobility of resources throughout the housing market, which the package promotes. Redevelopment is an attempt directly to excise an accumulation of the effects of poor mobility. The package as a whole is not actually inconsistent with redevelopment in that it tends to decrease the number of areas where redevelopment resources need to be used, and it makes possible the loosest market conditions for any given total size of the stock, thereby easing the problem of relocation.

### Expansion of Credit

It is not enough to say that credit scarcity for lower-quality areas will be rectified. Some indication must be given as to how this will be done. Direct federal provision of long-term loans was intro-

---

[10] It is possible, however, to find pieces of the package that are not complementary to every alternative. For example, code enforcement does not especially ease the task of redevelopment with regard to the housing of dislocatees. It may indeed underscore the need for some subsidizing of the demand for, or supply of, housing.

duced above, and this can be resorted to in an extremity. But if it is not an overall expansion of credit to housing but only a redirection within the housing field that is wanted, it may be possible to act through private sources. It was argued that loans for lower-quality areas are scarce partly because banks tend to evaluate their potential productivity on a client-by-client basis. Any one attempt to upgrade or replace a structure in such areas is likely to find its value enhancement restricted by the character of the surrounding neighborhood. These adverse neighborhood effects make any loan of this sort a poor risk. But if a neighborhood is certified as an urban renewal area for rehabilitation, this indicates to the bank that there are plans to upgrade the neighborhood as a whole. The neighborhood effects are to be reversed and may be expected ultimately to *enhance* the value of individual projects. This should increase the flow of private credit to those areas.[11] Such a flow will be further facilitated by recent extensions of FHA eligibility. And these can be supplemented finally to whatever extent is considered desirable by direct federal lending.

### Property and Income Tax Reform

The reform of property and income taxes is a major problem. The provisions that encourage the creation of slums are general ones, and modification, especially of the income tax, would have wide and complicated repercussions outside the field of land use. Adverse consequences elsewhere could make it undesirable to make the changes for land-use reasons. Probably a better case could be made for adapting the property tax to the earning ability of the property. Other suggestions concerning the property tax—for example, tax relief for upgrading or replacing slum property—are more controversial and probably require benefit-cost analyses to test their merit.

### Code Enforcement

Code enforcement, taken by itself, is problematic. It is an expensive program on any but a superficial level, and it is difficult to administer. Its consequences, even where successful, are not uniformly attractive. These problems stem chiefly from the ownership

[11] Grigsby, *op. cit.,* p. 310.

and occupancy characteristics of slum structures. In any dense slum area there are many separate ownership units that must be processed by code enforcers. Owner-occupiers are likely to be relatively poor and unable to afford the necessarily extensive improvements required without real hardship. If forced to comply, they may sell the property. Slum landlords are likely to be recalcitrant. Renovations, repairs, higher maintenance levels, and lower allowable occupancy levels almost always are unprofitable, especially if demand is still brisk and each landlord expects the environment to continue to exercise adverse neighborhood effects. Dilapidation, a population marked by poverty and some of its associated deficiencies of urban skills and community responsibility, and overcrowding combine to require such extensive remedial action that the cost sometimes equals or exceeds the value of the property. Landlords under these conditions frequently try evasion and, when apprehended, prefer to institute lengthy and difficult legal holding actions or simply to pay the resulting fines rather than comply. In the extreme they may prefer to relinquish their property to the city rather than incur large, fruitless expenses. Finally, where compliance *is* forthcoming, the result of the substantial sums paid by the landlord is an increase in rentals (in return for higher quality) and a decrease in occupancy, since overcrowding is prohibited. Both of these have the effect of dislocating slum dwellers in much the same way redevelopment does, although on a much smaller scale, since the quality upgrading, if any, does not go much above minimum code standards.

## Discrimination

Ending discrimination in housing against racial and ethnic minorities is an extremely difficult task, and it is certainly beyond the scope of this study to suggest a solution. Some methods like "blockbusting," which makes lumpy increments of dwelling units available to Negroes in former white neighborhoods, accomplish short-run gains at the expense of a lasting, long-run solution. A lasting solution would seem to require stable mixed neighborhoods. Massed white flights perpetuate segregation and maintain important constraints against housing market mobility—for both whites and Negroes. Open occupancy statutes (which must be passed by a high enough level of government—for example, the state—to discourage interjurisdictional moving) can contribute toward the goal by substantially increasing the cost and decreasing the expected gains to whites from their successive flights from integration.

# Rehabilitation as an Alternative Method of Urban Renewal

Rehabilitation is probably the most important urban renewal technique, after redevelopment, in the present program. It was originally conceived as a small-scale adjunct to redevelopment, but as political opposition to redevelopment has grown, rehabilitation has been escalated until it is a major part of the program. In its present intent, if not actual scale of operations, it should be considered at least partly as an alternative to development.[12] In present legislative proposals the role of rehabilitation is to be further expanded while that of redevelopment is to be explicitly cut back; a direct competitiveness between the two as the major foci of renewal is envisaged.

## Coordination of Rehabilitation and Code Enforcement Programs

For reasons to be made clear below, rehabilitation, to be effective, must be coupled with serious code enforcement efforts and a provision for liberal credit. The tandem works roughly as follows. Blighted dwellings may be voluntarily upgraded by private efforts if their owners decide that the benefits to be attained (in terms of a change in property value) would exceed the costs. Included in these costs would be any additional tax liability resulting from an appreciation in value.[13] If they are not voluntarily upgraded, it may be inferred that the costs are expected to exceed the benefits. To use Schaaf's notation, the criterion is to compare $V_2 - V_1$ with $C$, where $V_1$ is the pre-upgrading value of the property, $V_2$ is the post-upgrading value, and $C$ is the cost of upgrading.[14] Thus, where blighted structures remain standing, it may be inferred that $C > V_2 - V_1$.

[12] In A. H. Schaaf, *Economic Aspects of Urban Renewal: Theory, Policy and Area Analysis* (Research Report 14, Real Estate Research Program, Institute of Business and Economic Research, University of California, Berkeley, 1960), rehabilitation and redevelopment are analytically treated on a unit-by-unit basis as fundamental alternatives of renewal, with their appropriate relative use dictated by cost and benefit conditions.

[13] Or alternatively, calculate value change as excluding the backward capitalization of increased tax liability.

[14] *Op. cit.*, Chap. III.

## Code Inspection

The rehabilitation program now moves in. Code inspection establishes a bill of particulars in which each such structure falls below code standards. Unless they are rectified, the structure will be condemned and prevented legally from continuing to provide residential services. Thus, the use of code enforcement with its new requirement of compliance or loss to the government through eminent domain changes the relevant profitability calculation of the property owner. He can (1) comply, in which case he loses $C - (V_2 - V_1)$ with respect to his original position; or (2) relinquish the property to the government through condemnation, in which case he loses $V_1 - V_E$ (where $V_E$ is the price he receives through eminent domain); or (3) sell the property to a private party, in which case he loses $V_1 - V_p$ (where $V_p$ is the price attainable through private sale); or (4) retain ownership, fail to comply, and adopt a strategy of evasion, legal delay, or payment of fines while accepting the risk of ultimately having to comply or lose possession by one of the preceding routes—for which strategy he loses $H$ (the cost of legal harassment plus the expected loss from ultimate confrontation); or finally, (5) withdraw the property from residential use, in which case he loses $V_1 - V_N$ (where $V_N$ is the value of the property in its best nonresidential use).[15]

Options (1) and (3) suggest private upgrading, (2) guarantees public upgrading, (4) may or may not lead to upgrading, depending on the diligence with which the code is enforced; and only (5) precludes upgrading. But (5) is the least likely to be chosen, since allowable nonresidential use (given zoning regulations) probably reduces the value to nearly nothing; the owner loses almost all of $V_1$. For present purposes, if it is assumed that code enforcement is strict and that eminent domain establishes government purchase

[15] Schaaf, op. cit., formulates the new choice as containing only two options, (1) and (5), and $V_N$ is implicitly assumed to be equal to zero. Thus, if the owner complies, he loses $C - (V_2 - V_1)$; whereas if he does not, he loses $V_1$. He should comply whenever $V_1 > C - (V_2 - V_1)$, that is, whenever $V_2 > C$ (p. 10). In other words, application of code enforcement makes $V_1$ a sunk cost, utterly without relevance to the question of compliance. Compliance creates an asset worth $V_2$: it costs $C$. Schaaf's simpler formulation overstates the effect of code enforcement in mobilizing private incentives to upgrade and therefore fails to predict sources of difficulty in administering the program.

prices that disallow illegal slum profitability (so that $V_1 > V_B$ $\leq V_p$ and probably $V_E < V_p$), then private upgrading, either by the original owner or by a subsequent purchaser, is nearly assured.

## Availability of Credit

This assurance is based on the covert assumption that $C$ includes the private cost of financing the improvement—in other words, that credit will be available to the private owner if only he is willing to pay its charges. Institutionally, this has not been true of the private loan market. Credit has been extremely scarce for improving existing buildings in blighted and slum areas, as was noted in Chapter III. The federal rehabilitation program effects two changes in this situation.

First, while one of the reasons for unavailability of credit, or limited availability at very high interest rates, is the risk of default and the high cost of processing small loans, another is the prospective productiveness of the loans. In blighted areas, the physical upgrading of a single structure is not likely to mean much enhancement in its value, since its environment remains overwhelmingly adverse. As was noted above, when banks process loan applications singly, despite the existence of numerous plans for improvements in the same neighborhood, they are likely to be pessimistic about the productiveness of such loans. But if a neighborhood is certified as a renewal area, credit institutions know that the neighborhood as a whole is to be upgraded. Each improvement loan can be perceived in the context of a neighborhood whose upgrading will enhance the productivity of this loan. Thus neighborhood effects are mobilized to work *in favor of* every attempt to upgrade, and financial institutions are more willing to extend credit for private rehabilitation.

The second change effected by rehabilitation is direct federal participation in financing. Especially since 1962, the federal government has been empowered to arrange that property owners have liberal financing available to them. The FHA is authorized to grant Section 220[16] low-interest-rate mortgage insurance for upgrading projects. These loans sometimes permit refinancing of a pre-existing high-interest-rate, short-term mortgage, together with the cost of

[16] The Housing Act of 1949.

rehabilitation, in a single low-interest-rate, longer-term package. As a further help, these insured mortgages can be purchased by FNMA if private investors are no longer willing to hold them. Finally, a special federal fund of $50 million was set up in 1964 to make direct, extremely low-cost twenty-year loans for rehabilitation. This is a small amount relative to the size of the whole program, but it does add to the general loosening of credit availability by the government for the purposes of the program.

The federal government is not the only level of government involved in helping property owners who have been affected by code enforcement. Local government adds an important supplement in the form of strategically placed public improvements, like schools, streets, street lighting, sewage facilities, trees, off-street parking, community centers, parks, and other public amenities. These investments have the effect of consolidating expectations about general neighborhood upgrading, and so they not only supplement the spatial configuration of rehabilitation physically; what is perhaps more important, they trigger many of the contingent private incentives to participate. As always, each property owner believes that his costly participation will be warranted only if most others also participate. The substantial public investment stands as a tangible commitment to the plan.

An additional governmental neighborhood-enhancing factor is the likelihood that the program will be combined with spot clearance and replacement. Individual structures that are economically unfeasible to rehabilitate ($C > V_2$) and represent public nuisances can be taken over by the local public agency and demolished, the cleared site then being used for construction of new units or public improvements. The flexible use of spot redevelopment as a partner with rehabilitation further indicates the intention of overall neighborhood improvement and thus further helps to mobilize private compliance with the program.

One of the factors hidden in the $V_2 - C$ calculation above is the effect of the local property tax. It was argued in Chapter III that the administration of this tax tends to discourage property improvement, since liabilities are not closely tied to a property's income potential, but *are* closely tied to the value of capital improvements added to the property. It was argued above that reform of the property tax is probably desirable no matter what other public policy is adopted for slums. It would remove a barrier in the provoking-enabling process characteristic of the rehabilitation program. But it may not be politically feasible. Another device has been considered, and sometimes resorted to, as a partial substitute for reform. This is a tax exemption—partial or total—on any increase in property value resulting from participation in a rehabilitation program. In comparison with the more radical reform, this promotes *ex post* amelioration of blight that has already occurred, but does not serve as a continuous preventive of blight. Besides, it raises important questions of equity. Why should a property owner in one neighborhood be exempt from tax for undertaking certain repairs when a property owner in a different neighborhood is subject to tax on exactly the same repairs for exactly the same kind of structures? Nonetheless, its implementation of explicit rehabilitation programs suggests that it might pass the test of a benefit-cost analysis.

## Rehabilitation and Redevelopment Compared

The theoretical effect of a rehabilitation program is now compared briefly with that of redevelopment. Upgraded structures pass from a substandard to a standard level. Some increase in property values and in rents occurs as costs are passed upward to tenants. Some decrease in total units occurs as illegal overcrowding is corrected. Thus, because of both a rent increase and reduced crowding, some dislocation occurs.

### Relative Resource Costs

In comparison with redevelopment, the resource cost of raising the average quality level of the housing stock by rehabilitation is considerably less for three reasons: (1) existing structures do not have to be demolished; (2) the construction resources are added to structures that already embody some positive social value[17] (and thus do not have to be duplicated); (3) the increase in quality level is much smaller than under redevelopment. Thus, most of the elements of net project cost under redevelopment are avoided, as well as the cost of building anew structure values that had necessarily to be destroyed along with the undesirable part of the existing stock. Besides this, there is no significant regressive shift in the composition

---

[17] Those that do not will either be publicly replaced or will simply be retired without replacement or upgrading.

of the housing stock. Improvements are small enough to keep units within the reach of most of the previous occupants. Rental increases are payments for increased quality, and they are likely to fall short of the value of the improvements, partly because some of the outlays involved are like fixed costs (given the all-or-nothing option provided by code enforcement) and do not find full expression in prices if any profits had previously been earned. Neighborhoods, with all their established social networks, are kept intact. Indeed, the increased community awareness involved in the neighborhood coordination of effort required for rehabilitation often results in a serendipitous extension and deepening of these networks. These are net benefits.

In sum, neighborhood externalities are internalized by means of *coordinated* land use, substandard occupancy is decreased, qualitative improvements are kept within a narrow enough range to be relevant almost exclusively to the poor, and yet most of redevelopment's net project costs and neighborhood upheaval costs and the disadvantages of regressive income distribution are avoided.

### Disadvantages of Rehabilitation

This sounds overwhelmingly attractive. But there are disadvantages. Rehabilitation is far less appropriate for upgrading badly dilapidated dwellings than mildly substandard ones. For the former, $C$ comes too close to equaling or exceeding $V_2$ to be worthwhile. Demolition and replacement is the preferable alternative here. Where serious blight is concentrated, as it is in the case of slums, rehabilitation, if it is not paired with spot redevelopment, will leave the slum barely touched. Yet if the two are paired, even this will cause trouble. Much of the area will have to be razed relative to what can be saved. But the attempt to raze selectively both increases average demolition and site preparation costs (since total area clearance very likely has scale economies) and precludes the possibility of important changes in land use. This last point is a special instance of the second disadvantage. Rehabilitation allows for internalizing neighborhood externalities by coordinating land-use decisions but not by integrating them. Where radically new forms of land use are especially advantageous, area redevelopment can achieve them, but not rehabilitation—even with spot redevelopment.

The smaller degree of quality improvement is of course cheaper to obtain, but it is a different commodity. It begs the question to assume that the further quality improvement is not worth the cost. As an offset to the maintenance of existing neighborhoods with their low-income populations is the absence of subsidies to attract middle-income families back into the central city, and to provide adjacent expansion space for institutions to enhance the central city's commercial viability. In addition, the subsidy to the city's finances is not as great. Of course, the decreased burden on the poor may well be worth these sacrifices, but the choice between them must be made explicit.

Rehabilitation entails heavy costs in code enforcement and administration, since each property has unique problems that require some individual attention. As to financing, the total needs of redevelopment exceed those of rehabilitation on a per-unit basis, since a larger value of new construction is involved in the former; but a much smaller share of its financing must be in the form of federal subsidies.

In sum, rehabilitation means much lower resource and human costs than does redevelopment, and a smaller relative burden on the poor. But it eliminates far fewer units of slum occupancy and permits far less large-scale community planning. Unless one is willing to make gross evaluations in the absence of the detailed benefit-cost calculations, one can make only a tentative qualitative judgment at this point that the two methods would offer real advantages if flexibly paired together. Redevelopment works best in heavily concentrated slums, rehabilitation in the less concentrated blight of the so-called grey areas.[18] An exact balance between them, however, must be established by concrete benefit-cost analysis.

## Administrative Problems

Finally, some practical problems in the administration of rehabilitation will be considered. The theoretical advantages of rehabilitation have been widely discounted in view of alleged extreme difficulties in operating the program successfully. One observer cites data as of December 31, 1962, to show both that a very small percentage of the units that had been scheduled for rehabilitation

[18] See Robert C. Weaver, Godkin Lecture No. 2, Harvard University, March 30, 1965, cited in *Current* (June 1965), pp. 24-25.

were actually rehabilitated (16.9 percent) and that the total number involved was trifling relative to the remaining task. He sees this as evidence of an intrinsic inability of the program to meet the rehabilitation need, a need which he believes is likely to be met only from predominantly private sources. He accounts for the alleged failure of the federal program on the ground that many private owners imposed on by the program do not want to rehabilitate, and even among those who do, many cannot obtain satisfactory financing.[19]

This extreme pessimism seems to be based on a situation that was shortly to be changed significantly. The program accelerated after 1962, with the number of projects increasing from 170 in 1960 to 225 at the end of 1962 and to more than 400 by December 1964.[20] The proportion of completions increased to 33 percent by June 1964, with completion and work in progress equal to 53 percent of scheduled rehabilitation.[21] Moreover, one of the alleged explanations for the early difficulties of the program, the inadequate sources of financing, has changed importantly. Authority for FHA insurance, direct low-cost federal loans, and rehabilitation grants has been extended. So an early demise anticipated because of the program's halting start, may not be in the picture. Yet there are widespread doubts, not ideologically based, that rehabilitation may face important obstacles if it attempts to tackle a substantial part of the problem of blight.

On the one hand, code enforcement is not likely to be pushed very strongly. Since some capital losses will almost inevitably result from strict enforcement, there will probably be widespread evasion, legal delay, willingness to absorb legal fines, and ultimate willingness to allow really poor housing to fall into the control of local authorities. This would impose increasing administrative burdens and delays on the program. These delays and uncertainties would themselves make it extremely difficult to coordinate private action effectively and would further discourage private participation. Moreover, they would be likely to induce a considerable selling off of property

[19] Martin Anderson, *The Federal Bulldozer; A Critical Analysis of Urban Renewal, 1949-1962* (M.I.T. Press, 1964), pp. 148-49.

[20] U.S. Housing and Home Finance Agency, Urban Renewal Administration, "Cities Show that Rehabilitation *Can* Work" (mimeo. Preliminary edition of a proposed bulletin, September 1965), p. 1.

[21] "America's Cities," *The Economist* (London, Feb. 6, 1965), p. 549.

to private speculators, especially by the poorer property owners. In predominantly owner-occupied renewal areas, one of the goals of the program, stability of ownership and population, would thus be jeopardized. But any laxity in code enforcement designed to avoid such complications would seriously weaken the pressure for private efforts to upgrade. Noncompliance would be widespread and would even more decisively discourage contingent cooperation. Thus, private recalcitrance in the face of prospective capital losses, whether code enforcement is pushed rigorously or not, might be great enough to make administration difficult.

On the other hand, the provision of liberal credit may in a practical manner prove inadequate for any substantial increase in the scope of the program. Partly because private sources may remain relatively unattracted, and partly because of the poverty of the affected tenants and some of the property owners and the likelihood of residual capital losses, a substantial proportion of loans may have to be on terms that require federal subsidy. The federal government might be willing to commit its loan resources in an amount that would represent seed money for demonstration projects. It is less likely that it would be willing to extend outright subsidization to cover a considerable part of the overall task.

Finally, even if neighborhood improvement should be accomplished, it is not clear how long the improvement could be maintained. As has been noted above, existing components in the housing stock depreciate over time and filter downward to lower-quality occupancy, unless the tendency is reversed by continued adequate maintenance and repair. A rehabilitated neighborhood is not as high above minimum code levels as a redeveloped neighborhood. If the owners' and inhabitants' commitment to community coordination is only superficial, then the usual market forces will soon reestablish patterns of blight, and the neighborhood will again subside toward slum levels. The real problem is to reverse and *forestall* blight for intervals long enough to warrant the heavy overall costs of the program. Experience with the program so far offers no convincing evidence as to whether this will be possible.

To conclude, rehabilitation is an attractive renewal tool. To some extent it supplements, to some extent competes with, redevelopment. There is some presumption that a mix of the two would be desirable. The actual shares given to each would depend not only on their respective theoretical consequences but also on practical questions of political feasibility. And rehabilitation too, not redevelopment alone, would face political obstacles.

# Easing the Financial Difficulties of the Central City

The greater weight given to avoiding an adverse income impact on the slum dweller in the various alternatives to redevelopment typically results in a sacrifice of non-slum goals, such as the economic viability of the central city and the financial strength of the central city government. This, plus the conjecture in Chapter V that the way in which redevelopment subsidizes the central city government could distort the government function, suggests that a separate measure should be considered to effect such subsidization. It could be treated as a supplementary part of an overall package alternative to redevelopment. The one suggested in Chapter V was a federal blocked grant to the city government for general purposes chosen by the city.[22]

## Federal Grants to the City

An unencumbered intergovernmental grant would perform just that corrective function that the analysis of jurisdictional externalities called for to decrease suboptimal resource allocation in metropolitan areas. Without further distorting governmental resource use (which the alternative "profitability" criterion would do to some extent), the grant would decrease the portion of public services that would have to be financed by the inhabitants of the central city and lead to a better sharing by commuters in the cost of these public services. It would also to some extent decrease the "artificial" pecuniary motivation for jurisdictional mobility ("fiscal zoning"), thereby moderating forces leading toward metropolitan sprawl.

---

[22] Grigsby (op. cit., pp. 328-31) argues for dropping federal financing on a project basis. He would have the federal government give aggregate grants for the general purposes of slum clearance, conservation, code enforcement, etc., without the cities having to specify particular projects. Grigsby's modification is designed to improve the overall configuration of planning in these areas, however, not to decrease the more general kinds of resource distortions.

*Political Difficulties*

There is a difficulty, however, connected with the political implementation of such a program. This simple sort of grant system involves two analytic elements: (1) an upward shift in responsibility for raising revenues from the local to the federal level of jurisdiction (a proportionate "shared-tax" feature); and (2) a subsidization of central city jurisdiction by other local urban, suburban, and rural jurisdictions. It was argued that this particular complex was justified by the analysis here only under certain empirical circumstances—circumstances which might be present in some cases but not all, and in varying degrees. In other words, the practical implication of the analysis was that different cities might qualify for different degrees of help from this source, ranging from a full share down to zero. The degree warranted in each case could be established only by a thorough empirical investigation.

Unfortunately, this degree of operational subtlety is probably not feasible politically. All central cities, or indeed all cities, might have to share in the program in amounts based on criteria quite different from the foregoing (for example, population). This extension would blur the analytical justification for subsidy. It might, however, be defended on the ground that it would help all central city governments to offset some of the loss of leverage for internal income redistribution through political means that they have suffered as a result of suburbanization.[23]

But even this much extension might be too little for political feasibility, since it would involve subsidizing cities at the expense of other jurisdictions without very tangible and pressing justification for the large amounts involved. The mechanism chosen might be some sort of a shared-tax scheme, with revenue-collecting responsibility for *all* local jurisdictions being passed upward to the federal government to take advantage of the greater fiscal maneuverability available at that level. Sharing downward would be proportionate, so that no element of subsidy to the cities would remain. This would nonetheless help meet some of the problem, since it would decrease the *total* effect of local tax differentials on jurisdictional location, although it would leave the *marginal* effect largely untouched.

[23] See the discussion in Chap. V of the so-called "financial plight of city governments," which gave rise to *value judgmental* benefits and costs.

In sum, while general-purpose intergovernmental grants are analytically to be recommended as a supplement to any of the program packages discussed here, political realities may reduce their ability to meet particular circumstances. Their ultimate justification may turn out then to be based preponderantly on other considerations altogether.

## Proposed New Directions in the Present Program

It will be interesting to examine what new features have been enacted recently or proposed for the urban renewal program in view of this discussion about alternatives to redevelopment. In this context it should be noted that the present program has never consisted solely of residential redevelopment. It has included as well downtown redevelopment, rehabilitation, industrial redevelopment, and community renewal.

### Focus on Problems of Slum Dwellers

Most of the individual changes represent a shift in fundamental emphasis and would meet most of the criticisms discussed above. Under them, the focus of the program would be taken off physical land use and spatial and architectural planning and placed squarely on the problems of poor slum dwellers. Not only would slum dwellers not be allowed to become expendable pawns, whose plight is incidental to primary emphasis on physical planning, their welfare would be the primary goal of the program, with physical planning determined by their needs.

The change of emphasis is shown in the following:[24]

1. Too much of the recent urban renewal effort has gone into downtown commercial redevelopment at the expense of residential goals. More imaginative new attention and resources are expected to be directed toward the latter. No increase will be allowed in the 30 percent ceiling on resources for nonresidential projects.

[24] The following characteristics come largely from these sources: "America's Cities," *The Economist* (London, Feb. 6, 1965), pp. 550-54; Robert C. Weaver, Godkin Lecture #2, Harvard University, March 30, 1965, cited in *Current*, (June 1965), pp. 24-25; *New York Times*, "News of the Week in Review" (Feb. 6, 1966).

2. The mix of new construction on mass clearance sites has been much too heavily weighted toward middle-income and upper-income housing units. It is envisaged that substantial attempts will be made, by means of local public agency land disposition policies and recent extensions of eligibility for federal credit, to increase the proportion of medium-income and low-income units constructed.

3. Relocation has been too extensive, too disruptive, and too costly for the poor displaced households. Henceforth, the need for relocation will be reduced by increasing the incidence of rehabilitation projects relative to redevelopment, especially in the "grey areas" not hopelessly blighted. This will also help to preserve neighborhood communities from disruption. Where redevelopment (with mass clearance) occurs, the new emphasis on constructing units that are within the economic reach of the dislocated will also decrease net displacement and preserve the stability of neighborhoods. Whatever net relocation does occur as a result of redevelopment and rehabilitation will be allowed to work less hardship on the poor, and there is a hope that the program can be modified to actually benefit such families. Toward this end new standard units are to be available through construction, and rent supplements are to be available to the displaced to enable them to afford better quality housing.[25] Furthermore, to the extent that new construction and rehabilitation aims succeed in modifying the present pattern of housing stock changes, relative housing prices will move less regressively than heretofore.

4. Other needy elements in the population will be helped. Rent supplements will be requested for the elderly and handicapped, even those who have not been displaced by redevelopment.

5. The total welfare of impoverished groups will be the target of public policy. Housing will be integrated with the war on poverty. Under the Model Cities Program begun in 1966—a program that does not supplant, but supplements and possibly sets the stage for, further changes in the urban renewal program—an effort will be made to develop and demonstrate total programs for betterment by concentrating manifold efforts and resources on the populations of specific blighted areas. The housing part of the pro-

---

[25] And higher relocation grants to businesses will be available.

gram will consist heavily of rehabilitation. Tax revision and rig-
orous code enforcement will be adopted to encourage this. New
construction resulting from mass clearance will be largely at medium-income and low-income levels. Much of the program direction
will come from the neighborhood's own participation. Employment
opportunities arising from the program will first be offered on a
nondiscriminatory basis to neighborhood inhabitants. Heavy emphasis will be placed on public investment in schools, parks, play-
grounds, and health, community, and recreational centers, and in
providing continuous welfare, informational, and adult education
services. Federal funds will go only to a select number of cities
whose projects meet the broad program targets. For each such city
a federal official will coordinate all the federal housing, health,
education, and welfare programs impinging on target areas.

## Interjurisdictional Coordination

In addition to the change in orientation toward the poor, another new target has been mentioned—to adopt, as a condition for
federal grants, the requirement of greater coordination, or at least
cooperation, among the several jurisdictions within metropolitan
areas.[26] The importance of this was argued in Chapter II. Some attention may also be given to making direct federal grants to cities
for specific public facilities and services, but this is less likely, for
reasons mentioned earlier.

Other elements in the existing program will continue: some residential redevelopment, some aid for institutional expansion, and
some commercial downtown and industrial redevelopment.

## Significance of Changes

It is too early to predict the extent to which the shape of urban
renewal will be affected by the complex of legislative changes and
new administrative intentions. One can, however, remark its relevance for the analysis of this study. Whatever the actual effect
on resource allocation and income distribution, it indicates a willingness by the federal government to impose some national priorities on the hitherto extremely decentralized program. To some extent this makes a benefit-cost analysis of portions of the program

[26] "America's Cities," p. 554.

easier to carry out, since it helps the investigator to formulate differential weights for the various outcome dimensions. It also curbs to some extent the problem of the biased definition of the relevant population. The primary focus on the poor in blighted central city areas produces programs that involve far smaller interjurisdictional externalities. On the other hand, this same focus on the poor has given rise to a proposal for integration of various types of public programs, of which housing is only one. Social consequences are recognized as stemming from composite circumstances (as, for example, where adequacy of housing and responsibility in occupancy depend in part on educational, health, and employment opportunities). The need to analyze clusters of programs does increase the difficulty of carrying out benefit-cost studies, because it complicates the conditions under which *independent* variations can be assumed to have occurred.

That the urban renewal program may move closer to some of the alternatives discussed in this chapter does not make their analysis, or the more extended earlier analysis of redevelopment itself, superfluous. For one thing, it is not at all clear how far the program will go in these directions. For another, whatever the extent of the changes, both analyses are still important for determining the most appropriate mix of elements. They are also important in evaluating the program as a whole, since a comparison with the status quo or any other alternative must establish the various consequences resulting from a bundle of such several parts, and that is what these analyses attempt to provide.

### Role of Benefit-Cost Analysis

This brings us finally to the main theme of this study. Should benefit-cost analysis be carried out? Is it important to the formulation and modification of public policy? If the normative assumptions on which this analysis has been based bear any interest for the electorate, then the results show that intuition and *ad hoc* examination often miss the real nature of what may be gained and what must be given up. Waiting for the affected parties to come forward and declare their stakes will rarely succeed in correcting these errors. It will certainly not help policy makers to understand the relationships from which benefits and costs are generated and therefore how particular hypothetical modifications in policy are likely to change those benefits and costs. A benefit-cost analysis can genuinely help to do these things.

But benefit-cost analysis itself costs something for whatever help it renders. The complexity of certain factors, the broad scope of the study necessary to obtain crucial estimates mean that substantial resource costs are entailed. It is indeed possible that the benefits from using benefit-cost analysis may not be worth their cost. But this can be decided only by knowing something about what it can perform and what that performance costs. This study is offered to help clarify the nature of both the stakes involved in urban renewal and the stakes involved in gaining such clarification.

# Bibliography[1]

Abrams, Charles. *The City Is the Frontier,* Harper and Row, 1964.

Ackoff, Russell L. "Toward Quantitative Evaluation of Urban Services," in Howard S. Schaller, ed., *Public Expenditure Decisions in the Urban Community,* Johns Hopkins Press for Resources for the Future, Inc., 1963.

"America's Cities," *The Economist,* London, February 6, 1965.

Anderson, Martin. *The Federal Bulldozer: A Critical Analysis of Urban Renewal, 1949-1962,* Massachusetts Institute of Technology Press, 1964.

————. "Fiasco of Urban Renewal," *Harvard Business Review,* January-February 1965.

Bailey, Martin. "Note on the Economics of Residential Zoning and Urban Renewal," *Land Economics,* August 1959.

Berger, David. "Current Problems Affecting Costs of Condemnation," *Law and Contemporary Problems,* Vol. 26, Winter 1961.

Bloom, Max R. "Fiscal Productivity and the Pure Theory of Urban Renewal," *Land Economics,* Vol. 38, May 1962.

Blum, Walter J., and Allison Dunham. "Income Tax Law and Slums: Some Further Reflections," *Columbia Law Review,* Vol. 60, April 1960.

Borus, Michael E. "A Benefit-Cost Analysis of the Economic Effectiveness of Retraining the Unemployed," *Yale Economic Essays,* Vol. 4, Fall 1964.

Bos, H. C., and L. M. Koyck. "The Appraisal of Road Construction Projects: A Practical Example," *Review of Economics and Statistics,* Vol. 43, February 1961.

Brownfield, Lyman. "The Disposition Problem in Urban Renewal," *Law and Contemporary Problems,* Vol. 25, Autumn 1960.

Buchanan, James M., and Gordon Tullock. *The Calculus of Consent, Logical Foundations of Constitutional Democracy,* University of Michigan Press, 1962.

---

[1] These references are in addition to those given in the Appendix to Chap. III.

Chapin, F. Stuart. *Experimental Designs in Sociological Research*, Harper, 1947.

Chinitz, Benjamin, and C. M. Tiebout. "The Role of Cost-Benefit Analysis in the Public Sector of Metropolitan Areas," in Julius Margolis, ed., *The Public Economy of Urban Communities*, Johns Hopkins Press for Resources for the Future, Inc., 1965.

Clauson, Marion. *Methods of Measuring the Demand for and Value of Outdoor Recreation*, Resources for the Future, Inc., Reprint No. 10, February 1959.

Crutchfield, James A. "Valuation of Fishery Resources," *Land Economics*, Vol. 38, May 1962.

Dagen, Irvin, and Edward C. Cody. "Property, *et al.* v. Nuisance, *et al.*," *Law and Contemporary Problems*, Vol. 26, Winter 1961.

Davis, Otto A. "A Pure Theory of Urban Renewal," *Land Economics*, May 1960.

————. "Urban Renewal: A Reply to Two Critics," *Land Economics*, Vol. 39, February 1963.

Davis, Otto A., and Andrew B. Whinston. "The Economics of Urban Renewal," *Law and Contemporary Problems*, Vol. 26, Winter 1961.

Dorfman, Robert, ed. *Measuring Benefits of Government Investments*, Brookings Institution, 1965.

Downs, Anthony. "An Economic Analysis of Property Values and Race," *Land Economics*, May 1960.

Dyckman, John W., and Reginald R. Isaacs. *Capital Requirements for Urban Development and Renewal*, McGraw-Hill, 1961.

Eckstein, Otto. *Water-Resource Development: the Economics of Project Evaluation*, Harvard University Press, 1958.

————. "A Survey of the Theory of Public Expenditure Criteria," in National Bureau of Economic Research, *Public Finances: Needs, Sources, and Utilization*, Princeton University Press, 1961.

"The Effects of Housing on Health, Social Adjustment and School Performance," *Proceedings* of 39th Annual Meeting of American Orthopsychiatric Association, 1962.

Feldstein, Martin S. "Net Social Benefit Calculation and the Public Investment Decision," *Oxford Economic Papers*, Vol. 16, March 1964.

————. "Opportunity Cost Calculations in Cost-Benefit Analysis," *Public Finance*, Vol. 19, No. 2, 1964.

————. "The Social Time Preference Discount Rate in Cost Benefit Analysis," *Economic Journal*, Vol. 74, June 1964.

Fisher, Franklin M. "Income Distribution, Value Judgments, and Welfare," *Quarterly Journal of Economics*, Vol. 70, August 1956.

Foard, Ashley A., and Hilbert Fefferman. "Federal Urban Renewal Legislation," *Law and Contemporary Problems,* Vol. 25, Autumn 1960.

Foster, C. D., and M. E. Beesley. "Estimating the Social Benefit of Constructing an Underground Railway in London (with Discussion)," *Journal of the Royal Statistical Society,* Vol. 126, Part 1, 1963.

Gans, Herbert J. "The Failure of Urban Renewal: A Critique and Some Proposals," *Commentary,* April 1965.

Goldston, Eli, Allan O. Hunter, and Guido A. Rothrauff, Jr. "Urban Redevelopment—The Viewpoint of Counsel for a Private Redeveloper," *Law and Contemporary Problems,* Vol. 26, Winter 1961.

Greer, Scott. *Urban Renewal and American Cities; the Dilemma of Democratic Intervention,* Bobbs-Merrill, 1965.

Grigsby, William G. *Housing Markets and Public Policy,* University of Pennsylvania Press, 1963.

Groberg, Robert P. "Urban Renewal Realistically Reappraised," *Law and Contemporary Problems,* Vol. 30, Winter 1965.

Hammond, Richard J. *Benefit-Cost Analysis and Water-Pollution Control,* Stanford University, Food Research Institute, 1960.

Hansen, W. Lee. "Total and Private Rates of Return to Investment in Schooling," *Journal of Political Economy,* Vol. 71, April 1963.

Harsanyi, John. "Cardinal Welfare, Individualistic Ethics, and Inter-Personal Comparison of Utility," *Journal of Political Economy,* Vol. 63, August 1955.

Hirsch, Werner Z., Elbert W. Segelhorst, and Morton J. Marcus. *Spillover of Public Education: Costs and Benefits,* University of California at Los Angeles, 1964.

Hirshleifer, Jack, James De Haven, and Jerome Milliman. *Water Supply; Economics, Technology and Policy,* University of Chicago Press, 1960.

Hufschmidt, Maynard M., John Krutilla, Julius Margolis, and Stephen A. Marglin. *Report of Panel of Consultants to the Bureau of the Budget on Standards and Criteria for Formulating and Evaluating Federal Water Resources Development,* June 30, 1961.

Kelnhofer, Guy I., Jr. "Slum Clearance—Its Costs and Benefits," *The Tennessee Planner,* April 1955.

Kitagawa, Evelyn M., and Karl E. Taeuber, eds. *Local Community Fact Book, Chicago Metropolitan Area, 1960,* Chicago Community Inventory, University of Chicago, 1963.

Knetsch, Jack L. "Outdoor Recreation Demands and Benefits." *Land Economics,* Vol. 39, November 1963.

Krutilla, John V., and Otto Eckstein. *Multiple Purpose River Development: Studies in Applied Economic Analysis,* Johns Hopkins Press, 1958.

Laurenti, Luigi. *Property Values and Race,* University of California Press, 1960.

Leach, Richard H. "The Federal Urban Renewal Program: A Ten-Year Critique," *Law and Contemporary Problems,* Vol. 25, Autumn 1960.

Lichfield, Nathaniel. "Benefit-Cost Analysis in City Planning," *Journal of American Institute of Planners,* Vol. 26, November 1960.

————. *Cost-Benefit Analysis in Urban Redevelopment,* Real Estate Research Program, Institute of Business and Economic Research, University of California, Berkeley, 1962.

————. "Spatial Externalities in Urban Public Expenditures, A Case Study," in Julius Margolis, ed., *The Public Economy of Urban Communities,* Johns Hopkins Press, 1965.

Lichfield, Nathaniel, and Julius Margolis. "Benefit-Cost Analysis as a Tool in Urban Government Decision Making," presented at the Conference on Public Expenditure Decisions in the Urban Community, Washington, D. C., May 15, 1962.

Little, I. M. D. *A Critique of Welfare Economics.* Oxford University Press, 1950.

Maass, Arthur. "Benefit-Cost Analysis: Its Relevance to Public Investment Decisions," *Quarterly Journal of Economics,* Vol. 80, May 1966.

Maass, Arthur, *et al. Design of Water-Resource Systems,* Harvard University Press, 1962.

Mao, James C. T. "Efficiency in Public Urban Renewal Expenditures Through Benefit-Cost Analysis," *Journal of the American Institute of Planners,* Vol. 32, March 1966.

Marglin, Stephen A. *Public Investment Criteria: Benefit-Cost Analysis for Planned Economic Growth,* M.I.T. Press, 1967.

Margolis, Julius. "Secondary Benefits, External Economies, and the Justification of Public Investment," *Review of Economics and Statistics,* Vol. 39, August 1957.

McKean, Roland. *Efficiency in Government Through Systems Analysis,* Wiley, 1958.

————. "Costs and Benefits from Different Viewpoints," in Howard G. Schaller, ed., *Public Expenditure Decisions in the Urban Community,* Johns Hopkins Press, 1963.

Metropolitan Housing and Planning Council of Chicago. *The Road Back— The Slums,* Chicago, 1954.

Millspaugh, Martin, and Gurney Breckenfeld. *The Human Side of Urban Renewal,* Washburn, Ives, 1960.

Mitchell, George W. "The Financial and Fiscal Implications of Urban Growth," *Urban Land,* July-August 1959.

Mohring, Herbert. "Land Values and the Measurement of Highway Benefits," *Journal of Political Economy,* Vol. 69, June 1961.

Mohring, Herbert, and Mitchell Harwitz. *Highway Benefits: An Analytical Framework,* Northwestern University Press, 1962.

Mumford, Lewis. *The Culture of Cities,* Harcourt, Brace, 1938.

———. *The City in History,* Harcourt, Brace, and World, 1961.

Mushkin, Selma J. "Health as an Investment," *Journal of Political Economy,* Vol. 70, Supplement, October 1962.

Nakagawa, August. "Profitability of Slums," *Synthesis,* April 1957.

Nourse, Hugh O. "The Economics of Urban Renewal," *Land Economics,* Vol. 42, February 1966.

Pasamanick, Benjamin, ed. "Housing Environment and Mental Health," *Epidemiology of Mental Disorder,* Pub. No. 60, American Association for the Advancement of Science, 1949.

Plant, James S. "Some Psychiatric Aspects of Crowded Living Conditions," *American Journal of Psychiatry,* Vol. 9, March 1930.

Prest, A. R., and R. Turvey. "Cost-Benefit Analysis: A Survey," *Economic Journal,* Vol. 75, December 1965.

Rapkin, Chester. *The Real Estate Market in an Urban Renewal Area,* New York City Planning Commission, 1959.

Rapkin, Chester, and William G. Grigsby. *Residential Renewal in the Urban Core,* University of Pennsylvania Press, 1959.

Rawson, Mary. *Property Taxation and Urban Development.* Research Monograph 4, Urban Land Institute, 1961.

Redfield, Robert. *The Primitive World and Its Transformations.* Cornell University Press, 1953.

Reid, Margaret G. *Housing and Income,* University of Chicago Press, 1962.

Renshaw, Edward F. *Toward Responsible Government: An Economic Appraisal of Federal Investment in Water Resource Programs,* Idyia Press, 1957.

Reynolds, D. J. "The Cost of Road Accidents," *Journal of Royal Statistical Society,* Vol. 119, Part 4, 1956.

Rhyne, Charles S. "The Workable Program—A Challenge for Community Improvement," *Law and Contemporary Problems,* Vol. 25, Autumn 1960.

Rossi, Peter H., and Robert A. Dentler. *The Politics of Urban Renewal: The Chicago Findings,* Free Press, 1961.

Rothenberg, Jerome. *The Measurement of Social Welfare,* Prentice-Hall, 1961.

Salisbury, Harrison E. *The Shook-Up Generation,* Harper, 1958.

Samuelson, Paul A. "The Pure Theory of Public Expenditure," *Review of Economics and Statistics,* Vol. 36, November 1954.

Schaaf, A. H. *Economic Aspects of Urban Renewal: Theory, Policy and Area Analysis,* Research Report 14, Real Estate Research Program, Institute of Business and Economic Research, University of California, Berkeley, 1960.

Schorr, Alvin. *Slums and Social Insecurity,* Research Report No. 1, U.S. Department of Health, Education, and Welfare, 1963.

Schussheim, Morton. "Determining Priorities in Urban Renewal," *Papers and Proceedings of the Regional Science Association,* 1960.

Seeley, John. "The Slum: Its Nature, Use and Users," *Journal of American Institute of Planners,* 1959.

Sewell, W. R. Derrick, J. Davis, A. D. Scott, and D. W. Ross. *Guide to Benefit-Cost Analysis* (Resources for Tomorrow), Ottawa: Queen's Printer, 1962.

Slayton, William L. "State and Local Incentives and Techniques for Urban Renewal," *Law and Contemporary Problems,* Autumn 1960.

————. "Report on Urban Renewal," *Urban Renewal,* Hearings before the Subcommittee on Housing, House Committee on Banking and Currency, 88 Cong. 1 sess., November 1963, Pt. 2.

————. "Rehabilitation Potential Probed for Urban Renewal, Public Housing," *Journal of Housing,* Vol. 22, December 1965.

Steiner, Peter O. "Choosing Among Alternative Public Investments in the Water Resource Field," *American Economic Review,* Vol. 49, December 1959.

————. "The Role of Alternative Cost in Project Design and Selection," *Quarterly Journal of Economics,* Vol. 79, August 1965.

Stokes, Charles J., Philip Mintz, and Hans von Gelder. "Economic Criteria for Urban Redevelopment," *American Journal of Economics and Sociology,* Vol. 24, July 1965.

Strotz, Robert. "How Income Ought to Be Distributed: A Paradox in Distributive Ethics," *Journal of Political Economy,* Vol. 66, June 1958.

Turvey, Ralph. "On Investment Choices in Electricity Generation," *Oxford Economic Papers,* Vol. 15, November 1963.

U.S. Department of Housing and Urban Development, Urban Renewal Administration, *Urban Renewal Project Characteristics,* December 31, 1965.

Walker, Mabel. "Tax Responsibility for the Slum," *Tax Policy,* October 1959.

Walters, A. A. "The Theory and Measurement of Private and Social

Costs of Highway Congestion," *Econometrica,* Vol. 29, October 1961.

Weaver, Robert C. Godkin Lecture No. 2, Harvard University, March 30, 1965, cited in *Current,* June 1965.

Weisbrod, Burton A. *Economics of Public Health; Measuring the Economic Impact of Diseases,* University of Pennsylvania Press, 1961.

————. *External Benefits of Public Education; An Economic Analysis,* Princeton University, Department of Economics, 1964.

Wilner, Daniel M., *et al.* "Housing as an Environmental Factor in Mental Health: The Johns Hopkins Longitudinal Study," *American Journal of Public Health,* Vol. 50, January 1960.

Wilson, James Q. "Urban Renewal Does Not Always Renew," *Harvard Today,* January 1965.

————, ed. *Urban Renewal; the Record and the Controversy,* M.I.T. Press, 1966.

Wingo, Lowdon, Jr. "Urban Renewal: Objectives, Analyses, and Information Systems," in Werner Z. Hirsch, ed., *Regional Accounts for Policy Decisions,* Johns Hopkins Press, 1966.

Winnick, Louis. "Economic Questions in Urban Redevelopment," *American Economic Review,* Vol. 51, May 1961.

————. "Facts and Fictions in Urban Renewal," in *Ends and Means of Urban Renewal,* Papers from the Philadelphia Housing Association's Fiftieth Anniversary Forum, Philadelphia Housing Association, 1961.

Woodbury, Coleman, ed. *Urban Redevelopment: Problems and Practices,* University of Chicago Press, 1953.

# Index